NOW WRITE! NONFICTION

NOW WRITE! NONFICTION

Memoir, Journalism, and Creative Nonfiction

Exercises from Today's Best Writers and Teachers

Edited by SHERRY ELLIS

JEREMY P. TARCHER/PENGUIN
a member of Penguin Group (USA) Inc.
New York

JEREMY P. TARCHER/PENGUIN
Published by the Penguin Group
Penguin Group (USA) Inc., 375 Hudson Street, New York, New York 10014, USA •
Penguin Group (Canada), 90 Eglinton Avenue East, Suite 700, Toronto, Ontario M4P 2Y3,
Canada (a division of Pearson Penguin Canada Inc.) • Penguin Books Ltd, 80 Strand, London
WC2R 0RL, England • Penguin Ireland, 25 St Stephen's Green, Dublin 2, Ireland (a division of
Penguin Books Ltd) • Penguin Group (Australia), 250 Camberwell Road, Camberwell, Victoria
3124, Australia (a division of Pearson Australia Group Pty Ltd) • Penguin Books India Pvt Ltd,
11 Community Centre, Panchsheel Park, New Delhi–110 017, India • Penguin Group (NZ),
67 Apollo Drive, Rosedale, North Shore 0632, New Zealand (a division of Pearson
New Zealand Ltd) • Penguin Books (South Africa) (Pty) Ltd, 24 Sturdee Avenue,
Rosebank, Johannesburg 2196, South Africa

Penguin Books Ltd, Registered Offices: 80 Strand, London WC2R 0RL, England

Most Tarcher/Penguin books are available at special quantity discounts for
bulk purchase for sales promotions, premiums, fund-raising, and educational
needs. Special books or book excerpts also can be created to fit specific needs.
For details, write Penguin Group (USA) Inc. Special Markets, 375 Hudson Street,
New York, NY 10014.

Library of Congress Cataloging-in-Publication Data

Now write! nonfiction : memoir, journalism, and creative nonfiction exercises
from today's best writers and teachers / edited by Sherry Ellis.
p.   cm.
ISBN 978-1-58542-758-1
1.   Authorship—Problems, exercises, etc.   2.   Exposition (Rhetoric)—Problems,
exercises, etc.   3.   Report writing—Problems, exercises, etc.   I.   Ellis, Sherry, date.
PN147.N69   2009   2009037013
808'.02—dc22

Printed in the United States of America
9   10

Book design by Gretchen Achilles

THIS BOOK IS DEDICATED TO
DENISE GESS

CONTENTS

MEMORIES AND INSPIRATION

CHARACTERIZATION

PLACE

REVISION

AUTHOR'S NOTE

During the three years since the fiction version of *Now Write!* was published, several writers and teachers have mentioned how helpful the book has been. I've received feedback that the exercises helped writers break through impasses and add depth and layers to their writing. Also, there are writing groups that have used these exercises to provide weekly structure to their meetings. It is with this feedback in mind that I decided to collect nonfiction writing exercises for this second book in the Now Write! series.

GET WRITING

MICHAEL STEINBERG

Three Things That Stopped Me in My Tracks: An Exercise in Discovery and Reflection

MICHAEL STEINBERG has written and edited five books. In 2003, *ForeWord Magazine* chose *Still Pitching* as the Independent Press Memoir of the Year. He's also founding editor of the anthology *The Fourth Genre: Explorations in Nonfiction,* and coeditor of *The Fourth Genre: Contemporary Writers of/on Creative Nonfiction.* Currently, he's writer-in-residence at the Solstice/Pine Manor low-residency MFA program.

Writers often talk about the sensation of discovering "what we didn't know we knew." It's a shorthand phrase that describes the unexpected surprises—ideas, insights, and/or feelings—that we didn't plan on encountering. And if these discoveries are compelling enough, they can resemble what fiction writers and poets describe as epiphanies or moments of self-illumination.

Part one of this exercise is designed to help you become more attuned to catalysts—incidents, observations, encounters, situations—that can, if you're paying attention, trigger these unexpected discoveries. And part two asks you to use those discoveries to take your writing a step further.

EXERCISE

Part One: Three Things That Stopped Me in My Tracks

Write three separate entries or notations that describe three things that stopped you in your tracks. To get the maximum benefit out of this exercise, do each one at least two to three days apart.

For example, say on the tenth of this month you found out that your best friend was badly injured in an automobile accident; on the twelfth, the temperature unexpectedly plunged from the seventies to the thirties—and something unusual happened because of that; and on the fourteenth you found out that something you were looking forward to with great anticipation—an encounter, an interview, an appointment, etc.—got canceled and/or put on indefinite hold.

If you did your first notation on, say, Wednesday, then do the next on Friday, and the third on Sunday. Just describe the specifics of what you saw and/or what happened. Then, write a short note to yourself explaining why this particular thing caught your attention.

These notations can be as long or short as they have to be. They can be serious, sad, playful, puzzling, exhilarating, disappointing—and so on. It'll depend on what three things you write about, and the mood you're in when you write them.

Let's say, though, that you can't find three things that stopped you in your tracks this week. Maybe you can only find two. In that case, go into your memory bank and write about an episode, incident, encounter, etc. Pick one that has been nagging at you for a while.

Part Two

Now let's see if we can't make some sense out of these three seemingly random happenings.

First, read your notations back to yourself, with an eye toward discovering some common thread or pattern—no matter how far-fetched or speculative—that links all three. There are lots of possibilities here.

Maybe, for example, the common link is a running motif of some sort; maybe it's a feeling of déjà vu; or, maybe these three things have reminded you of a problem that's still unresolved.

In any case, when you come up with a connection (trust your subconscious; it'll be there if you look for it), write a thoughtful *paragraph or two of speculation/reflection/analysis*—where you try to determine exactly *what* connects the three things that stopped you in your tracks. Then write about *how* and *why* you think they're connected.

In the process of writing this, hopefully, you'll discover something you didn't know you knew. And, in the best-case scenario, it will become rich material for you to write about in more depth and detail.

JAY KIRK

The Dying Goat

JAY KIRK'S nonfiction has appeared in *GQ, Harper's, The New York Times Magazine,* and *Chicago Reader,* and has been widely anthologized. He teaches in the Creative Writing Program at the University of Pennsylvania, and is the author of *Kingdom Under Glass,* to be published in the fall of 2010.

Good nonfiction writing is, largely, about the conviction of one's impressions. Your honest "take" on the world. I often tell my students to mind not only the details, but, in particular, the *weird* details. It is not the fact that you notice your nonfiction subject has "dark shaggy hair" that makes him a memorable character, but the fact that a yellowed curl of fingernail left from his morning's ablutions clings to the fabric of his shirt just southeast of that little embroidered Izod alligator. The same goes for the more soulful aspects of your writing: the deeply personal, subjective impressions you make about your characters, your situations, your prejudices, the vagaries of your own mind. You must give yourself permission to put down the really true stuff, which, at first, might seem inappropriate, obscene, or, again, for lack of a better word, "weird." But there is much truth in the strange; sometimes it's the only way to reassess the ordinary. Of course, it's frightening to risk the truth, mainly for fear that somebody might read what we've written and take it badly or, worse, think badly of us—that our observations and hard-won insights are bizarre or creepy. That's why, to really get the ink flowing, I often console myself with the morbid thought that, in all likelihood, when I die nobody's gonna remember me, so why the hell not write what's true? Only once we let go a little can we get down to the lonely business of what we really think. So, embrace your mortality and write better! I know, it's kind of depressing, but it works.

EXERCISE

Here's one of many variations on this exercise that I like to call "The Dying Goat."

Pretend/imagine that you are a goat. You are a goat that has been separated from the rest of your goat community. You are lost in the wilderness. As you stumble through the wilderness, in your goat-like panic, you prick yourself on the thorn of a honey locust. Don't let its name fool you: the thorns are evil, five-inch suckers, very nasty. The puncture wound is deep and, in your best, medically unprofessional assessment, lethal. You will probably bleed to death, alone, out here in the wilderness. You quickly go through Elisabeth Kubler-Ross's five stages of grief and come to accept your demise. Then, in your indefatigable need to express yourself, as a writer of truth, even in the hour of your own inevitable death, you find a well-nubbed twig and dip it in the puddle of your blood. What are your final words?

You can use this as a starter for an automatic writing, as an opportunity to revise your list of subjects/story ideas worth writing about, about which you've previously felt too shy or polite or otherwise constrained to write about yet, or you can use this exercise as a way to purge yourself of the Big Think ideas you've been too humble as of yet to share with the rest of the world. The main idea is to *let go*, for starters, and give yourself permission to bridge the gap between your real thoughts and real ink. I find that by simply pretending I'm on my deathbed, with a notepad and quill pen, I can often tap deeper into those buried truths if I exorcise the demon of self-consciousness. Whatever it takes, write as if your next words are your last.

If this doesn't work, try writing a practice suicide note. I write them all the time, and leave them scattered around the house for my wife to find. If it does work, however, and you find yourself on a roll, and want to flesh out the scenery, this exercise can also serve as a warm-up to better things. In your efforts to bring greater verisimilitude to your dying inner goat's last words, you can visit the library, and there, while reading up on the nature of goats, and while poring over atlases to vivify your portrait of the sort of wilderness in which a goat might become disoriented, rifling through botanical prints of the honey locust and whatnot, perhaps you will come across a more valid nonfictional angle. If so, be mindful of the absurd. It is not, after all, the exclusive realm of fiction alone.

ROBIN HEMLEY

Your First Kitchen

ROBIN HEMLEY has published eight books of nonfiction and fiction, most recently *DO-OVER!*, in which a forty-eight-year-old father of three returns to kindergarten, summer camp, the prom, and other embarrassments. His awards include a 2008 Guggenheim Fellowship, two Pushcart Prizes, and many others. He currently lives in Iowa City and teaches in the Nonfiction Writing Program at the University of Iowa.

These are two exercises I usually give my students on the first day of class, regardless of level of expertise, but they can be modified for a smaller, more informal group. A minimum of two people are needed—one to prompt and the other to list and then write. As one of the exercises builds from the other, I think they should be considered linked.

EXERCISE

First of all, after we've made our introductions, I ask my students to close their eyes. No peeking, though there are always a couple of distrustful souls and/or cheaters who want to open their eyes. But I make it clear that no matter what, they must keep their eyes closed until I tell them to open them again. Then I tell them that we're going to go around the room and I'm going to ask each of them to describe a different detail of the room in which we're seated. I tell them that writers have to be good observers (though I, in fact, am a terrible observer, but I don't tell them that).

The first few people I choose have a seemingly easy task. Someone describes the floor, or the desks, or the windows and the door. Also inevitably there's some controversy regarding EXACTLY how many windows are in the room, the color of the carpet, the number and shape of the lights hanging from the ceiling. I encourage the students to chime in with their own picture of what the classroom looks like, whether it disagrees or not with what others think. I try as much as possible to write down these observations on the blackboard, which is often green.

As we go around the room, I try to squeeze out finer and finer details from them—the NO SMOKING sign at the back of the room, the pencil sharpener by the door, the overhead projector, the pull-down maps at the front of the room with old maps of the Soviet Union. You see, already I'm transforming this exercise into my own idealization of what a classroom should look like—circa 1970. It's not surprising that people often get the details wrong, but what's fun is when someone invents an object that's not even in the room. I once had a student swear there was an American flag on a pole at the front of the classroom—of course, it was simply a figment.

Finally, after we've exhausted the descriptions of the room, I ask students to keep this picture in mind as much as possible and then to slowly open their eyes. Most of the time, the students are stunned as they try to reconcile the picture in their mind with the actual room. In this way, I'm able to introduce students to the idea that one's memory, imagination, and expectations weigh heavily on the nonfiction writer. Best to understand that we are not tape recorders or cameras, and the goal of our writing is not to transcribe but to filter the world in the way that humans filter the world through their very subjective minds.

We also talk about salient details—if we were going to describe this classroom, we would not include every detail listed on the board because that would be tedious and would bore the reader. So I ask the students to pick out three or four details that exemplify the room to them, that seem most evocative of the feeling of this room (most often, institutional and oppressive). The salient details tend to overlap from one person to the next, but they can vary quite dramatically. It all depends on what you're trying to get across by using these details.

After we're done sharing the salient details, I ask the students to close their eyes again. Now I tell them I want them to go back in time and remember their first kitchen, or at least the kitchen they remember most vividly from childhood. Man or woman, young or old, we all have kitchens in common, and kitchens contain more than food. They're the places the family congregates, where guests gather, where family dramas occur. I ask my students to imagine this kitchen and then we do a slow inventory of the kitchen. I ask them to stay within the bounds of the kitchen. They can note doors and windows, but they shouldn't be led away from the kitchen. I ask them to imagine how big the kitchen was. How many windows and doors? Were there plants on the windowsills, soap, dishwashing liquid? What about the refrigerator? What did that look like? Open up the fridge and see what's inside. What's in the vegetable bin? How does it smell? Take a look in the freezer. How about the stove. Anything cooking? Are there people there? Who? Are they talking? What are they saying? Take a look under the sink, in the cupboards, the pantry. What does the light fixture look like? Are there dead bugs trapped in the overhead light? What other appliances are there? Do you have a favorite glass you drink out of? And so on . . .

After I've spent seven to ten minutes rebuilding, or remodeling, their childhood kitchens, I ask them to open their eyes and write down everything they saw. I allow them to write for twenty minutes or so, and then I ask them to read their pieces. I make sure that EVERYONE who wants to read gets a chance to read—they all want to read their pieces. In many cases, the exercise has brought back images they hadn't thought about in years—invariably, this will be the case unless a student still lives in the house in which he or she was born. But even in a case such as this, most kitchens go through a remodel at some point or another, so chances are good that the student will be able to write a compelling piece about the kitchen before the remodel. As students listen to one another read, I ask them to write down the salient details—the details that best evoke this childhood kitchen.

These exercises paired in this way almost never fail—of course, if you have no writing buddies, if you live on a spit of land in Newfoundland or Alaska visited once a month by a supply ship or plane and you can't entice the pilot to do this exercise with you, I will allow you to modify it. Go ahead and write down the details of your writing room—best do this with your eyes open. You probably won't miss anything, but at least you'll notice minutiae that perhaps you had previously taken for granted—a cobweb, a can of diet Sierra Mist on the floor, a dried bat skeleton (you're going to have to spend a little more time cleaning, I'm afraid). Now share the details with yourself and tell yourself the salient details. After this, you're ready to remember your first kitchen, and to write about it and see what's called up from your deepest memories.

Together these exercises cogently demonstrate the roles played in our writing of memory, the imagination, and observation.

GRETCHEN LEGLER

The One-Inch Window

GRETCHEN LEGLER is a professor in the Department of Humanities at the University of Maine Farmington. Her works of nonfiction include *On the Ice: An Intimate Portrait of Life at McMurdo Station Antarctica* and *All the Powerful Invisible Things: A Sportswoman's Notebook.*

In Virginia Woolf's memoir, *Moments of Being*, she speaks of wanting to see and understand the "patterns" behind what she calls the "cotton wool" of daily existence. These glimpses into "moments of being," she writes, are the special gift given to the writer. But they don't come entirely without effort. There is a "shock receiving capacity" that the writer needs to cultivate, a kind of patience and willingness to see beyond the ordinary, or to see the extraordinary in the mundane. This "shock receiving capacity" is best developed through meditative acts. Oftentimes writers are so focused on production that they neglect the necessity of being still so as to be filled.

How can a writer cultivate this sense of stillness and focus? How can a writer prepare herself to receive those "sudden violent shocks" that Woolf spoke of, those shocks that reveal the patterns of truth that lie behind the surface of life? I have found several ways to do this, but the most enjoyable is to work with what I call "The One-Inch Window." The exercise has its origins in Anne Lamott's book *Bird by Bird*, where, in giving advice to those with writer's block, she counsels writers that they need not be overwhelmed by the responsibility for the "whole picture"—the whole story—but only for the part of the story they see through a one-inch window.

EXERCISE

1. First, make a one-inch window by cutting or tearing a small square in the center of a note card or small piece of paper. I tell apprentice writers that this is something they can carry in a pocket, in their writer's notebook, or in their wallet to remind themselves of the need to focus. It is not only a tool that you can literally apply to the world around you by holding it up to objects, but it is also a philosophy of seeing in a focused, minute sort of way. Practice putting your one-inch window on various surfaces and objects. What you will always see is part of the whole, and that part in amazing detail. At this point, a writer could go on and simply create a written one-inch window by focusing on and recording literally what is in the window—part of an eyelash and furry face of a dog, one petal and part of the stem of a tulip, the deep red-bronze knot in a plank of wood.

   I've found that often the tendency, especially with beginning writers, is to think that there is not enough in the one-inch window to write about, and the impulse is to strike out almost immediately into larger territory, or into metaphor. But it is important that one sticks with ONLY what one sees in the window. Sometimes, there is also a tendency to turn the exercise into something of a riddle—describing the thing in the window without naming it. That is also unnecessary. I encourage writers to describe what they see through the window very literally: what does it look like, what color is it, what texture is it, what does it smell like, feel like, taste like, etc.

2. A related exercise that creates different results is to "describe" what is in the window not in words, but with the tools of another kind of artist—pastels, watercolors, colored pencils, crayons, and markers. I call these "visual one-inch windows." What one is after here is not the literal manifestation of what one sees in the window, but the essence of the thing—the patterns. Let's say that you prop your one-inch window up against the side of a large Granny Smith apple, capturing in the window one rounded edge and a bit of the bottom, where it curves into the Formica countertop that it sits upon. Focus on color and line. There is a specific color of green, there are curves, there is the contrast where the curves meet the line of the countertop, there is the shiny texture of the skin, there is shadow, and the contrast of the smooth organic apple with the cold white of the Formica. Now re-create this essence visually. One does NOT need to be a talented artist to do this exercise; in fact, that is part of the point—to let the imagination play in a realm where there are no expectations. The point is only to see deeply and then represent what you see. Your visual one-inch windows may be totally abstract and unrecognizable to others, but that is the point. What do YOU see beyond the cotton wool of daily life?

CHRISTINE HEMP

Writing Your Way in the Back Door:
The Painting as Entry

CHRISTINE HEMP is currently finishing a memoir titled *The Land of Forgetting*. Her essays and poetry have been heard on NPR's *Morning Edition*, and she teaches at the Iowa Summer Writing Festival. Hemp lives in Port Townsend, Washington.

William Carlos Williams's dictum about *things* being the life of poetry holds true in creative nonfiction as well. The essay teeming with "stuff" is much more memorable than one that floats in abstraction. A piece about love doesn't end up in our cells unless it is grounded in the softness of your lover's neck as it disappears into the collar of his sweatshirt. Or what about that scab you picked while you were crying on the phone to the man you knew would leave you by spring? Just like the strong poem, the strong piece of prose is rife with metaphorical power—from your mother's out-of-tune piano to the orphan sock that keeps showing up in your tangled underwear drawer. When we turn to things, the truth comes at us through the back door, and we are surprised by ideas and emotions we didn't know we possessed.

To take it a step further, *disparate* things—unlikely juxtapositions—help us to write our way into new and unexpected "aha" moments. For example, in her essay called "Seeing," Annie Dillard sits on the bank of Tinker Creek watching a tremor near a muskrat burrow, and then she sees a ripple in the water that suggests an underwater creature. We follow her gaze, but in the middle of her nature reverie, she introduces something else: "The ripples continued to fan upstream with a steady, powerful thrust. Night was knitting over my face an eyeless mask, and I still sat transfixed. A distant airplane, a delta wing out of nightmare, made a gliding shadow on the creek's bottom that looked like a stingray cruising upstream. At once a black fin slit the pink cloud on the water, shearing it in two." The jet's shadow is the last thing we'd expect in a meditative piece about what it means to see, but it pushes the essay toward another level of understanding, a different perception of creature in nature. It's like a black diagonal slash through an otherwise pastoral landscape painting. These disparate things thump against one another, so that a third and unforeseen insight reveals itself in the process.

One of the assignments my nonfiction students love best involves art. I take them to the art museum and ask them to choose one painting in the collection that they are attracted to, but also makes them feel uncomfortable. We sit and look at our respective paintings for ten minutes or so. Then we write. For fifteen minutes—nonstop. Not as an exercise in art criticism, but as a kind of "climbing in" to the painting—exploring its colors, its objects, its creator, anything that comes to mind. These are often the shiniest essays of the week, and I believe it is because the disparate "things" in the paintings—the color orange, a dead cow in a tree, a man in a blue coat—smack against one another.

When we concentrate on the *thing*, rather than the mere emotion or idea, we enter through the back door, stumbling into the fecund pantry rather than the tidy, acceptable ideas of the front foyer. In fact, not only is the writing stronger, we also discover that what poet Richard Hugo calls the "triggering subject" is rarely the true subject. The things—the shadow of the plane on Tinker Creek, the angled barn, the blue horse—lead us into a larger meditation. They help us write our way into the true subject, something much more compelling than we could have predicted.

EXERCISE

Embark on a private field trip to your local art museum, or go on-line to the Museum of Modern Art—or the Louvre—and choose an unfamiliar painting that makes you mildly uncomfortable. Look at it—really look at it—for ten minutes without doing anything else. Then write for fifteen minutes without stopping. Be sure to include the painter's name, the date, the title of the painting, and the medium. "Richard Diebenkorn," "1975," and "oil on canvas" can prove invaluable, and they place the work in space and time. Discuss the scene, the colors, the textures, the shapes, the composition, and maybe even speculate about the painter, letting your own associative synapses go wild.

Take a break. Then pull a sentence out of your freewrite that includes a specific element of the painting: a triangle, a shade of green, or a nude figure, and start there. Now compose an essay that tangles with the notion of relationship—with a house, a person, a tree, a city, an animal, an idea. Use the components of the painting to illuminate your own arguments with yourself and your exploration of this relationship. See if you can fasten several disparate things together in your piece to create an adhesive for a larger epiphany. Allow the work to surprise you, as if a new you had walked in your own back door.

KATHLEEN SPIVACK

Words as Inspiration

KATHLEEN SPIVACK is the author of six books of prose and poetry. Her most recent book is *The Moments of Past Happiness*. Her essays have appeared in the *Atlantic Monthly, Kenyon Review, The Harvard Review*, the *Virginia Quarterly Review, The Massachusetts Review, North American Review*, and in many anthologies. Ms. Spivack is currently working on a personal literary memoir about Robert Lowell and his circle: Sexton, Bishop, Plath, and so forth. She teaches in Boston and in Paris.

I often work in countries where English is not the first language. Words, our ways of naming things, assume supreme importance. They carry intentionality: pebbles thrown out into a pond, the ripples spreading further. I have always liked to read dictionaries for pleasure, trying to memorize strange words and how to use them.

Writing in my first language, English, is no longer only the language of every day, but something to be savored. I meet it on the page, a precious private tryst. It is my lover, with all the secrets and code words that weave the fabric of our relation. "*Let me tell you how it is.*" In intimacy one briefly enters a borderland of gesture and murmured sounds. But at the truest moments of passion, whether in ecstasy or fury, our own words in our original language, the ones

with the real power, those exact words that define what we are feeling, leap up and singe us.

EXERCISE

This exercise is so simple: you just have to like reading and to have
a pretty good dictionary. One might begin with an idea, a glimpse
of something, an image, or a larger inclusive grouping of events
about which to write. But it is not always easy to find the way in;
there are so many possibilities. When working on a topic, any word,
or collection of words, might be the starting point. It's like entering
a labyrinth. Finding your way out is more difficult though. That's
between you and the Minotaur.

1. Open an English language dictionary (if you are writing in
   English). I prefer the weight of an actual book on hand because
   it lends itself easily to random wandering and associations,
   lazily turning the pages. Reading a dictionary lures me the
   way the old libraries with their tottering card catalogs, their
   yellowing milky odor, and open stacks used to do. They invite
   one to search further and deeper, each random word leading
   to another, touching the pages of books shelved alphabetically
   until one day maybe you'd be found, locked in the underground maze of a great library, skeleton propped up at a little
   corral—books stacked high and a fresh one open before you.
   Writing is a bit like that, isn't it?

2. Now you're in front of the opened dictionary. Eyes closed,
   put your finger on a word: random page, random word.
   Then read about this word: origins, meaning, usage, and so
   forth. Place the word on your tongue. Let it dissolve.

3. Write the word down at the top of a sparse white page.

Your word is a bit of sun caught in a sunflower: it is petal and center, aura and corolla.

4. Let your mind wander outward from that word center. Think of your project, what it is you intended to write about. Can this word be a touchstone, even if you don't actually use it?

Enter its whole universe of meaning, the alpha and omega: memory and starting point.

Your word is a first step, a walk, an opening: it is your journey. If it is a long project, you might write down several words before starting, letting them resonate.

5. Now write two pages. Less. Or more. Usually by the end of the first paragraph I have an idea of the piece. Words become sentences, letting themselves be shaped. At the end of the writing time, I might write down a few key words to remind myself where I want to go the next day.

Many writing prompts include something like this. All it needs is one word to get the imagination going. Writers and teachers working with schoolchildren on their writing often use a "basket of words." The poetry magnets, so popular with refrigerators, also start with words, each one definite, stark, and yet associative. In France, where I have been teaching during the past years, words are national treasures, to be cherished and protected.

If we have the words, with their many layers of meaning, we can witness and give voice. Living outside my own language has helped me appreciate the sensibility and structure of English as well as those of other languages. It has made me listen carefully to words and their meanings, their flaws, absences, and failures. There are words and there are also concepts for which individual languages have no words. That subtle area, which dictionary and thesaurus try to map, longs for exploration.

6. But by now we have digressed, and your writing still waits for you. Open the dictionary again. Touch another word. Listen to its sound. Let it whisper its secrets, its past, and what it has to say to you right now.

TOM LUTZ

Writing About Images

TOM LUTZ is the author of *Doing Nothing, Cosmopolitan Vistas, Crying,* and other books, and has written for the *New York Times, Los Angeles Times, Chicago Tribune, salon.com, New Republic, ZYZZYVA, Exquisite Corpse, Black Clock, belief.net, American Literary History,* and other newspapers and journals. He lives in Los Angeles, teaches at the University of California, Riverside, and is hatching plans.

My friend Dorothy Braudy, the painter, decided several years ago to put together a show based on her family photographs, a kind of memoir on canvas. She picked through a century's worth of photos and began with a very early Kodak snapshot of her knickers-clad father and his two siblings taken around 1904. She appears as a toddler in the eighth or ninth of what became some forty paintings that chronicle her growth into adulthood in the late 1970s. I would stop by her studio every couple months and watch the paintings take shape, seeing them evolve from early sketches, which often involved a re-cropping of the original photo, through more formal sketches, to the filling in of detail and coloring, the reworking and retouching toward the final versions. Each time she told me stories about the people in the paintings, a few of whom I had met, many of whom were already dead and gone, the stories becoming more elaborate as time went on and this exercise in memory did its work. The paintings have an extraordinary interest as a narrative sequence, and they are extremely compelling as visual objects. Braudy is a true California artist and her colors are exceptionally vivid and bright, to an extent I began to think of as related to literary magical realism. When she asked if I would write an essay for the show's catalog, I jumped at the chance.

I had spent very little time writing about painting before this time, and as I sat with each canvas, sticking one at a time on an easel and writing, I was amazed at what happened: I saw more. I discovered things about the paintings that I had been completely blind to despite my long involvement with them. Visual echoes, body postures, color patterns, brushstrokes, facial expressions, compositional decisions, human relations among the different subjects all emerged that, although they all must have had some effect on me, I was far from recognizing before sitting down, computer in lap, to examine them in prose.

Immediately afterward I brought the exercise to my nonfiction workshop: I projected an image on the wall (it was a striking photograph of a very young Wallace Thurman) and asked my class to write about it. I gave no further instructions. Some students immediately began telling stories—some realistic, some fantastic—while others invented a character study (none recognized Thurman, a somewhat obscure Harlem Renaissance writer). A few wrote about the image as an image, some about shapes and lighting. In discussing the various ways people approached the image, the workshop participants had an experience similar to mine, in that the projected photograph opened up, revealed possibilities for seeing, and for writing, that weren't immediately apparent.

I have since developed a more elaborate version of the same exercise, a kind of "20 Questions" approach.

EXERCISE

Take a painting, or a reproduction of a painting, set it in front of you, and try to write about it from as many different perspectives, and in relation to as many contexts as possible. For instance, say the painting was Edward Hopper's *Nighthawks at the Diner* (a decent copy can be found at www.artchive.com/artchive/H/hopper/nighthwk.jpg.html).

1. Describe the scene.

2. Tell the story of the woman at the counter.

3. Tell the story of the waiter.

4. Describe the painting in compositional terms.

5. Describe the artist's use of color.

6. Describe the brushstrokes.

7. Tell the story of the painter and imagine his intentions for this painting.

8. Describe the emotional impact of the painting on a viewer.

9. Describe the first time you saw this painting.

10. Describe what this painting suggests about the American nighttime city of its era.

11. Analyze why this painting has remained such an important, iconographic image.

12. Describe how this image does or doesn't jive with your own experience in a similar place.

13. Describe and discuss as many of the other details as possible: the men's hats, the bar stools, the coffee, the cigarettes.

14. Discuss the play of light and dark in the painting. Is it related to film noir?

15. The painting is from 1942. What was happening then in the world of art?

16. Tell a different story about the woman.

17. The United States was at war in 1942. Is this evident?

18. Tell a story from your own life that the painting suggests or prompts.

19. Describe another image that this one evokes for you.

20. Describe the process of writing these various pieces.

Obviously many of these questions and prompts are specific to the Hopper painting, and many are easier to reproduce for realist, figurative paintings than for more formalist, abstract paintings. This exercise has some value not simply in relation to visual images, it seems to me, but as a way to think about attention and fullness, and about the relation between analysis, description, and multiple narratives. The next step, of course, would be to try to arrange or weave how these various perspectival pieces fit into a piece.

CELESTE FREMON

Anna's Shrapnel:
Recognizing the Revelatory Detail

CELESTE FREMON is an award-winning freelance journalist, and the author of *G-Dog and the Homeboys* and the upcoming *An American Family*. She is also the creator and editor of WitnessLA.com. She teaches journalism at USC, and is a Pereira Visiting Writer at University of California, Irvine.

"Show, don't tell" is the mantra of every good nonfiction writer. (Every good fiction writer, too, while we're at it.) And one of the primary keys to the art of *showing-not-telling* is the revelatory detail—the small but telling fact or action that brings a character more fully to life, takes a scene to a deeper level, illuminates a previously hidden theme in a narrative. These days, when I talk with students about how best to hunt down and make use of their own revelatory details, I first tell them about Anna and her shrapnel.

Anna Politkovskaya was a famous Russian journalist and nonfiction writer who was honored throughout the world for her powerful stories documenting the effect of two Chechen wars on ordinary Chechen people. Whenever Politkovskaya was asked to accept yet another writing award, before she left her Moscow apartment, she'd tuck a piece of shrapnel in her purse to use when giving her acceptance speech. She admitted it was bothersome to justify the shrapnel's presence to airport security officers. But she felt the hassle was worthwhile because, when it came to giving her audiences a window into the everyday reality of living in a war zone, nothing beat the sight of that shrapnel. The small, twisted piece of metal was the revelatory detail that bypassed the intellects of her listeners and engaged them at a more fundamental level with the story she was telling.

Politkovskaya understood the concept well because, for years, she'd employed the same technique in order to breathe life into the difficult stories she investigated in her columns, features, and books. Since much of my writing requires me to persuade readers to care about stories relating to gang violence and other "unsympathetic" criminal justice–related topics, I found Politkovskaya's determination to cart around that shrapnel to be an instructive reminder that the right object or action, if used skillfully, can carry a great deal of thematic and/or informational weight when one is attempting to construct a compelling narrative.

For this same reason, I love the story that mystery writer Michael Connelly tells about his own first encounter with the art of the revelatory detail. (Connelly was a journalist before he hit the bestseller lists with his Harry Bosch novels.) He was working as a crime beat reporter in Fort Lauderdale, Florida, and was assigned to follow a local homicide squad, which meant going to crime scenes. At murder sites, Connelly noticed that the squad's taciturn sergeant had the habit of pulling off his eyeglasses and resting one end of the glasses in his mouth when he squatted beside a body and contemplated the city's newest crime victim.

Connelly thought little about the quirk until his last day with the squad. He was in the sergeant's office when the exhausted cop again took off his eyeglasses and laid them on his desk. This time, as Connelly glanced at the glasses, he spotted something interesting. There was a deep groove in one of the arms of the sergeant's specs.

All at once, Connelly got it. Whenever this tough-acting sergeant was confronted with a new homicide, he kept his outward cool, but expressed his all-too-human internal distress in one, nearly imperceptible way: he clenched his teeth on the plastic arm of his glasses. Hence the groove.

Connelly says that the groove epiphany has informed his writing—both fiction and nonfiction—ever since. Through that little groove, he was able to comprehend how a seemingly trivial but emotionally significant detail can deliver a very large wallop. For Connelly, the groove was analogous to Anna's shrapnel.

EXERCISE

Exercise One: Go to a public place where you are able to observe lots of people. Write short descriptions of five or ten individuals whom you observe, in each case using a single physical detail, characteristic, or telling action.

For instance, is that man's hair stiffened with hair gel or with old sweat? What does that woman's choice of footwear tell you? Notice the solitary teenage girl who, while reading, stirs her tea, then takes the hot spoon and presses it to her lips.

Exercise Two: Think back to an important experience in your own past—either happy or traumatic. Pick a single physical detail or action that embodies your feelings about that experience and describe it.

One more tip: when I'm researching a story, I always bring my digital camera to use as an additional note-taking device. Later, when I'm back in front of the computer, I often find that the camera has recorded a wonderfully revelatory detail that my eye has missed.

ROBERT ROOT

Stepping into Photographs

ROBERT ROOT is the author of *The Nonfictionist's Guide: On Reading and Writing Creative Nonfiction* and *Following Isabella: Travels in Colorado Then and Now*, and the editor of *Landscapes with Figures: The Nonfiction of Place*. He is also coeditor of *The Fourth Genre: Contemporary Writers of/on Creative Nonfiction* and Interview/ Roundtable editor of the nonfiction journal *Fourth Genre*. A professor emeritus of English at Central Michigan University, he teaches creative nonfiction in the low-residency MFA Program in Creative Writing at Ashland University.

Writing, as writers and writing teachers know, is a means of discovery. Putting words on a page generates more words eager to be set down, and the words you intend to write revise themselves many times before they are first physically recorded. Writing isn't simply transcribing thought; writing taps involuntarily into memory and imagination to provoke language that generates thought. That's how spontaneous writing spurs discovery and, consequently, why, in my own writing and in my classes and workshops, I use a variety of strategies to get writing going before conscious or conscientious composing takes place. One highly effective strategy involves what I've termed "captioning" or "stepping into photographs." The exercise I'm going to describe is variable but effective in helping you see how a writing prompt can get you started on the discovery of subject matter, visualization of scene, setting, and characterization, and producing either a discovery (zero) draft or a first draft of a writing project.

EXERCISE

If I ask you to select one personal photograph that you possess to write about, which photo or photos come immediately to mind? Chances are, you have photos in your billfold, on your desk or dresser or refrigerator or wall, as a screensaver or cell phone image, that you've already selected and positioned where you can review (re-view) them from time to time.

Phase One: Whichever one you select as you sit thinking about it, don't look at it now but start writing about it. Try to conjure the image in your mind's eye and begin by simply recording what you remember is in the photograph in the most objective language you can muster, as if you were a random viewer describing the picture rather than an individual for whom *that* particular picture has meaning. Be as thorough as you can about the setting and the participants and whatever you think a complete stranger might deduce from the evidence of the image. Finally, try to write a caption in six to twelve words that identifies the content of the photo as an outsider might interpret it.

Once you've been thorough as a spectator or reporter of the photo, shift gears and begin writing as a participant or an intimate of the photo. Why did you think of this photo? What do you think the photo shows? What does it record for you or why is it meaningful to you? Depending on the photo, sometimes the images as seen by an intimate and by an outsider are nearly identical—what the photo shows is that transparent—but sometimes the image as interpreted by an insider is completely different from what a stranger sees. Try to write a caption of the photo that identifies in six to twelve words its particular significance for you.

The chances are good that you've already unearthed feelings, memories, interpretations, attitudes about the subject of the photo that either you didn't know you had or you hadn't examined before. Generally a fount of other memories and emotions and ideas will start flowing as you're writing, giving you a lot to work with if you choose to work with it further. But there's more to be done with this approach.

Phase Two: If you haven't looked at the original photo while you've been describing and captioning it from memory, take a look at it now. Scan it slowly and carefully. What's in the photo that you didn't remember being there? What's not in it that you thought was there? Does the actual viewing of the photo support your interpretation from memory? If there are discrepancies—there likely will be—what significance do they have? What do they tell you about why you interpreted the picture the way you did, why the picture has the meaning it has for you? Write about what you see and feel about the physical photo for a while.

Phase Three: Look closely at the photograph and, closing your eyes, imagine it not as a photo but as a physical location. Push out the borders of the photo until they expand beyond your peripheral vision. If you're in the photo, step into it and take up your position; if you aren't, step into it as an invisible presence. Find a place to stand and look around, back at the photographer and beyond the photographer. Set the scene in motion—what happens before the photo is taken? What happens after? Notice how the participants interact, how setting feels to all your senses, how you feel about being there. Walk out of the frame, resume your writing position, open your eyes, and write.

It's possible to benefit from one, two, or all three phases of this exercise. It's worked for me and my students with memoir, travel narrative, essays of place, nature essays, and reportage. I think the relationship between the visual and the verbal in writing is very elemental.

S. L. WISENBERG

The Brain Map

S. L. WISENBERG often combines personal writing with research and reporting to form segmented and lyrical essays. She is the author of two works of creative nonfiction: *Holocaust Girls: History, Memory & Other Obsessions* and *The Adventures of Cancer Bitch*, as well as a short story collection, *The Sweetheart Is In*. She codirects the MA/MFA in Creative Writing program at Northwestern University.

How many times do we jot down ideas on scraps of paper—the backs of shopping lists and ATM receipts, on sticky notes that lose their stickiness, and the like? Too many, in my case. And, of course, we lose them, both the papers and the ideas. This exercise is a way to pin down all those stray ideas for essays and other creative nonfictions, and to have them in one identifiable place; in other words, to give them the respect they deserve so that we can use them. This exercise basically is an inventory of what's inside your head at the moment. You can refer to it later whenever you're stuck for a subject. It has a number of steps, so please set aside at least forty-five minutes for it.

Please note that the symbols are arbitrary, but they are mysteriously important because they help turn a piece of paper into a map. You can do this with a pencil or pen, but feel free to use colored pencils, crayons, markers.

EXERCISE

1. Get a piece of unlined paper, typing or larger. Write the date on the top.

2. For five minutes, draw plain circles randomly on the page. Next to each, write the name of a place you know and care about. The places can be large (former Soviet Union) or small (back of the bushes in your childhood home).

3. Now for five minutes, draw circles and color them in. Next to each, write the name of a place you've never been but can imagine. Examples: Paris with Gertrude Stein, Vietnam.

   If you're a very precise person, you might object that you don't know everything or nothing about a place. If you know a little bit about Vietnam, for example, you could color in the circle just a little bit.

4. For five minutes, draw squares and next to each, write a subject you know about and care about. Examples: fly-fishing, Art Deco.

5. For five minutes, draw squares and—you guessed it—color them in. Next to each write a subject you don't know much or anything about but think must be interesting. Examples: cloistered life, footbinding.

6. Take five minutes and draw triangles. Next to each, write the name of someone you know well or know a lot about. Examples: your mother, Stalin.

7. Now, of course, it's time to take five minutes to draw triangles and color them in, writing next to each the name of a person or group you don't know well but think must be interesting. Examples: surfers, maternal great-grandmother.

8. Now you have a piece of paper covered with shapes and writing. If you're working alone, close your eyes and point. Take the subject or name that your finger lands on and write it on the top of a clean piece of paper. Start listing: What I know about _____, and what I don't know about _____. Keep going, freewriting for five minutes.

9. Do this three more times. If you're working with a partner, exchange maps.

    Person A chooses a topic from B's list and says, "Tell me about _____." Each person does this three times, then each writes for ten minutes.

10. Keep this map. Tape it to the wall near your computer or to the inside cover of your notebook. Refer to it whenever you're stuck. Add to it from time to time. Experiment with weaving together two different, seemingly disparate topics.

DENISE GESS

The Five Stages of Grief

DENISE GESS is the author of two novels, *Good Deeds* and *Red Whiskey Blues*, and the nonfiction book (with William Lutz) *Firestorm at Peshtigo: A Town, Its People, and the Deadliest Fire in American History.* Her personal essays have appeared in *Philadelphia Stories, The Sun,* and *Remarkable Reads: 34 Writers and Their Adventures in Reading.* She's working on a collection of essays, *Bad for Boys.* She is associate professor of creative writing at Rowan University.

Many years ago, folk singer Janis Ian wrote and recorded "Jesse," a song later rerecorded by Joan Baez. Ian's slow tempo and whispery, plaintive tone—"Jesse, come home/there's a hole in the bed/where we slept/now it's growing cold"—resonates with grief. The way Ian sings it suggests that Jesse hasn't left for another girl, but may be dead. In singer-speak, Ian's "phrasing" creates the tone of self-delusion without losing listeners' sympathy. We feel the singer's loss more through her denial of it.

Baez's version of the same song, delivered in a quicker tempo with clipped, bold enunciation, still suggests loss, yet Baez's tone emanates from a different stage of grief. Unlike Ian, Baez seems to be bargaining with a lover who might still be persuaded to return home, who might, in fact, be listening to her on the other end of a phone line.

Much of the subject matter of creative nonfiction (especially the personal essay and memoir) is born out of the writer's desire to explore personal loss or yearning. Like Ian's song, the visceral effect of an essay or memoir on the reader depends upon the author's relationship to the grief and the author's "phrasing."

The following exercise is designed to help you fearlessly sink into the difficult stages of grief as a means to help you identify the diction, syntax, and rhythms of each of these stages when you write. When you can hear it, only then are you able to change it, to learn which tones are difficult to sustain, inappropriate for your subject matter, or too off-putting.

EXERCISE

First, familiarize yourself with the stages of grief (denial, anger, depression, resignation, and acceptance). Devote some thought to how your perception alters when you're experiencing each stage. For instance, if you're writing an essay about the loss of a job that sent you into bankruptcy, you might want to begin writing your personal essay from depression, the third stage of grief. Write at least two paragraphs.

Now read those paragraphs out loud. Be honest with yourself. What do you notice about your sentence lengths? Your diction? Your tempo? Is it repetitive (depression often is)? Loaded with abstractions and clichés? Could you read the sound of depression for more than two paragraphs? For the length of a book? Why or why not? How does your emotion affect your tone, the material, and your reaction as a reader?

Repeat the exercise until you've applied each state of grief to the same two paragraphs. Note the changes in your language and rhythm from one state of grief to the next. Ask yourself the same questions. Better yet, have a friend read your words to you. Pay attention to your visceral reaction. Are you annoyed with what you hear? Why?

You will often find that the one emotion you are trying to avoid in your personal essay or memoir is precisely the one you need. Perhaps you've been avoiding anger, yet when you embrace it, you're able to write with humor. Don't hold too fast to the belief that the creative nonfiction writer must keep anger at bay. Essayist William Hazlitt built a career on his cantankerous yet un-bitter tone. Of course, you may scare the reader (and yourself) with unmitigated rage. Or disgust yourself with the drone of depression. Or be pleasantly surprised with the amusing jazzed-up rationalizations of denial and resignation. But you'll also hear—perhaps for the first time—that the key to creating compelling tone is not how well you hide your grief, but how well you "phrase" it.

BARRIE JEAN BORICH

Life in One Page

BARRIE JEAN BORICH is the author of *My Lesbian Husband*, winner of an American Library Association GLBT book award, and the creative nonfiction editor of *Water~Stone Review*. She is a core faculty member of the MFA in Writing Program at Hamline University's Graduate School of Liberal Studies in St. Paul, Minnesota, and a member of the MFA faculty of Hamline University.

One of the differences between writing a fictional narrative and writing a memoir narrative is in nonfiction we must decide what details of an already existing story are worth bringing to the page. I often liken the process to walking down a rocky beach in order to extract the few bits of polished glass and agate from the greater mass of uninteresting detritus.

The Life in One Page Exercise, which I have used over many years in many forms, is designed both to promote early generative drafts and to direct the eye toward revision—i.e., toward the agates embedded in the greater wash of the unedited life story.

PART ONE—20 MINUTES

Using no more than one handwritten page, WRITE YOUR ENTIRE LIFE STORY. Start at the top of a blank page with your birth and, once you've reached the bottom of the page, end with the present day. Expect to summarize and leap over great important events, years, even decades, because the idea is not to see how far you can get in one page, but rather to get to the present day in no more than one page.

PART TWO—5 MINUTES

Read through what you've written and place an asterisk next to any moment or area that needs more attention. Place as many asterisks as you see fit, anyplace you think you may have more to say.

PART THREE—10 MINUTES

PICK ONE asterisk. Bring a story, moment, scene, or event to mind that includes this asterisk point. Then close your eyes and meditate on some PRECISE MOMENT of that event. With your eyes closed, peruse each of the five senses, as they pertain to your chosen narrative moment. Notice the visual elements of that moment. Notice the audible elements of that moment. Notice the textural elements of that moment, and the ground of that memory (for instance, were you standing, sitting, or stretched out on bare earth? On the top floor of a skyscraper? etc.). Notice the odors and fragrances of that moment. Notice the tastes of that moment, and if there is no discernible taste, then notice the feeling of the inside of your mouth as you remember this moment.

PART FOUR—5 MINUTES

Open your eyes and, as quickly as possible, without thinking, make simple LISTS of concrete, sensory details you remember about this moment. Don't worry about whether these details are relevant. Just brainstorm, and write them down.

PART FIVE—15 MINUTES

Write a page or so in which you focus on transforming your moment into a scene, giving precise attention to physical, concrete, and action-based detail.

I have adapted this exercise, over many years, from exercises I saw presented first by writers/teachers Patricia Hampl and Sheila O'Connor.

KATHRYN DEPUTAT

The Composite

KATHRYN DEPUTAT has taught and coached Boston-area writers for more than seventeen years, in both academic and nonacademic settings. Her poetry and articles have appeared in various publications, including *Spirit of Change* and *Natural Awakenings* magazines. She is the author of *Love's Way: Reflections and Practices*, and publishes regularly on LovesFreeway.com.

Facing a blank page can be the most daunting moment for a writer—even when one knows one's subject and general direction. Preconceived ideas can certainly cause their own trouble. When we overthink our subject or material, we are much more likely to turn out overly linear, ordinary prose than we are something fresh and original. To optimize the writing session and its yield, it is best to loosen one's grip. It's fine to know the field, if you will, in which you aim to stroll, but best to maintain complete freedom of movement within that field: to truly wander. The Composite serves like the rungs of a ladder or scaffold, while allowing freedom of movement within its structure.

The components of The Composite, assembled in advance, anchor us all along the way so we are never grasping at air. When we reach, there is something there, ready. By way of the scaffold, we remain in touch with our ground, and traversing a blank space becomes not only possible but easy.

EXERCISE

1. Begin with a specific topic (moment, person, place, condition) in mind, e.g., "the cost of oil," or "family breakfasts," or "my falling-out with Alice," or "the bed"—whatever will best access the anecdote (in the case of memoir) or essay you are setting out to write. Alternatively, you can begin with no topic in mind and let one arise as you proceed through the exercise.

2. Find an image (photograph, newspaper or magazine clipping) that draws you, and bring it into your writing space. Note: It is usually more evocative, surprising—more of a stretch for the writing muscle—if the image is not necessarily related to your topic.

3. Make a list. Write the first thing that comes to mind in response to the following prompts whether or not it relates to your topic:
   - an expression or phrase (yours or another's)
   - a day of the week (one of the seven)
   - a sound
   - something you associate with a grandparent/elder
   - something in your refrigerator
   - a sensation (emotional, physical . . .)

4. Glance at the image (from number 2) and notice what catches your eye, where your glimpse lands. Write "It's the . . ." (with "it" being that which you glimpsed) and continue writing without stopping for twenty minutes. As you write, bring in the items listed in number 3. You might bring in more of the

image or what it evokes, or you might not. Note: Do not force anything! Let the various components insinuate themselves into the piece, let them suggest direction, content, leaps, etc. Let them anchor and guide you.

For continued or additional writing, simply generate a new list from the suggested prompts, or vary the prompts themselves (e.g., a piece of music, a smell in the "room," the weather, an unexpected sound, a fruit . . .). No matter the elements, the exercise will yield powerfully grounded, fresh, and surprisingly integrated prose.

LEE ZACHARIAS

Riffing

LEE ZACHARIAS has recent nonfiction in *Shenandoah, Prairie Schooner, Pleiades, Crab Orchard Review,* and *The Best American Essays 2008.* Author of *Helping Muriel Make It Through the Night* (short stories) and the novel *Lessons,* she is professor emeritus of English at the University of North Carolina Greensboro.

When I began writing nonfiction I had several essays I wanted to write—about my father's suicide, about the impact her mother's early death had on my mother, about a brain-damaged boy in the neighborhood where I grew up. These were the things that presented themselves to me as subjects— they seemed important, and I knew a lot about them—but as I went on writing, I discovered that some of the most exciting nonfiction comes out of material that didn't seem important, out of the over- looked detail. Focusing on a particular image and letting it show me a meaning I hadn't previously understood proved generative not only in terms of material but also method—it freed me from the plodding sincerity of so many strictly narrative personal essays.

This discovery was made particularly acute when a friend asked if I would write a bitter essay about marriage for an anthology. Because my husband and I have been together more than thirty years, this struck me as (a) an odd request, and (b) not a very good idea. But as soon as I said no, I began to think about the wedding dress I used to keep underneath my bed. My mother had preserved the gown I wore to marry my first husband when I was very young;

for lack of anywhere else to put it, I stored it beneath the bed, dragging it from one apartment to another, afraid that I would hurt my mother's feelings if I got rid of it. I hadn't thought about that dress in years, but immediately I knew I wanted to write an essay titled "The Bride Beneath My Bed," which turned into a nonlinear third-person account of my dissociation and reconciliation with a former self, an essay structured more like a jazz riff than a narrative even though it tells a story.

Because many students come to nonfiction in the same way I did, with a few subjects for personal essays already in mind, subjects that almost invariably lead to straightforward narrative, often very good narratives but narratives that can lock the student into one way of thinking about structure, I sometimes challenge them to discover other subjects and other methods by asking them to write a page that grows out of a word they choose from a list. My list is generic, and their first task is to associate a specific image—or series of images—with the more general word; in fact the student should choose his or her word because it evokes a vivid and specific image. The noun *tree*, for example, might be the ginkgo tree outside a fifth-grade classroom, the tree the fifth grader stared at while the teacher went on with the geography lesson and the student picked at a scab on her arm and wondered whether her father would be gone again when she came home that afternoon. Or it might be the pine tree out back where crows congregate each evening, or the one where biologists have discovered the red-cockaded woodpecker they thought extinct. The page the student writes might be a personal narrative based in memory, a free association, an observation, a meditation, a scientific exploration, or some entirely new form. What I like about this exercise is that it doesn't lock the student writer into a particular approach.

The list of words that follows begins with nouns and moves on to verbs and adjectives, but students are free to transform their word into any other part of speech. Teachers might want to add or substitute words that seem appropriate to the particular experiences and interests of their student body. The student's assignment is to write at least a page that centers on the specific image or images that the student associates with the word he or she has chosen. (If the student has trouble getting started, the teacher might suggest beginning with an assertion, e.g., *The bride beneath my bed lives in a blue house with an awning.*) What results may be an entire short essay or may lead to a longer piece. In choosing the word and letting it speak to him or her, the student has already discovered the title.

EXERCISE

SOME WORDS TO RIFF ON

window	fish	box	key
spider	track	wagon	pocket
tree	fence	snail	dust
map	rug	closet	snake
hole	letter	river	bowl
thorn	chair	bicycle	corner
cemetery	path	stain	pill
jar	train	basement	music
stairs	bush	lake	porch
bride	groom	barn	book
crack	rain	scar	picture
shop	blanket	hill	house
fan	car	garden	shadow
bucket	horse	roof	bird
mirror	cup	gate	grass
eye	egg	stone	fire
spin	run	sing	push
open	dance	break	lose

peek	free	fear	climb
fall	whisper	drip	taste
dig	win	drop	smell
close	shout	give	take
steal	choose	jump	build
skate	spy	cut	smell
burn	hate	tease	whir
bully	squeak	float	sink
call	cook	fly	count
sour	ragged	hot	clean
dark	red	sweet	rough
loud	bitter	pretty	wet
smooth	soft	mean	quiet
cold	ugly	hard	blind
big	sharp	tall	tiny
uninvited	iridescent	wrinkled	dirty

MYRA SKLAREW

What Am I Going to Say?

MYRA SKLAREW is the former president of the artists' community Yaddo, professor emerita of literature at American University, author of three chapbooks and six collections of poetry, including *Lithuania: New & Selected Poems* and *The Witness Trees*, as well as a collection of short fictions, *Like a Field Riddled by Ants*, and essays, *Over the Rooftops of Time*.

A student whose thesis committee I serve on has written a novel. His way has been to push through it hard all the way to the end. It hasn't accumulated its full emotional weight but he has the shape of its story. I know that some novelists like to work this way, getting a draft however unfinished and then fleshing it out later. John Gardner (*Grendel, The Sunlight Dialogues, The Art of Fiction*) once told me that he would walk around sometimes for two years, letting his characters tell their stories, reveal themselves, never putting down a word, and then one day he would start to type and he'd stay at it night and day for several months until the work was done.

Perhaps because I started life as a poet I approach the writing of nonfiction and fiction as a poet might, working from dreams and images, discovering as I go. The real excitement is not so much gaining mastery over material that I already know, but finding out things that I haven't yet known, making odd juxtapositions that help me to see things in a new way. Metaphor, analogy, association are the tools in this mode. This approach may seem strange, particularly when writing nonfiction that has to do with science and medicine, but consider Lewis Thomas's wonderful essay in *Lives of a Cell* on the complexity of liver function. He'd rather be told at 37,000 feet in the air that he was now in charge of flying the plane than asked to take over the function of his own liver.

In *Writing the Australian Crawl*, William Stafford tells us that "intention endangers creation." He speaks of "that feeling you have when you go along accepting what occurs to you." He wants to "witness for a wilder, unplanned" process. The truth is that each of us must find our way as writers. And even if we think we've discovered a route for one piece of writing, the next one may require an entirely new approach.

EXERCISE

If you write initially on your computer, turn the monitor screen setting to its lowest setting so that you aren't able to see what you are writing. If you are writing by hand, don't reread what you have written until you are finished. If you always start by using the computer, try writing with a pen or pencil on a sheet of paper, the tactile pleasure of that. If you always begin with pen and paper, you might wish to start this exercise by using the computer.

Think of this as an experience where you are going to see what is there, much as you might step out into a field or a subway or into a strange house or a street in a city you've never visited before. Trust that there is something to be found there. And just begin. Give yourself ten minutes or so to write freely without judging the worth of anything you are writing. Bill Stafford said that there is no such thing as writer's block; just lower your standards and keep on going! Here's an example: a subway station, urine smell, clothes of

a homeless man, dark walls, people pushing, sounds of heels click-
ing up an escalator, thought of falling down the escalator. Deadlines, joint pain, doctors, bud of a tree, crocus, March, dream of a
place I haven't seen in forty years.

Take a look at what you have written. If several images or ideas
or characters or objects emerge, accept all of them, whether or not
they seem to have any coherence. Does what you have written seem
to have an emotional basis without any particular visual or tactile
images? Or do you find visual images, sounds, odors without any
emotional counterpart? What are you drawn to, curious about in
the words you have written?

Follow out any of the areas of the writing that you want to explore further. This time let yourself associate to any part of your
known life or memory that bears on what you have written initially.
Example: All the subway images. Yesterday while I was waiting for
the subway that was very late because of track maintenance and
doubling up of cars, I stood with close to a hundred people when
we all witnessed a man lying on the earthen-colored tile floor across
the tracks from us. We watched two teenage girls go over to the
man and shake him. They were far enough away that we couldn't
hear what they were saying to him. Was he dead? He didn't move.
One of the girls tapped on his shoulder and then skipped over him
and scooted away.

On our side of the tracks, no one moved or spoke or called for
help. After a while, a tall thin man tried to get the man to sit up.
Every time he pulled him into a sitting position, the man fell over.
Then he dragged the man by his feet a short distance. There was a
huge crowd on that side of the tracks. No one else came to help.
Now the tall man lifted the other one to a standing position and
held him up and tried to move away from the tracks with him. They
made poor progress but eventually moved out of sight. Suddenly a
Metro employee came by. Someone assures her that the situation is

under control. It is clearly not. She goes away. I think of Elias Canetti, his writing in *Crowds and Power*, the kinds of things people do or don't do when they are part of a group; things they do or not when they are on their own.

Now I remember that a week ago I drove through a community I haven't seen for forty years. Why did I go there? What did I hope to find there? I had tutored babies, helped them in their language development so they would have a better chance once they got to public school. When the Civil Rights Movement got into full sway, some in that community didn't want me to come there anymore. Now I drive up and down the little streets. Some of the original wooden houses still stand. What had I hoped to see? The little girl I'd worked with who became the "teacher" in the community? Her aunt who took care of her and taught me so much about their lives? The person I'd been all those years ago?

Now I remember a story a friend told me about sitting down on a stone bench in the subway station, annoyed that a man beside her took up so much space, stretched out across the whole bench. Then she suddenly thought he might be dead. . . .

Now we have pieces of stories. I don't yet know what relationship they bear to one another. I'll have to figure that out after a while. But I'm beginning to be interested. Time to go back and write again, not editing what I've written so far but to explore what else might be hovering there. And that might point me to some core that could unite all these pieces. So I look briefly at what I've written to see what a new starting place might be. One of the first words I wrote when I was free-associating was "Deadlines." That word seems resonant: deadlines, dead lines. And it came just after the fear of falling down the escalator. So I am entering a liminal space, going from the world above ground into an underground, known through myth and history to carry certain dangers: see Dante's *Inferno*. See *Orpheus and Eurydice*. I have a fear of falling down into that world, getting there too hurriedly. Without preparation.

So this is a beginning, something that started from a few words. There is more to tell and much more work to be done to turn this into a work of creative nonfiction. But it's something I never intended to write about, didn't even know it was hovering there. Try it yourselves: it's the best work one can imagine.

TRUTH IN NONFICTION

"What Was That Like?" Or,

How to Find a Subject

MADELEINE BLAIS is the Pulitzer Prize–winning author of *The Heart Is an Instrument; In These Girls, Hope Is a Muscle;* and *Uphill Walkers.* She is a professor of journalism at the University of Massachusetts in Amherst.

Whenever I am stumped for something to write about, I recollect the story told by my neighbor in western Massachusetts, Roland Merullo. Shortly after one of his books was published, a newspaper reporter from a big-time paper called to request an interview. The two met for coffee. The reporter went through the usual polite inventory of questions about where Merullo got his ideas (I am always tempted to answer, "Why, at the Idea Depot. Nice men in orange outfits climb long ladders to retrieve them from the top shelves") and about his writing schedule and whether he composes on the computer or makes an outline: the usual softballs. But then the reporter asked something more probing, wittingly or not. He had looked over Merullo's résumé, seen the places that had shaped him, and he wanted to know what it had been like for Merullo to grow up in Revere, Massachusetts, a honky-tonk sort of place, a heavily blue-collar, very Italian suburb of Boston with its own dog track, and then to leave it and spend his high school years at Phillips Exeter Academy in New Hampshire, known as a breeding ground of the ruling class and the setting of the novel *A Separate Peace*, where no more than sixteen students per class sit at a round table with a teacher. One place is rationed and ragtag, but at least it has yeast; the other posh and cosseted, but not the same kind of edge.

"What was that like?" the interviewer wanted to know, and Merullo found himself feeling defensive. It was as if he had to choose, as if one place had been good, one bad, and there could be no middle ground.

Merullo's answer was curt and evasive. He mumbled something unmemorable and then steered the conversation back toward the new book, about which his feelings were more certain. Later, he saw his discomfort as a gift, a sign that the reporter had tapped into something complicated, something worth revisiting and confronting in a deeper way.

Ever since I became familiar with this story, I began to examine the times when I give a short answer to a question when I know a longer one would be more honest. I call these "Merullo moments." Anytime you are in a similar position and a question fills you with that rush of ambiguity and confusion, you have, at least potentially, entered rich territory for your writing. It doesn't matter what the question is so much as how it hits you, and if it hits you in the deepest part of yourself, at the intersection of memory and misgiving, of Private Property and No Trespassing signs, it just might be the subject of your next essay, or even book.

A few years ago, I used this technique consciously when I wrote my own memoir, exploring in depth the questions that strangers had felt entitled to ask me all during my childhood.

EXAMPLES

"How old were you when your father died?"

"Do you remember him?"

"Did your mother ever remarry?"

"Why not?"

The short answers are five, maybe, no, and ask her.
The long answers occupy 264 pages of a book called *Uphill Walkers*.

EXERCISE

Make a list of three questions for which there is a short answer and a long one and write out long responses. Sample recent questions students in my memoir class report having grappled with: What was it like . . .

1. growing up in the United States with Iranian parents?

2. spending your childhood in Alaska?

3. dancing competitively from first grade through high school?

4. to lose your father to suicide when you were eight years old?

5. to have a father who is a famous right-wing talk show host, who communicates with you in code on air, always with a negative message?

6. to grow up with eight kids in your family?

7. to pass yourself off as Latina when you are not?

8. to go back to college at the age of fifty-five?

9. to be the mother of twins?

10. to play a Division One sport?

Merullo's long answer became a brilliant essay entitled "My Two Heavens," in which he captured what was wondrous about both places and what he lost by leaving Revere for high school, but also what he gained. It was measured and elegant, nonjudgmental and nuanced. It took its time, and got it right.

Afterward, in the cool light of reflection, you, too, can take his lead and ponder the deep questions and at last give an answer that is as expansive and as forthright and as meticulous as you wish from the bully pulpit of your own prose.

LISA KNOPP

Perhapsing

LISA KNOPP is the author of four collections of essays: *Interior Places; The Nature of Home; Flight Dreams: A Life in the Midwestern Landscape;* and *Field of Vision*. She is currently working on *Three Rivers*, essays about the Mississippi, Missouri, and Platte rivers. Knopp is an associate professor of English at the University of Nebraska-Omaha.

At some point, all of us come to a roadblock or dead end, a spot in our creative nonfiction where we don't have access to the facts we need to tell our story or to sustain our reflection with depth and fullness. If only it was ethical to just make something up, we might think, to just elaborate a bit on what we know. But of course then, we wouldn't be writing creative nonfiction. It might appear that our only choice in such cases is to either abandon the topic for a lack of information or write it without fully developing it.

In *Woman Warrior*, Maxine Hong Kingston offers another choice. In the first essay, "No Name Woman," Kingston explains that when she started menstruating, her mother told her a brief cautionary tale about her father's sister in China, who became pregnant even though her husband had been away for years. On the night that the baby born, villagers raided the family's house and farm. The aunt gave birth in a pigsty, and then killed herself and her baby by jumping into the well from which the family drank. Kingston's father was so shamed by his sister's behavior that Kingston was forbidden to ever mention her in his presence.

But because Kingston believed that her aunt's ghost was waiting by the well, perhaps trying to pull her niece down as a substitute, Kingston needed a deeper, fuller understanding of her aunt's life. The only information Kingston had, however, was the bare-bones story that her mother had told her. So, Kingston chose to speculate an interior life for her aunt. I call this "perhapsing." Notice in the following passage from "No Name Woman" how Kingston uses "perhapsing" to imagine an identity for the man who impregnated her aunt:

"*Perhaps* she had encountered him in the fields or on the mountain where the daughters-in-law collected fuel. Or *perhaps* he first noticed her in the marketplace. He was not a stranger because the village housed no strangers. She had to have dealings with him other than sex. *Perhaps* he worked in an adjoining field, or he sold her the cloth for the dress she sewed and wore. His demand must have surprised, then terrified her. She obeyed him; she always did as she was told." [Italics are mine.]

The word "perhaps" cues the reader that the information that Kingston is imparting is not factual but speculative. Kingston doesn't need to use "perhaps" in every sentence because we can see that one "perhapsing" leads to another. We can also see that when Kingston presents facts ("He was not a stranger because the village housed no strangers. She had to have dealings with his other than sex."), she does not begin those sentences with a "perhaps."

Elsewhere in the essay, Kingston uses other words and phrases to alert the reader when she's moving from fact to conjecture:

"*It could very well have been*, however, that my aunt did not take subtle enjoyment of her friend, but, a wild woman, kept rollicking company. Imagining her free with sex doesn't fit, though."

"*She may have been* unusually beloved, the precious only daughter, spoiled and mirror gazing because of the affection the family lavished on her."

By perhapsing, Kingston presents motives, actions, justifications, and the specific details that add the richness, texture, and complexity absent in her source's account without crossing the line into fiction. Kingston believed that by remaining silent about her desperate and defiant ancestor, she was participating in her aunt's punishment. By perhapsing, Kingston freed both herself and her aunt from the traditions that bound them.

EXERCISE

Take a passage in one of your essays that could be made richer and fuller through the use of speculation. If, for instance, the person you're profiling can't or won't say why he started playing the banjo when his wife left him, "perhaps" some likely motives. If a stranger said something curious and cryptic to you, "perhaps" some possible meanings for his/her words. If you and your family don't know why your grandmother inserted such a peculiar clause into her will, "perhaps" some plausible motives. Other words and phrases that you may use besides "perhaps" include *maybe, suppose, if, what if, might/could have, possibly, imagine, wonder, perchance.*

JENNY BOULLY

Breaking from "Fact" in Essay Writing

JENNY BOULLY is the author of *The Book of Beginnings and Endings;
[one love affair]**; and *The Body: An Essay.* She teaches at Columbia
College Chicago.

In the spring of 2006, I had the opportunity to hear essayist John
D'Agata read from his yet-to-be-released second book. At the
end of the reading, when audience members should ask, and
are invited to ask, the author about the author's work, audience
members instead wanted to hear D'Agata's views about the recent
controversy surrounding James Frey's *A Million Little Pieces*. A certain audience member disagreed with D'Agata. She insisted that
Frey had done something terribly wrong and that writers of "nonfiction" should stick to the facts. D'Agata responded by asking why
should essayists have to live, artistically, within the confines of rules
that say what they can and cannot do? Why should essayists have
to live within a fence, he asked, and moreover an electrified fence?
Although his rebuttal was humorous, it was also quite true: one
wrong move, and the essayist or writer of nonfiction can be killed
by a reading public that has misconceived notions of what it is to
be an essayist.

It seems as if we are living in an era when, more than ever, the
public is persecuting artists. The public wants to hold these artists
accountable; the public, it seems, wants less art and more "fact." I
put quotes around the word fact, as I do "nonfiction," because, as

a writer of what people term "nonfictions," I can hardly say that I understand just what "fact" is or what "nonfictions" are. I do know, however, that the most difficult part of my job as an instructor of experimental essay writing is teaching my students how to break away from the belief that essay writers must live with and abide by strict rules, rules that artists are allowed to break without having to answer to anyone.

I always remind my students of the beautiful beginning of Annie Dillard's *Pilgrim at Tinker Creek*, and the horror an audience somewhere at some conference expressed when Annie Dillard said that she didn't own a cat.

When I took my first poetry workshop as a freshman in college, my instructor told us that in poetry, we lie to tell the truth. When essayists "invent," however, their writing is seen as a criminal act. In many ways, the essayist forbids herself invention, metaphor, or embellishment because she "wants to get the story right."

How do we own, if we ever do, our experiences, and more importantly for essayists, how do our experiences own us?

Emerson, fascinated by having heard a panharmonicon, wrote that essay writing ought to be like a panharmonicon; of the essay, he writes: "Here everything is admissible—philosophy, ethics, divinity, criticism, poetry, humor, fun, mimicry, anecdotes, jokes, ventriloquism— all the breath and versatility of the most liberal conversation, highest and lowest personal topics: all are permitted, and all may be combined into one speech."

How is it, then, that "essay" came to be associated with writing that is not allowed to be versatile? How is it that when most of us think of "essay," we think of writing where many things are not admissible?

The following exercise is intended to help the essayist not necessarily disengage from facts, as facts are fascinating subjects for essays, but to foster and encourage thinking "outside the fence."

EXERCISE

Dream-life, the daydreaming-life, and the imagined-life can sometimes be experienced so profoundly that they feel real to us. Some of our thoughts, when they approach a frequency that can be called "obsessive," may be the perfect "experience" to write about for this exercise. The challenge of this assignment is to accept these experiences as something real and to write about them as if they were real. You can write a dream journal, but try not to ever mention that what you're writing are dreams! You can move in and out of dreams in your essay. You can write a scene or outcome that you keep imagining in your head. For example, do you often think about getting something you really want or, conversely, getting something you don't want? You may want your obsessive joyful thoughts to mingle with your obsessive painful thoughts. Whatever you ultimately choose to write about and however you want to write about these "experiences," never point out in your essay that these are experiences lived outside of the physical world. The challenge here is to let this essay live in that physical world without your challenging its validity or right to exist as real.

Letting the Experience Choose You:
The First Step in Writing the Personal Essay

SUSAN M. TIBERGHIEN, an American writer in Geneva, Switzerland, is the author of three memoirs, and the recent acclaimed nonfiction book *One Year to a Writing Life: Twelve Lessons to Deepen Every Writer's Art and Craft*. Tiberghien teaches at graduate programs, C. G. Jung Centers, and writers' conferences for the International Women's Writing Guild. She directs the Geneva Writers' Group and Conferences.

Writing the personal essay is both inventive and fulfilling. Inventive, because the writer becomes storyteller and poet. And fulfilling because in this artful crafting of personal experience, the writer shares its meaning with the reader. Phillip Lopate describes the personal essay as a conversation between the writer and the reader, "one individual speaking to another who wants to listen." The writer shares an experience that resonates for both the writer and the reader. The question is "Which experience?"

EXERCISE

In my workshops, I teach four steps to writing the personal essay.

1. First, choose a personal experience. Montaigne, named the father of the essay, wrote in the sixteenth century: "Every-

thing has one hundred parts and one hundred faces, I take one of them . . ." So choose one experience and write it down.

2. The second step would be to show the experience. Dramatize it, in a second draft. Think about the elements of storytelling: specific details of setting and characters, dialogue, tension, revelation.

3. The third step would be to polish your words, highlighting the meaning of the experience, in a third draft. Think about the elements of poetry: imagery, rhythm and sound, compression.

4. Then put it aside. Let it gestate. Rilke writes in his *Letters to a Young Poet*: "Everything is gestation and then bringing forth." After a while, go back to it for a last draft.

Here we will look at only the first step, with the exercise "Letting the Experience Choose You." How do we take one of the hundred parts, of the hundred faces? How de we choose an experience? You don't choose, you let the experience choose you. Ask yourself, what experience wishes to be shared? Sit quietly, close your eyes, go within. Try to empty your mind and wait for the experience to come on its own. Something you experienced—a person you met, a place you visited, an event, an insight, an emotion—something that happened recently or something that happened many years ago. Take your time. When the memory surfaces, hold it a moment in your imagination. Like a photographer, imagine taking a picture of it. Focus and take a snapshot.

If you are in a workshop, share the experience with the person sitting next to you. First one and then the other. Are you able to get their attention? If you start too early in the experience, you lose the momentum. If you give too many details, you lose the attention of the listener. If this happens, start again. Go within and wait for another memory to surface. All of us have experiences that resonate. When they come into our attention on their own, these are the ones to share. These are the ones that take us from the personal to the universal.

If you are not in a workshop, then jot down the experience in a short paragraph. Try to capture it in a few sentences without thinking about it too much. Next take a breath, stretch, and reread what you have written. Is there something there? Does it catch your attention? Are you inspired to continue writing about it? If not, start anew. What experience, what memory, calls to you?

Once you have caught the experience, or rather once the experience has caught you, start to write it. You are not yet crafting (steps 2 and 3), you are freewriting, letting the experience lead you. Do not erase, do not cross out. Follow the words. The experience may shift and lead you elsewhere. Write one or two pages, for ten minutes. This is the first draft of your personal essay.

Here is an example of how this exercise works. Several years back, I noted my seven-year-old grandson's disappointment at the train station south of Paris where I was coming for a visit. He was hoping to arrive in time to see the train. Instead the train was early and when he arrived there was only his grandmother standing alone on the platform. I wanted to imitate the train's whistle for him to make him happy, but I realized that trains don't whistle in France. This experience often surfaced when I sat down to write. It seemed too trivial for the subject of a personal essay. Yet it kept calling, "Write about me, write about me." Finally when I let the words flow out on paper, I found myself writing not about my grandson's disappointment but about my longing for that American train whistle, the whistle I had not heard for over thirty years in France. About the longing for home.

These are the experiences that will touch the reader because they have touched us. Writers and readers, we share the same core of humanity, of universality. As writers we learn to be receptive to those experiences that tap into this core. Our personal essays then become conversations with the reader, "one individual speaking to another who wants to listen." Gifts to both the writer and the reader.

SHARA McCALLUM

The Collage Essay

SHARA McCALLUM is the author of two books of poetry, *Songs of Thieves* and *The Water Between Us*. Her personal essays have appeared in journals such as *The Antioch Review, Creative Nonfiction, and Witness,* and elsewhere. She lives with her family in central Pennsylvania, where she teaches creative writing and directs the Stadler Center for Poetry at Bucknell University.

The *Oxford English Dictionary* defines collage as "an abstract form of art in which photographs, pieces of paper, newspaper cuttings, string, etc., are placed in juxtaposition and glued to the pictorial surface; such a work of art." The history of the form, or at least references to it in English, begins in the Modernist period, and collage has been associated with such Surrealist painters as Picasso. Another example, and one to which I am especially partial, is the work of Romare Bearden. In its simplest form, collage can be practiced by anyone and is often thought of as a "cut and paste" technique in which different *parts* are selected and assembled by the artist to make a *whole*.

My own introduction to making collages took place in my early childhood. My mother saved magazines (and everything else); cutting images, words, and phrases out of magazines to make "pictures" was something my sisters and I often did. For me, it was the only visual artistic expression for which I remember feeling I had any kind of a knack.

Collage—and this is important to remember when considering

whether we can ever write a "collage"—is a visual medium. This means that the simultaneity of the visual field, the possibility of viewers ("readers") making connections based on the point at which they enter the field and how they scan the canvas, is lost to the writer.

Still, to use collage as a writer is to map onto your essay (or poem, as I've used this technique also in writing poems) the semblance of continuities and discontinuities associated with the art form. As well, using collage as a tool for drafting (and revising) work allows meaning to gather by the *relation* of things presented, as opposed to locating it primarily within the narrative or the implied logical progression of incidents, ideas, and images offered in an essay. In this way, then, the collage essay is a consciously meandering form of play within an already meandering and playful form.

There are many ways to approach writing the collage essay. What's more important to me than providing the steps I do below is to encourage the idea that you might use collage as a way to capture the tidy-messiness, the orchestrated-disorder inherent to relating and understanding one's own experience—and that you might discover something about your essay's "subject" as you assemble the essay, rather than before you've written it.

In the interest of offering an exercise that can be followed, here is one way you might approach the task.

EXERCISE

Write about an object (or more than one object), preferably one in front of you. Be descriptive but allow the object to take on whatever symbolic meaning it might. If your writing leads you to a memory or an incident connected to the object, write about that as well.

Write about at least five separate incidents (not events but rather moments) from your life that feel somehow related. If these vignettes are from different periods in time in your life, all the better.

Write about a place (or more than one place) that holds sway over you. You don't have to understand why this place feels important, and in fact it might be better if the place is one to which you are inexplicably drawn. Again, be descriptive but allow other elements of your imaginative life to take over as they may.

Write three different declarative statements that feel true to you. For example, define big ideas (God, race, sex, death, etc.).

Write three different questions to which you genuinely don't possess the answer.

After you've finished with each step, use a scissors to cut out each part and then arrange these in different orders so that they play off of one another. In order to see the different possibilities for your essay, it's important to physically cut out and arrange the parts (not just use your Word program's "cut" and "paste" options). For a canvas, I like to use the floor of a room so I can stand above the different strips of paper before me and easily move pieces around.

You may choose not to include each part (I usually don't) and you may find that there is too much discontinuity in what you've written for your taste, in which case you can write more to figure out the relationship between the different parts you have so far. In any event, I hope what results will be the draft of an essay that will surprise you with what it has to say.

DINTY W. MOORE

Just Add Water:
An Experimental Mini-Essay in a Can

DINTY MOORE is the author of *Between Panic and Desire; The Accidental Buddhist; Toothpick Men; The Emperor's Virtual Clothes*; and the writing guide *The Truth of the Matter: Art and Craft in Creative Nonfiction*. He teaches creative nonfiction at Ohio University.

Many writers habitually compose memoir-based nonfiction as if someone had once ruled "all childhood stories must be told in chronological order." Though there is obvious utility to relating events in the order in which they occurred, this tidy approach can also be very limiting. Often, it is the juxtaposition of events that gives one's childhood memories meaning, and sometimes the odd juxtaposition becomes a gathering place for discovery and fresh insight. Logic, in other words, is not the only way into the truth.

The following exercise *forces* incongruity. It also teaches the importance of detail—nouns and verbs, specific moments and particular things.

Finally, the exercise encourages the writer to trust "chance" to a certain extent. Seasoned writers often marvel over some element or another that just seemed to show up, unbidden, in their writing, yet ended up being alive, surprising, and richer than where the author was headed. This, of course, is the unconscious reaching up and through the rational mind, but at times it seems random and capricious. If some oddity of detail or language appears in your writing, and it works, then keep it there, and be thankful. You don't have to know why!

The first draft that results from the eight steps listed below may result in a finished experimental mini-essay. I have assigned this to students who subsequently published the (revised and polished) version. But at the very least, it almost always generates rich and fruitful raw material.

(Important note: As hard as I know this will be to do, this exercise works best if you *do not* read ahead. Don't read step 2 until you've assembled your index cards and pencil. Don't read step 3 until you've completed step 2. Trust me, it works.)

EXERCISE

Large index cards are best for this exercise, but they may not always be available, so separate sheets of paper will work as well. This can be done alone, but works even better with writing partners or small groups. You may want to set a timer—give yourself about five minutes for each step.

1. Assemble four oversized index cards (or four separate sheets of paper).

2. On the first card: <u>Describe a smell from your past</u>. Don't worry whether or not it is a significant or important smell; all that matters is that it remains in your "memory bank" ten or twenty or thirty years later. Describe the smell, the quality of the odor. Is it sour or sweet, smoky or clean, sharp or dull? Does it remind you of anything? Keep this to around four or five sentences.

3. On the second card: <u>Describe part of someone you love</u>, but just a *part*. Stick to one physical aspect—your mother's hair, your aunt Lula's elbows, your little brother's teeth. Be specific. Instead of "Dad had rough hands," describe the texture of the palms, the shape of the fingers, the bruises or cuts, the caked oil in the seams. No more than six sentences.

4. On the third card: <u>Pick a quote from your past, something you heard all the time when you were younger</u>. It can be significant—a parent's correction or sharp criticism—or seemingly insignificant—a dumb joke your older brother made every time you sat down to eat chili. It can be anything at all. The only requirement is that you heard it often and that it remains in your memory bank, for whatever reason. Do NOT illuminate, describe, or elucidate. Just give us the quote:

   "Drink your milk. You want to have strong bones, don't you?"

5. On the fourth card: <u>Construct a disjointed list of thirty words, primarily nouns, or nouns with some slight modification</u>. Each of these words or phrases describes a remembered something in your past. For instance, my list looks like this: "Ringo. Sled. Uncle Clem's wooden leg. Cooked cabbage. Howdy Doody. Bugs. Sycamore tree." In this instance, it is *not* important to give enough information for the reader to fully understand. Just make your list. No phrase more than four words long. Thirty words. (It often works best to write forty-five words and then cross some out.)

   When you have completed the five steps above, take the four cards and shuffle them in random order.

7. At the top of each card, write a number—1 through 4.

8. To the first card, add this title: "Why I Am Who I Am."

9. You have now written an experimental essay, in collage form. Read it out loud, including the title, and the numbers at the top of each card. Marvel at the unexpected connections and odd logic.

MAUREEN MURDOCK

Finding Truth

MAUREEN MURDOCK is a psychotherapist, writing teacher, and author whose work has been translated into a dozen languages. She is the author of the bestselling book *The Heroine's Journey*, as well as the newly revised *Fathers' Daughters: Breaking the Ties That Bind*; *Unreliable Truth: On Memoir and Memory*; *Spinning Inward: Using Guided Imagery with Children*; and *The Heroine's Journey Workbook*. She has just completed a memoir about madness and addiction in the family and teaches memoir writing at the San Francisco Writing Salon and UCLA Extensions Writers' Program.

Adaptation is from my book Unreliable Truth: On Memoir and Memory. *(Seal Press, 2003).*

In her essay in *The Anatomy of Memory*, Toni Morrison writes that the deliberate act of remembering is a form of willed creation. Few of us aside from historians try to find out what actually happened during a particular event, because, quite frankly, we don't have time or the desire to research. We dwell instead on the way the event appeared to us in our memory and why it appeared in that particular way.

Memory is a way of creating one's identity. And that's exactly what a memoirist does when she chooses a particular memory for illumination—she re-creates her sense of identity. The memoirist takes a slice of life, a remembered image, and chews on it, munching slowly if not perhaps deliberately, to extract as much nutrition—as much meaning—from it as possible. She does more than relive the experience; she tries to make sense of the relationship between the remembered image and the feelings contained in the image that have caused her to safely store it away for later review.

The job of the memoirist is to find her truth, not so much to determine the factual accuracy of what happened; that is history, a testimony, perhaps even an interesting tale. The memoirist, instead, both recounts an event and muses upon it. What meaning, what value do I attach to how my life has unfolded? How did this happen, how did that happen? Not why did this happen. That is explored in psychotherapy, which is not my focus here. However, finding out the truth of what happened can certainly challenge one's sense of self.

EXERCISE

1. In order to choose a remembered event, start by writing down the first fifteen years of your life in fifteen minutes. Set a timer and write as quickly as possible; don't take your pen off the paper. This is called a "freewrite." Just write whatever comes to mind in whatever order it appears. Don't worry at this point about punctuation or paragraphs. Just follow your pen. Don't censor and don't judge. Don't ask, "Did this really happen?" Assume that it did.

2. When you have finished, read what you have written and pick one incident you want to learn more about. Circle it. You may have two or three events you'd like to explore, but for the purpose of this exercise, choose the one that holds the most interest for you. Now focus on the memory. Notice how you enter the memory. What are the colors you remember, the sounds, the smells, the tastes, the textures, your feelings? What is unusual about this incident? What is novel? What is

humorous? Start with one image and use all of your senses to reexperience it. Write that memory with as much sensual detail as you can capture. Allow the reader to enter the scene with you. Write for fifteen minutes.

3. After you recount the details of the memory and read what you have written, notice what the underlying story is. Is there tension in the piece? Is there a pivotal event? What is the emotional essence of your remembrance? What does this incident reveal about you or another person involved in the memory? What do you now know about yourself that you didn't know before writing this piece? How do you feel about that? What more do you want to find out? Spend a few moments writing down your thoughts about the memory you've captured.

JUDITH KITCHEN

Worth 1,000 Words

JUDITH KITCHEN is the author of two collections of essays, a novel, and a book of criticism. She lives in Port Townsend, Washington, and serves on the faculty of the Rainier Writing Workshop Low-Residency MFA at Pacific Lutheran University.

A photograph is both a pseudo-presence and a token of absence. . . .
—SUSAN SONTAG, *On Photography*

Traditionally, photographs have been used in nonfiction as confirmation. Placed in the middle of the biography, they confirm events, give face to people we've met in print. Scattered throughout the memoir, they attest to the truth of what we're being told. This exercise is intended to move beyond the realm of confirmation, making the photograph a part of the text itself.

They say a photograph is worth a thousand words. Well, this exercise forces you to cut out those thousand words and find another thousand words that cannot be replaced by the image itself. Your job, then, is contemplation. Speculation. Meditation. You must surround this photograph with the thoughts and feelings that well up in you as you examine it for what it might reveal—about yourself, your memories, your assumptions, what you know you simply cannot know. You must probe its contents, and then move beyond its boundaries, thinking about what it doesn't say, what isn't in the frame.

EXERCISE

The exercise is simple. Begin with a photograph—one that has some personal meaning: maybe a photo of your mother before she was married; your grandfather standing next to his father, a man you never knew; a place where you used to go on vacation; an album you found at a garage sale, a stranger's life sold for a dollar; your childhood pet; yourself at the age of seven, your lost tooth grinning up at you; an odd snapshot from the box on the shelf, someone you vaguely remember, but who?

Now come at the photograph from many angles. Look at it as a physical object. What is there? Look at its subject. Who inhabits its spaces? Examine the emotions it evokes. Ask it questions. What is your relationship to this scene? Who is taking the photograph? And don't forget to observe what is not there—sometimes absence is what it is all about.

Keep in mind that you may know the people in it, or the story behind it, but that your reader does not come to the photograph with any prior knowledge. Your job is to make it matter to readers as much as it matters to you—and in the way that it matters to you. You can write *about* the photograph, but not mere description, since you must keep in mind the thousand words that the photograph could make redundant. If you want to tell its story, you will need to find words that do it justice. Bring to your reader what looking will not provide—the smells, the sounds, the texture of the day. You can write *from* the photograph, using it as a starting point, expanding on it until it comes alive for the reader, as it has for you. You can write *to* the photograph, speaking directly to the person there (even to your earlier self), or you can write it into being, telling its story right up to the moment of the camera's click. You can write *around* the photograph, or comment *on* it, moving in and out of its physical presence, making it a central part of your written text—necessary to it, and yet somehow removed from it as well.

Put in enough descriptive words that, even without the photo, the reader would "see" its sepia tint, the color of rusty water; or the odd angle of the shadow on the old man's face; or the serrated edge of the white frame that cuts across your uncle Henry's silhouette, stranding him half-in, half-out of the scene—as he seems to be in your memories, only half present, kind of ghostly. But move beyond description into the "tone" of the moment. Capture how it felt to slide down that slide, how high it seemed as you climbed those steps that, now that you look at it, was really not very high at all. The exhilarating, free-from-adults playground world. Wonder about your mother as a young woman, before you were born: What were her dreams? Where did they go? Why did she cut her river of hair? Give that stranger a life he may never have lived, but one that connects him to you in the odd, imaginative space that exists between you now that you own a piece of his life. Think about what is gone, how things have changed, what the photo holds for all time. Think about the nature of time.

What this exercise does is unlock your meditative voice and give it a focus. It allows you to step in and out of the "present" of your piece, saying "perhaps," and "I wonder if," and "Now it seems as though." By directing your own attention to the object itself—the photograph—you become a narrating sensibility; in other words, you find a "voice." The reader comes to know you by the way you have been thinking, and that is the very essence of nonfiction essays and memoir.

Find just the right title—something to give what you've written a context, a position or a stance from which you are looking. The final thing you should do is decide whether or not your words actually need the photograph to complete the text; it may just be that you no longer need it at all—that you've written the thousand words that are worth one photograph.

KATHRYN RHETT

Crucial Events

KATHRYN RHETT is the author of *Near Breathing*, a memoir, and editor of the anthology *Survival Stories: Memoirs of Crisis*. She has published personal essays in *Harvard Review, Michigan Quarterly Review*, and *River Teeth*, and elsewhere. She teaches creative writing as an associate professor at Gettysburg College, and in the low-residency MFA program at Queens University of Charlotte.

In my parents' generation, people say they remember exactly what they were doing when they heard the news that President Kennedy was shot in 1963. I always found that interesting, an event so important to the entire population of the United States that it literally seemed to have stopped people in their tracks. Born in 1962, I grew up being conscious of many crucial events, of course. But until September 11, 2001, I didn't experience any single event as one of collective crisis for the country.

On that day, I was teaching memoir class, at 1:10 in the afternoon. Many of us had just spent the past hour or so watching graphic television footage on a large screen in the library, and I couldn't imagine how class could go on as planned. Yet I had to convene the class. There were rumors of a plane crash at Camp David, twelve miles away, and campus guidelines had just been issued instructing us to "maintain normalcy" and encourage students to stay on campus, as they might not be able to "travel out of the immediate area." In class, I saw rows of sober faces, and when

I asked about their mornings, there were tears, then silence. So I asked my students what they wanted to do—and they wanted to hold the workshop we had all prepared for the night before. They wanted a sense of normalcy and security. Many of them lived near Manhattan and had parents who worked in the city. That day, I did not ask them to write anything, but I did a few weeks later.

The next year, and the next, I asked my students to write accounts of that day, an assignment that engaged them all and resulted in powerful narratives. But then I stopped. Enough already. In the spring of 2006, in my personal essay class, though, a student happened to write an essay that included a description of September 11, 2001, along with the statement, "That was the day everything changed" (Kathryn Holly Bruns, for the record, Gettysburg class of '06). Considering this statement in workshop, the class erupted into discussion as to its veracity. I run a very focused workshop. But this discussion wanted to happen, and I let it go on for a few minutes. At the end of our next class, I assigned them to write for ten minutes, giving a detailed narrative of the day, and then reflecting on the question, Is that the day everything changed?

Several students developed their exercises into essays, and they were a powerful mix of narrative and reflection. Why not write your account of this day, before the details fade?

This exercise connects to another one, called Five Points on a Line, that I use in memoir class. Students are asked to make a personal time line, with just five important events. I ask them to include events that were important in determining how they see themselves, or as changing their way of thinking (versus what we consider to be important public events, such as winning the big game, or graduating from school). Then I ask them to write a paragraph about each of these events.

EXERCISE

Write about the day of September 11, 2001, using as much sensory description and remembered dialogue as possible. Where were you when you heard the news? Who else was there? Describe what you saw, heard, touched, tasted, and smelled. Try to remember that actual day, before all of the facts were available.

Then, reflect on the impact of the day, now that more is known. Did everything change that day? Or did some aspect of life change?

The events of 9/11 are crucial in our national history, and they may or may not feel crucial to you as well. After writing about 9/11, consider the crucial events in your personal history. If you had to choose five, and only five, events that contributed to your identity, represented a crossroads, presented a lifelong complication, or changed your way of thinking, what would they be? Plot them on a time line, with dates and brief descriptions. Now write a paragraph about each one.

Maybe the 9/11 paragraph, or one of your five points paragraphs, will lead to an essay or memoir. Writing time is precious. Why not write about what is vital to you?

RENE STEINKE

A Past Embarrassment

RENE STEINKE is the author of the novel *Holy Skirts*, which was a 2005 National Book Award finalist. She is also the author of the novel *The Fires*. Her nonfiction has appeared in *Bookforum*; the *New York Times; Vogue; O, the Oprah Magazine*; and in anthologies. She teaches writing and literature at Fairleigh Dickinson University and lives in Brooklyn.

W hat's the most embarrassing thing that ever happened to you?" asked a friend one night at a dinner party. We were an intimate group, and the stories that followed were both hilarious and sad, often illuminating a piece of a person's personality that I had either not noticed or not understood before. Often, when writing creative nonfiction, students have trouble finding the significance in incidents from their own lives, partly because they're protecting some image of themselves. Stories of embarrassment are entertaining (when they work) because the teller allows himself to play the fool—that's the given. Often that makes for more insightful and engaging prose for at least two reasons: (1) something usually HAPPENS when you get embarrassed, often something funny, and (2) the storyteller becomes interested in juxtapositions, wild inconsistencies, and ironies, rather than "lessons" or pristine portraits of themselves.

EXERCISE

1. Write about something embarrassing that happened to you in the past. Be as objective as possible, almost as if you were writing about someone else. Use as many concrete details as you can summon, EVEN DETAILS THAT SEEM TRIVIAL AT FIRST.

2. When you're finished, ask yourself: Why exactly was that incident so mortifying? Why do I remember it? LOOK AT WHAT YOU WROTE AND SEE IF YOU CAN FIND LINKS TO OTHER FORCES THAT WERE AT PLAY IN YOUR LIFE AT THE TIME. SEE IF YOU CAN SEE ANY CONNECTION TO YOUR LIFE NOW. WRITE ABOUT THESE CONNECTIONS.

    In my own work, I've found this strategy helpful.

    FINDING THE HUMOR IN A PAST EMBARRASSMENT ALLOWS FOR THE DISTANCE I MIGHT NEED TO MAKE SENSE OF THE INCIDENT.

    In "What Coco Ate," an essay I wrote for the anthology *Dog Culture*, I list the grotesque assortment of things my boyfriend's dog ate when I took him for walks, and my at first uncomfortable relationship with this creature. In "Lone Star," an essay I wrote for *Vogue*, I discuss something I rarely if ever mention to my adult friends, the fact that I was a teenaged Wranglerette (a kind of half-time dancer at football games) and how this experience made me, for a time, obsessed with a kind of overblown, gaudy beauty. In both cases, creating distance between my past and present selves helped me to find the drama, but it also allowed me to see how the awkwardness was usually a sign of something more profound beneath the story.

PHILIP GERARD

Beyond a Shadow of a Doubt

PHILIP GERARD is the author of three novels, four books of nonfiction, eleven documentary scripts, and numerous essays and short stories. He chairs the Department of Creative Writing at the University of North Carolina Wilmington and coedits *Chautauqua*, the literary journal of Chautauqua Institution, in New York.

As teachers and students of creative nonfiction writing, we often talk glibly about "sticking to the facts," an honorable intention. But we can too easily assume those facts. That is, many of the things we think we know for sure turn out to be untrue—they didn't happen that way at all. Or more frequently they are unprovable—we simply don't have the evidence to say for sure that a certain fact *is* a fact, rather than merely a likely surmise based on incomplete information.

So I like to start my students out the way I start out whenever I take on any new project—as a reporter. Putting aside all preconceptions and received wisdom, all the stories we've heard from family historians and all the local myths, what do we really know for sure? And just as important, *how* do we know it?

We discuss levels of reliability in evidence. Take a simple example. How do we know a certain deceased person is buried in a particular place? Well, there's a tombstone, a student will say. Yes, someone else will remind us, but aren't there cases in which tombstones were erected over empty graves? And aren't tombstones sometimes moved without the body being exhumed? And in earlier centuries, didn't "resurrection men"—we would call them grave robbers—sometimes steal bodies and sell them to medical schools and doctors?

And what if there isn't a headstone at all?

We finally agree that a tombstone is at best a likely indicator—more reliable in some contexts than in others. A contemporaneous map of the cemetery that indicates that the grave we have identified by its tombstone is indeed where it was located when the interment occurred; perhaps a trustworthy witness who knew the deceased and left some testimony; a photograph of the funeral showing close relatives of the deceased, witnessing by their presence that they believe that is the person's final resting place. But short of exhuming the body and carrying out DNA tests—which may themselves be inconclusive—we can never actually know for sure. We can be fairly sure, maybe sure enough to count it as true, but as writers we need to recognize that we are bridging that last little gap between the absolutely provable truth and the likely truth with a leap of faith. Faith based in logic and experience and probability, but faith nonetheless. And a good part of our reliability as writers will rest with our coming to terms with an ethic regarding proof: at what point do we have enough evidence to accept a claim of fact and to present it to the reader as such?

This is not an idle exercise, just as the example above is not trivial: one of the most powerful religions the world has ever known rests on the proposition that a man was not in his grave. Closer to home, scholars cannot agree on where Christopher Columbus is buried. And the FBI is still looking for teamster boss Jimmy Hoffa. In each case, the fact of the matter of a final resting place is crucial to knowing the ending of the real story.

EXERCISE

Using any sources you need: *Try to prove one fact beyond a shadow of a doubt.* The fact should be significant enough to matter for some reason related to the writing. For example, if you are writing a family memoir, try to prove your grandfather did or did not take part in a certain World War II battle while he was in the service. Or try to prove where your mother was on a certain historically significant day. Present your sources and explain why you trust their accuracy.

Remember: an interview relies on memory and is not in itself sufficient proof. Contemporaneous accounts—newspaper stories, diary entries—are more likely to be reliable, but even they can be mistaken or deliberately falsified. So rather than take a single person's words as proof, you need to discover service records, other witnesses, souvenirs, photographs—enough evidence that a reasonable person could agree that your "fact" is true.

What seems at first blush a rather easy exercise usually turns into a maddening and fascinating process, as students turn up one source after another, often contradictory, each spiraling closer to the fact—and also leading to productive detours, as students examine the very nature and reliability of the evidence. Yet in the end there's almost always some necessary leap of faith—the spark crossing between the last absolutely provable thing and the next thing, which is what you set out to prove. It can be a minuscule leap, but the gap it crosses is always an abyss. In an early draft of a book, I once wrote of a young soldier who had fought at the battle for the Rhine in 1945. I had the unit roster, after-action reports, casualty lists for the duration of the war, his service record, and many other corroborating pieces of evidence. Yet he was not there. Turned out he had been wounded in an earlier battle and was recuperating in a Paris hospital. His name never showed up on the casualty lists because in the adrenaline rush of bombardment he never even felt his shrapnel wound until it had become infected the next day, after all the reports had gone in. The next battle generated its own reports, and so he simply fell into the gap between reports.

So we always must face the question in our own writing: How "hard" are facts, and at what point do you accept evidence for a fact as incontrovertible? Is it ever possible to be 100 percent sure of a thing? And how do we write "nonfiction" based on such a shifting, elusive reality? The answer we come up with—our reporter's ethic—in an important way also defines our aesthetic.

REBECCA BLEVINS FAERY

Creativity and Authority

REBECCA BLEVINS FAERY directs the First Year Writing Program at the Massachusetts Institute of Technology in Cambridge. She also teaches advanced courses in creative nonfiction and publishes essays in a variety of journals. She is working on a collection of essays—a kind of collage memoir—of the Vietnam War era.

A specter haunts the creative nonfiction classroom: the *personal*. Students often find it so liberating to be told they don't have to write in a stilted "academic" voice—you know what I mean, that voice that has no body, that *is* nobody, that speaks, or pretends to, from *out there*, or worse, *up there*—that they fall into the trap of writing only and obsessively about themselves. Maybe it's a pendulum swing, but it's part of the creative nonfiction learning curve, as I see it, to get the pendulum to move off that far point of writing mired hopelessly and solipsistically in the self and back to engagement with the world, which is the real work of the writer. Such engagement can of course take many forms and be expressed in many ways, including the strictly personal essay. But writers of nonfiction turn their attention to everything from the moon and stars to the makeup of the dust under their feet, and when the subject of your scrutiny is something you need to find out about, some serious investigating is in order. That does not, though, mean leaving behind your own voice and personality. That's the challenge of writing creative nonfiction of this sort—encouraging and helping you to do writing that takes up a subject that matters

93

to you, a subject on which you have had enough experience, gathered enough information, and thought deeply enough to have the *authority* to have something to say about that subject without abandoning a vivid personal voice and presence and all the play of language that we expect of creative nonfiction.

The task I forever face in teaching creative nonfiction, then, is helping apprentice writers to move beyond "I feel" and "I am" and "I did" and so on. Those stances can of course be a powerful ground for an essay, but they aren't a stopping place. Virginia Woolf, in "The Modern Essay," says *personality* is "the essayist's most proper but most dangerous and delicate tool." Why it is the nonfiction writer's most proper tool should be self-evident: nonfiction is writers themselves—crafted, of course, into textual selves that may have only a glancing resemblance to the people writing—speaking more or less directly to readers, those imagined others to whom we address our words.

But Woolf was right in her word choice: personality, when indulged in to excess, is dangerous. It can lead us to believe that because *we* experience something as interesting, others will find it interesting, too, and we forget the writerly task of *rendering* the experience in such a way that we make it interesting to readers. That is the gesture that moves writing away from the genres of diary or letter or personal journal and into the world of readers. It is, finally, the gesture that makes a recorder of experience into a writer of creative nonfiction.

The delicacy with which the tool of personality must be wielded can abash the seasoned as well as the novice writer. I used to say that no one but Madonna, that self-packaged and self-promoted icon of celebrity, could talk only about herself and count on the world to be interested. Now Madonna, I suppose, is passé; perhaps the right icon of the moment is Paris Hilton, who claims celebrity not because of any accomplishment but just because she claims it, and in startling her audience with the audacity of her personal revelations, she stirs interest, titillates, commands attention. Most of us have read nonfiction books and essays that fall into that trap. To reach beyond the self, to use experience in a way that transcends that experience—that is the challenge of nonfiction.

The task, then, of the writer is to *be present* in the writing, to connect in a personal way with the reader, without being herself or himself the sole subject of the writing. The writer sees, questions, reads, searches, observes, converses, wonders, and above all *thinks*. Things happen; he or she goes places, puts two and two together, pieces a quilt of incident or evidence that reveals to readers a picture, with luck a new picture, of the world, in all the particularity with which the writer has experienced it. The nonfiction writer is a conveyor, a medium, a lens.

Many excellent contemporary essayists are masters of this art: Michael Pollan ("Why Mow? The Case Against Lawns," "An Animal's Place"), Anne Fadiman ("Mail"), Jonathan Franzen ("My Father's Brain," "Sifting the Ashes"), to name only a few. To move out of the quicksand of the merely personal, then, you must read writers who do very well the real work of nonfiction writing, which is curiosity satisfied by engaging deeply with a subject. About midway through the semester, after my students have written several unrestricted essays on subjects of their choosing, I ask them to write what I call an "investigative essay."

EXERCISE

This exercise asks you to choose a subject that is compelling to you, that you want to know more about, and that you believe you can make some point or other about, even if the point is simply a question. You must set to work finding out enough about your subject that you can write about it with *authority*. Remember that an investigative essay is *not* a "research paper" in the sense you may be used to thinking of that genre in school. It must be an *essay*: your voice, your perspective, your persona must be evident in the piece, and, as in the more strictly personal essay, your lived experience can be included in the piece, as appropriate or desirable.

Long experience with this exercise has convinced me that writing this kind of essay prepares you well for writing you are likely to be asked to do in other circumstances, for whatever subject, and later in your working lives. You may sometimes be asked to write without using the vertical pronoun, but making your authority, and above all your investment in what you write, evident in your work will always be recognized and appreciated. The pleasure in telling your own stories, in pursuing subjects of your own choosing, and then *essaying* into those subjects in prose vivid with the essayist's "most proper and yet most delicate and dangerous tool" not only teaches you about writing creative nonfiction, but also prepares you for writing in which the surface markers of creativity are not so fully evident. The success I have had with this exercise is one of the reasons I consistently argue for the value of teaching creative nonfiction, whether or not you as an apprentice writer will do that kind of writing when you leave the creative writing classroom.

And while I have your attention, wouldn't it be nice if we could find a term for the kind of writing we do that doesn't define it by what it is *not*?

MEMORIES AND INSPIRATION

JOHN MATTESON

Simultaneity: Stepping Out of Line

JOHN MATTESON is a professor of English at John Jay College of Criminal Justice at the City University of New York. He is the author of *Eden's Outcasts: The Story of Louisa May Alcott and Her Father*, which was awarded the Pulitzer Prize in Biography in 2008. He is at work on a biography of Margaret Fuller, to be published by W. W. Norton and Company.

One of the significant limitations on writing as opposed to other creative media is its linearity. Painters can represent several actions in the same, frozen instant. Opera composers can have multiple singers perform different melodies simultaneously. Sculptors, choreographers, and architects all work in the luxuriant space of three dimensions. The writer, however, never has anything more than the line. We can only work with one word, phrase, or sentence at a time. If we want to add something resembling the depth and texture that other artists take for granted, we have to somehow manipulate our single dimension to create an illusion of multidimensionality.

One means of accomplishing this effect is to successively narrate events that have taken place simultaneously—to revisit the same moment as it unfolded in different places or from different perspectives. The trick is to do this without creating a clunky, meanwhile-back-at-the-ranch sensation in your reader. One way of accomplishing a more interesting effect of simultaneity is to describe two chains of events that begin far apart but gradually come together, building toward a climactic force.

I attempted something of this kind in a book that won me a Pulitzer Prize: *Eden's Outcasts: The Story of Louisa May Alcott and Her Father.* The scene takes place as Louisa journeys to a Union army hospital in Georgetown to begin work as a nurse—at the same time that the Union army is fighting the catastrophic battle of Fredericksburg. The first set of events I narrate is innocent and even heartwarming, as Louisa bustles about preparing for and at last departing on her trip. The second set involves a grimmer business: the futile slaughter of thousands of Union soldiers. Louisa and the soldiers, of course, have a common destination: the Union Hotel Hospital. However, the different paths they must take create a fruitful contrast, as well as a mood of tension and expectation. Here's an excerpt:

> *Louisa received her orders on the morning of December 11. She had not been assigned to the Armory Square, but to a less desirable institution in Georgetown known as the Union Hotel Hospital, a place Louisa learned to refer to in jest as "The Hurly-Burly House." Louisa was to report for duty as soon as possible, and the rest of that Thursday was spent in a whirl of activity. Abba, Anna, and May, back from Syracuse, all helped to stuff Louisa's traveling bag with all there was of home that such a bag could carry. Sophia Hawthorne looked in to see whether she could help. There were too many hands for the necessary tasks. Someone remembered to make tea but, in the confusion, put in salt instead of sugar.[1] Bronson was away that day making school visits; for all the documents show, he and Louisa may not even have had a chance to say goodbye. Proud as he was of his daughter's decision, he also knew that she was going to a dangerous post; he told someone that he was send-*

---

1. L. M. Alcott, *Hospital Sketches*, 55.

ing his only son to war.[2] Louisa was equally aware that she might never see the family again. She maintained a brave face until the very last, but when it was time to go, she began to cry. Everyone broke down. Already knowing the answer, she asked her mother as she held her close, "Shall I stay?" "No, go! and the Lord be with you," was the reply.[3] As Louisa turned to catch a last glimpse of Orchard House, she saw her mother waving a handkerchief. May, along with Julian Hawthorne, escorted Louisa to the Concord train station.[4] Louisa rode to Boston, where she spent one last civilian night with her cousin Lizzie Wells.

Friday was, if possible, more frantic than Thursday had been. Always eager to economize, Louisa scoured Boston to obtain the free rail pass to which her military appointment entitled her. Each official referred her to another, usually in some building on the side of town from which she had just come. She crossed and re-crossed the city, clashing with languid and indifferent bureaucrats seemingly intent on denying her the essential documents.[5] She got the last of her papers in order, just in time to join Anna and her husband for a hasty farewell dinner. The couple accompanied Louisa to the station so that theirs might be the last in a series of numbing goodbyes.

The sun in that dark season had already faded as Louisa sank into her seat on the train. Abruptly, after two days of furious bustle, hours of empty time lay ahead of her—time to check over her tickets, put them in a safe place, then lose and rediscover them again; time to count the small fund some family friends had given her to buy necessities for herself and modest gifts for her patients. She had time to gaze out onto the darkening landscape as city gave way to open fields. Feeling lonely, she let her seatmate draw her

2. Saxton, *Louisa May*, 277; Stern, *Louisa May Alcott*, 112.
3. L. M. Alcott, December 1862, *Journals*, 110.
4. Ibid.
5. L. M. Alcott, *Hospital Sketches*, 56–61.

into a long conversation about "the war, the weather, music, Carlyle, skating, genius, hoops, and the immortality of the soul."[6] Any topic was fine as long as it kept away the blues.

The train did not take Louisa directly to Washington. In New London, Connecticut, she transferred to a steamship, which carried her through the night to New Jersey. A rank novice at seafaring, she spent a wide-eyed night imagining that the boat was about to sink and wondering how she would save herself if it did. When, to her mild astonishment, the boat landed safely in Jersey City, she made her way to the train for Washington. Although the places through which she passed were unknown to her, they evoked clear emotions. As the train puffed its way through Philadelphia, Louisa regretted that she did not have time to stop and seek out her birthplace in Germantown. In Baltimore, her train passed not far from the spot where, two springs before, a mob of Southern sympathizers had attacked the Sixth Massachusetts regiment on its way to Washington. As she remembered the riot, Louisa's temper rose as if the assault had just happened, and she felt "as if I should enjoy throwing a stone at somebody, hard."[7]

Louisa's journey ended as it had begun, in early evening. As her hired carriage drew her through the streets toward Georgetown, she caught her first glimpse of the unfinished Capitol dome and gazed in wonder at the White House. On her arrival at the Union Hotel Hospital, she received the welcome of Mrs. Hannah Ropes, the hospital matron. The kindly woman noted Louisa's arrival in her journal that night: "We are cheered by the arrival of Miss Alcott from Concord—the prospect of a really good nurse, a gentlewoman who can do more than merely keep the patients from falling out of bed."[8]

6. L. M. Alcott, *Hospital Sketches*, 62.
7. L. M. Alcott, *Hospital Sketches*, 66.
8. Hannah Ropes, *Civil War Nurse: The Diary and Letters of Hannah Ropes* (Knoxville: University of Tennessee Press, 1980), 112.

All through the time of Louisa's journey, quite unknown to her, events had been unfolding in a fatefully simultaneous fashion. The new commander of Lincoln's Army of the Potomac, Ambrose Burnside, had decided to attempt a strike against Lee's Army of Northern Virginia before the coming winter would bring a pause to significant maneuvers. On the eleventh of December, the very day that Louisa received her orders, Burnside's engineers were hastily laying pontoon bridges across the Rappahannock River, and the Army of the Potomac prepared to cross into the evacuated town of Fredericksburg. The next day, as Louisa scoured Boston in search of an official to authorize her train pass, Union soldiers vandalized the Virginia town, smashing china and wrecking furniture. That night, as Louisa's train plunged into the night south of Boston, blue-coated amateur musicians played raucous versions of patriotic tunes on pianos that had been dragged into the streets of Fredericksburg, and officers gazed anxiously up at the strongly fortified Confederate positions above the town, wondering if Burnside's battle plan would lead to victory.[9]

Their worst doubts were confirmed the next day. On the damp, leaden Saturday afternoon of December 13, 1862, while Louisa's train was steaming through Pennsylvania and Maryland, Burnside sent fourteen separate brigades up the sloping hillside known as Marye's Heights. Near the top was a stone wall. Behind it, an entire corps of Lee's army lay waiting. When the rebels opened fire, their fusillade was as thick and rapid as machine gunfire. Of the thousands who answered the order to charge, not a single Union soldier came within thirty yards of the wall. Using a strangely placid simile, Union corps commander Darius Couch later described watching the brigades "melt like snow coming down on warm ground."[10] After nightfall, in Georgetown, Louisa first

---

9. Rable, *Fredericksburg!* 177–84.
10. Ibid., 238.

turned down the blankets in her upstairs room at the Union Hotel Hospital. Forty miles to the southwest, on the sloping ground above Fredericksburg, the bitterly cold air was filled with the despairing cries of literally thousands of wounded men. Louisa had completed her journey to the Union Hotel Hospital. For many of the Fredericksburg wounded, a journey to the same destination was about to begin.

EXERCISE

Choose an event that has two parties and that moves toward a climactic intersection. Examples may include two former rivals coming together for a reunion, a pitcher and a batter in the moments before a crucial pitch, or a criminal and his intended victim on their way to an explosive encounter.

1. Consider the event from the perspective of one of the parties. It usually makes sense to begin with the one whose participation carries less emotional charge, though your taste and the atmospherics of the scene may sometimes call out for the opposite approach. What preparations does the first party have to go through? What are her or his thoughts and feelings?

2. Looking ahead, consider how those preparations, thoughts, and feelings might contrast with those of the other party; you may want to set up some implied comparisons that you can complete as you narrate the other half of the event.

3. Write the first half of the event, following the first of your two parties through the time leading up to the intersection.

4. Write the second half of the event, reinforcing the sense of simultaneity by alluding occasionally back to what your first

party was doing at the same moment. As you do so, as you see fit, highlight similarities and contrasts between the two halves of the story. The extent to which you can do this will vary, depending on the facts with which you are working. As you write (and revise), ask yourself what each side of the story is helping the reader to understand about the other half.

In this exercise, I have suggested that you narrate the first side of the event from start to finish before turning to the other side. There may be situations in which you may prefer to cut back and forth more frequently between the two narrations. Your choice in this regard will be influenced both by your material and by the subtleties of mood you are hoping to create. More frequent back-and-forth movements will likely raise the level of tension in your narrative, though readers may also find this approach more distracting. In either event, treat the form only as a framework for your creative innovation; always make sure that it is helping to liberate your writing, not imposing additional strictures upon it.

DANIEL NESTER

Make Your Own White Album

DANIEL NESTER is the author of *How to Be Inappropriate*, a book of essays and humorous nonfiction; *The History of My World Tonight* (poems); as well as *God Save My Queen* I and II, collections on his obsession with the rock band Queen. His work has been anthologized in such places as *The Best American Poetry*; *The Best Creative Nonfiction*; and *Third Rail: The Poetry of Rock and Roll*. He teaches writing at The College of Saint Rose in Albany, New York.

> *We tell ourselves stories in order to live.*
> —JOAN DIDION, *The White Album*

One of my favorite comments about how to put an essay—a truly personal essay, one that reflects the essaying, or the trying out, of ideas in writing—comes from Michel de Montaigne (1533–1572), the inventor of the form himself. "Let attention be paid not to the matter," he writes in his essay "Of Books," "but to the shape I give it." What Montaigne means, I think, is that the form of the essay, the way the essay reflects the consciousness of the writer, is just as important, if not more, than what is addressed. Robert Creeley echoes Montaigne almost four hundred years later, as quoted in Charles Olson's 1950 essay "Projective Verse": "Form is never more than an extension of content." What Creeley meant, in part, is that, when writing poems in the twentieth century, one thing to take under consideration is that the old, received forms might not apply to both what we are writing about, or content, as well as the language we are using, or form.

One challenge writers have in writing a personal essay, in an era in which many things are happening at once, many tasks, many thoughts are being examined, is how to cover more than one time line, more than one set of events, and still have the essay reflect their own state of mind. One solution I've found is imitation, in the sense that writers copy (you might say "sample") the structure of the most successful or interesting essays. What follows is one of the more successful assignments I've given myself and my students over the years.

The writing assignment, in a nutshell, is to imitate the outline of Joan Didion's landmark 1979 essay "The White Album." You do this writing in a succession of shorter "mini-essays." The trick is to write these in an order that is different from what will appear as your final version, then reassemble them. The result will be your own "White Album."

EXERCISE

1. **Pick a time period** (*from twelve months to five years) in which your life was at a crossroads, you were about to experience a great change of place or mind-set, or you were otherwise experiencing some sort of transformation.* For some, such as Joan Didion, it is a longer period, in which the outside world as well as her personal life was in a major upheaval. For a college freshman, it may be senior year of high school; for others, it might be the death of a child or when they came out of the closet as a gay or lesbian.

2. **Write a series of short "mini-essays"** *that focus on different parts of your time period.* Make them three hundred to five hundred words each. Write them in this specific order as you move along. They are as follows:

1. *A Day in the Life.* Tell a story from your time period when you feel your life was changed in a significant way—this cannot be an "Official Day" (graduation, prom, sports event, wedding, funeral; you will get to that later). Give the exact calendar date, to the best of your recollection (day, month, year).

2. *Yearbook Entry.* Take out some sort of list or directory from your time period: your senior-year high school yearbook, a Buddy List/friends from AIM/MySpace, your childhood street. Think of a way to randomly pick from this list: every other person, every twentieth; two, four, six houses down from you on your street. Write down their names, any official information (address/AIM), and a paragraph or memory about them. If you do not remember a person, try to explain why he/she has not lasted in your memory.

3. *Road Trip Story.* Tell a story about a road trip you took during your time period. This can be anything from a school field trip to a debauched trip to a resort.

4. *Important Things List.* A list of items—ideas, objects, posters, belongings, medicines, drinks, or drugs, prescription or not, that were important to you in your time period.

5. *Hit Parade.* Find the top five songs on the charts from the week of either the Big Day or the Day in the Life. List them, plus impressions of those songs that stick in your mind.

6. *Official Day.* Describe a major event in your life that was in fact formal or official—a prom, wedding, graduation day, funeral, acceptance or denial from college.

7. *Home and the News.* A description of your home during this time period: your family (all of the names, full), a descrip-

tion of your bedroom. Plus: describe stories or events using two forms of media from the Day in the Life. Try to use both a newspaper or magazine and TV or Internet. Summarize the story and discuss how it might have related or directly related to your own situation.

8. *Preparation for the Big Day/Day in the Life.* Describe the days leading up to the Big Day or the Day in the Life. Tear away or cut out parts from those parts you have already written, if necessary.

9. *Icon Story.* Summarize and commentate on a story that was in the news—a specific figure in the culture—from your time period. Focus on one person, one event with that person if possible, and explain why you picked it; without, of course, saying you "picked it."

10. *Friend.* Tell a story from your time period about you and a friend, something you did that is memorable to you.

3. **When you are finished writing all the sections, re-order your mini-essays.** Don't worry about writing any transitions, not yet at least. Here's the order:

1. *Introduction*

2. *A Day in the Life (1)*

3. *Home and the News (7)*

4. *Official Day (6)*

5. *Icon (9)*

6. *Friend (10)*

7. *Yearbook Entry (2)*

8. *Important Things List (4)*

9. *Hit Parade (5)*

4. **Write the Introduction and Conclusion**. Look at all these stories, how they are ordered. What can you say about yourself? What larger statement can you make about this scrapbook, this White Album of your life? Try writing about yourself in the third person, perhaps even in the present tense. Here's some writing prompts for your introduction and conclusion.

- The narrator of this story is like _____.

- This is the time of my life when _____.

- The actions here took place between _____ and _____.

- I had a job/I did not have a job. I made _____ a year/hour.

- I had/did not have a girlfriend/boyfriend/wife/husband/partner.

- Most of my time was spent doing _____.

- What do I miss most from this time? _____. What do I miss least? _____.

- This story shouldn't be told because _____. This story should be told because _____.

- Which actor/actress should play the narrator in this story? _____.

- What is the color of this story? _____.

- What does this story smell like? _____.

- What section of the library does this story belong? _____.

- During the time of this story, I met the following famous people or important local figures: _____.

- I believed in God/I didn't believe in God. I still believe in God/I don't believe in God now/I still don't believe in God.

- The narrator of this story is like me in the following ways: _____.
- The narrator of this story is not like me in the following ways: _____.
- The headline on the front page of this life story's newspaper read:_____.
- What did I expect to happen in my life? _____.
- What really happened? _____.
- If I passed the narrator of this story on the street, I might have thought to myself, "_____."
- What would I say to the narrator of this story? _____.

Remember: writing these mini-essays out of order is the whole trick. For many writers, this is one of the only ways to write an essay that is disjointed thoughts—and time line–wise, that reflects the disjointed states of mind we all have in certain times of our lives; one that, as Montaigne or Creeley might say, gives a form or shape to our content.

5. **Other tips**. Read Joan Didion's essay before you start and keep it at your side as you write the sections. Think of how you will tell your stories. Make up titles for each section. Do research. Interview people from this time. Use other people's words, sources, literary works.

HONOR MOORE

Into Memory

HONOR MOORE is author of *The Bishop's Daughter*, a memoir, and *The White Blackbird: A Life of the Painter Margarett Sargent by Her Granddaughter*. Her three volumes of poems are *Red Shoes*, *Darling*, and *Memoir*.

I have used this exercise in groups, and I have used it writing memoir when I find myself on the periphery rather than at the heart of the matter at hand. It's important to do this exercise as a kind of binge—prompting yourself to write without pausing to revise, to surrender to the terrain of memory, the images and voices as they come.

EXERCISE

First Fragment

Move your mind back into the past, back past the recent past, back before your body was as it is now, back to a place where the light is different because it has been transformed by memory.

You are in a room with several other people. Or you are somewhere outdoors with several other people, some of whom you recognize, some of whom you do not. You become aware of the temperature, of the quality of the light, of some distortion in the sound—either something that should be loud is very soft or something that should be hard to hear is roaring.

You rest there for a moment. What is the largest person wearing? Can you see the sky? Is it day or night, cold or hot? Do you love anyone here? Something is happening, and you will remember it only if you write it down, so begin to write it. Start with an evocative phrase like *"I am still young"* or *"A door opens."*

As you write, stay connected to the sensual reality, temperature, time of day, become aware of the others, let them come more firmly into focus. When something sudden happens, something that changes everything, take note of it. Perhaps you couldn't tell, back there in the past, how this would change things, but it has.

Write this in the first person, present tense as if you are there then.

Write for forty minutes.

Second Fragment

You are still in the world you re-created in the first fragment, and so, in this fragment, bring forward at least one element from the first. If the first fragment was a painting, this would be another painting in the same series. Bring forward its colors, its light, but let them transform as you write this fragment.

There was someone in the previous fragment whose story did not get told, who might contradict your version of events. Bring that person into focus. What does he or she feel like in his or her skin? Is it easy for her to walk? Is it difficult for him to bend? What does the world look like out of her eyes, sound like through his ears? Colors are very intense for this person. Perhaps he is responding kindly to you; perhaps she is contemptuous of your very existence or eager to protect you from something you believe you need no protection from at all.

In what you write now, write from that person's point of view— bring her/him to life, honor his or her point of view. You may narrate a piece of the same event as in the first, or an event that happened before or after the event in fragment one. Write this in the third person, past tense.

Write for thirty minutes.

Third Fragment

There is someone else in the world of your fragments, someone to whom you don't speak—either you don't speak to this person at all, or you can't speak to him or her honestly. This person is either outside the frame altogether, or present as a reluctant witness to what you think and feel. The history of your circumstance with this person is that he or she won't look at you or acknowledge your reality, and you can't forgive this.

The poet Adrienne Rich has written: *"How did we get caught up fighting this forest fire,/we, who were only looking for a still place in the woods."* Meditate on how these lines relate to the relationship.

Write this fragment in the form of a letter to that person about whom you have these inchoate and angry feelings, a letter of forgiveness. Perhaps you must write through the whole disastrous mess again, seeing it, against your will, from that other person's outrageous and unfair point of view. Just because this is a letter does not mean that you should abandon sensual detail, your powers of description and narrative. If you want, begin with the words *"It surprises me that you opened this."*

Write this in the first person, past tense.

Write for thirty minutes.

Fourth Fragment

Stay in the world of your previous fragments, but this time, you are at a remove from events, writing a conclusion to the story, but adding a fact or a slant that is new or scandalous. You are breaking a taboo, a custom, or a heart. If you'd like you can begin with the words *Night has finally come, but even from this distance . . .*

Write for twenty minutes.

PAUL LISICKY

On Propriety, Or the Fear of Looking Foolish

PAUL LISICKY is the author of *Lawnboy* and *Famous Builder*. He's taught in the graduate writing programs at Cornell, Sarah Lawrence, Fairfield, and Antioch Los Angeles. He currently teaches at NYU and in the MFA program at Rutgers-Newark. A new novel, *The Burning House*, and a collection of short prose pieces are forthcoming.

> *The new rebels might be artists willing to risk the yawn, the rolled eyes, the cool smile, the nudged ribs, the parody of gifted ironists, the "Oh, how banal." To risk accusations of sentimentality, melodrama. Of overcredulity. Of softness.*
>
> —DAVID FOSTER WALLACE

Students of memoir are often instructed to write out of their deepest fears. They're told that any worthwhile personal narrative is born out of some kind of confrontation with shame, a head-to-head battle with a fact that one would rather not admit to. I'm sure that doesn't come as news to you. The very form of memoir—the sense of inquiry and meaning-making at the core of it—hastens the kind of disclosure that often leads to uncomfortable, sometimes devastating questions about self, the people we've held dear, and the values we might have built our lives upon. Not to mention the people who might have hurt us along the way.

But I'm proposing a new way to think about this matter. I think we tend to understand this instruction in conventional ways. We might think it asks for a confession. Or writing about an incident that might make us potentially unlikable, even morally unattractive. I'd be the last one to tell you *not* to write the scene of your most embarrassing choice because it's not as bad as you think it is, or that it's already been written by someone else. (Those of you who have submitted your work to editors, literary agents, and the like have probably heard that one.) At the same time, however, I'd like to encourage you to consider what you might elide from your work out of propriety, or the fear of looking foolish.

I'm reminded of a panel I attended at the Dodge Poetry Festival last year. The subject of the discussion was shame; four prominent poets talked about how they dealt with—and made use of—shame as part of their craft as poets. Interestingly, no one said the expected. Not one poet talked about the difficulty of writing about an early sexual experience—though at least three of these writers had written openly about such things. They talked about the fear of seeming trivial, of writing about matters that might not be seen as culturally approved.

One panelist, the wonderful Toi Derricotte, talked about writing a series of poems about her late pet goldfish. (I can already see you rolling your eyes, but listen first.) Toi has written a body of remarkable work, in poetry and nonfiction, about her relationship with her difficult mother, about the challenges of living as a person of mixed-race heritage, about class and identity, and many of the most imperative social issues of the day. And yet she told us that no subject was nearly as wrenching as writing about her goldfish. The truth was, she missed that goldfish; she couldn't not write about that goldfish; she was impelled. But wouldn't the reader think she'd lost her mind? And wouldn't some think she was focusing her attention in directions too insignificant to be socially responsible? (I think this condition is something that many—particularly women—labor inside of. It's easy to forget, from our twenty-first-century perspective, how subversive it was for Virginia Woolf to write about the domestic life from the perspective of a woman. In other words, to take seriously the drama inherent in Clarissa Dalloway's plan to buy flowers for her party.)

But think about the great work such risks have yielded. If Toi had listened to that externally directed voice, she wouldn't have embarked on that series of tonally slippery, grave poems that think about attachment and wordlessness. Through that vehicle of the fish, she found new ways to think about love, mourning, and growing older, which never would have happened if she'd tried to refract those issues through more acceptable lenses.

But it's not just content that's at issue here, finally. All of us are prone to elision when it comes to matters of style. I'm thinking of the fear of the purpled, the cheesy, the overboard. Of melodrama. Of sentimentality. Those fears should be taken seriously by any writer; I wouldn't begin to minimize those concerns, but they become a problem if they start to enervate our work and shut it down in terms of range. I think about some of my recent students who labor so hard—and with all good intentions—to create the aura of ironic, playful indifference that characterizes some of the indie bands they listen to on their iPods. No warmth of tone, no rise and fall of pitch. That coolness takes part in another kind of conventionalizing, the kind that's often difficult to see, because it's trendy. It's too much in the atmosphere. Control, control, control—how often is that the hidden subject of our writing? How often are we trying to be someone else on the page? How often is the means of our expression away from us, a vague notion we're reaching toward, and not quite inhabiting, because it doesn't embody our speech patterns, or the particularity of our seeing, or the objects and people we authentically cherish? How much ends up in the ether of the hard drive before it ever gets a chance to be work that's definingly ours, not just another competent version of a story that's already been reproduced a hundred times?

EXERCISE

1. Think about something that you love and haven't written about before out of the fear of embarrassment. A childhood hobby, an adult hobby: your secret life as an accordion player, or tole painter, or collector of Matchbox cars—anything. Write a single scene in which you're taking care to enact your participation in your love for this thing. Be faithful to description; make use of all your senses: sight, sound, smell, taste, and touch.

2. Think about your writing style, and the patterns of expression you typically take out of your work. Go back to the above scene after a week has passed and allow some of those patterns to emerge on the page. If you're attracted to long, qualified sentences, use a few. Remember that they might very well contribute to a voice that's necessary to the scene.

3. Extend the initial scene by writing about an incident in which someone else tries to dissuade you from your interest. How can the speaker talk back to that force, to resist it, through an action?

LAURIE STONE

Finding Stakes

LAURIE STONE is the author of three fiction and nonfiction books. She has been a longtime writer for the *Village Voice*, the *Nation*, and *Ms. Magazine*; has received grants from the New York Foundation for the Arts, Yaddo, and MacDowell, among others; has been writer-in-residence at Thurber House, Muhlenberg College, Old Dominion, and Pratt; and has taught in the creative writing programs and Graduate Theater Department of Sarah Lawrence, Ohio State University, Fairleigh Dickinson, Fordham, Antioch, The Paris Writer's Workshop, the St. Petersburg Literary Seminars, as well as many other distinguished institutions.

I often tell students there is no such thing as an intrinsically interesting subject. There's no such thing as an intrinsically uninteresting subject, either. A story isn't compelling because it happened in real life. We get hooked on the narrator's understanding of cause and effect and the narrator's assessment of the relative size of things. A story about sex with your father can put readers to sleep if it turns into a sermon, an advertisement for beliefs, a trial, or a twelve-step recipe for conversion. On the other hand, a story about a paper cut can zap readers down a rabbit hole of wonderment if it opens up the body for contemplation or muses on the fragility of flesh to protect us from damage.

To find stakes in a story, a writer needs to become destabilized, pursuing an investigation that leads to questions more than resolution. Like fiction, creative nonfiction is driven by dramatic narrative—scenes, dialogue, description that conjures interior states. For me, the important distinction between fiction and nonfiction narrative is the teller's sincerity. Fictional narrators can be simpletons, braggarts, and liars, but memoirs and other first-person nonfiction accounts depend on the narrator's willingness to investigate ambivalence that can't be resolved.

Where are there stakes for you? This is something the individual writer needs to discover, and that desire for self-knowledge is part of the pleasure and passion fueling first-person writing. Remember, though: the reader doesn't care about you and never will, no matter what you've lived through or believe is unique. The reader wants a story that the reader is made to feel is about the reader. As the writer, you serve as the reader's experimental lab animal, going about the business of being human and opening up a window on how we really behave and feel.

To create the illusion that experience is universal, the teller needs to become vulnerable. You need to be willing to step away from protection of any kind and control the impulse to protect others from the way you see. You need to be willing to look disheveled—not so pretty, not so nice, and not so sure of things. If you don't edit the picture you are contemplating in order to win love, acceptance, and social footing, you find that human feelings aren't pure. At its best, memoir bears witness to the contradictory nature of human emotions, revealing that there is pleasure in pain, ugliness in beauty, relief in failure, boredom in love.

Let's not confuse stakes with walking on the wild side or confessing a sooty fall. Much has been said about James Frey's book *A Million Little Pieces* and the revelation that he falsified events. His book may be fiction disguised as fact, but more important, it's dishonest writing without stakes. Wanting to generate amazement, he concocted a Mount Everest of abasement in order to ramp up the macho of surviving that much peril. The result flatters him. Finding stakes for Frey would mean discovering a story worth telling about *not being* especially macho.

An example of the distinction between showing off and finding stakes arose in a recent workshop. Howard Stern came up, and the group agreed that when Stern spanks a hooker's bare ass on TV, he's in his comfort zone. Nothing is being staked. When, however, he talks about having a small penis, there are substantial stakes, because he's detaching himself from the privileges of maleness, which include protecting the male body from public scrutiny.

How do you locate stakes in your story? By not making events bigger or smaller than they are in order to look good. Destabilization is the power position in creative nonfiction—and there is also a measure of restabilization in being the one who nudges the reader away from comfort zones. Kafka said, "Books should be an ax for the frozen sea in us." What a violent image from a man who often felt himself to be a worthless insect! There's internal contradiction that can't be resolved for you! Internal contradiction is the first place to look for stakes.

EXERCISE

Scar story

This is a natural subject for stakes because it involves a dramatic collision (between your body and something else), a lasting mark, and loss of safety and control.

Tell the story of how you came to have a particular scar. Pick one that has the potential to show you reacting in contradictory ways, perhaps scared and fascinated or in pain and relieved. Don't worry if contradictions don't surface right away. As you write, slow yourself down and investigate your memories in a moment-by-moment way to see if they contain some property of tension. Do not say the injury hurt. That is asking for pity, and the reader doesn't want to be told what to feel. The reader wants to feel sucked into your vivid re-creation. Show us how the trauma made you feel *from the way you tell* us the story.

Guilty pleasure story

Write about a guilty pleasure, such as enjoying soap operas or squirting whipped cream into your mouth from the can. Maybe you enjoy hearing stories about other people's failure. This is an investigation of pleasure that you don't think you are supposed to feel. Describe the guilty pleasure and how it functions in your life. Is it a secret? How do you keep it private? Describe the pleasure in detail, so we see your enjoyment. Show us your discomfort with the pleasure through an action rather than by summarizing or analyzing. Tell us about a time you told someone about your guilty pleasure. Perhaps someone caught you. That's the drama to unfold. Do not cringe in your prose or ask for forgiveness. Do not apologize, translate yourself, or ask for love. You can, however, describe your cringing in a dry-eyed, matter-of-fact way. Nothing is more destabilizing (and exciting) to the reader than the writer's unflappable tone while slipping on a banana peel, or discovering a strange tattoo, or finding yourself half-naked on the street.

REZA ASLAN

Metaphorical Memories

REZA ASLAN is assistant professor of creative writing at the University of California, Riverside, and the author of *No god but God* and *How to Win a Cosmic War*.

Your memories are lies you've convinced yourself are true. Science has proven that every time you recall an event in your past you actively *re-create* that event in your brain. You reshape it, give it new details, create new significances. And, in doing so, you irrevocably alter the facts of the event so that often what you remember is far from what actually happened.

Your brain is not a video camera. But for writers, this is a good thing. Because what matters most in good writing—particularly when writing about the self—is not always *what do you remember?* but rather *why do you remember it the way you do?* It is, in other words, not your memories that make for a good story, but the metaphors embedded in your memories.

EXERCISE

Take a few moments and write loosely about your earliest memory. Make sure to jot down as much detail as possible and rely on all of your senses. What colors are involved in the memory? What smells? What sounds? Pay particular attention to any odd details that may or may not seem out of place because these are often the most significant aspect of the memory. If you are driving in a car, is the passenger seat empty? If you are lying in your crib, are the lights on or off?

Once you have jotted down all the important details, write a short paragraph narrating the memory in first person. Now stop and pick out the *metaphors* embedded in what you've written. The dark stairwell whose top you cannot see. The tinny music coming from another part of the house. The smell of chopped onions wafting from the kitchen. It is from these seemingly insignificant details that the significance of your story arises.

Now, relying on the metaphors you've highlighted to provide sense and significance to the memory, write a scene narrating your first memory in either first or third person.

NATALIE KUSZ

A Vague Recollection

NATALIE KUSZ is the author of the memoir *Road Song*, and has published essays in *Harper's*, *Threepenny Review*, *Real Simple*, and other periodicals. Her work has earned, among other honors, a Whiting Writer's Award, a Pushcart Prize, and fellowships from the NEA, the Bush Foundation, and the Bunting Institute of Radcliffe College. A former faculty member of Bethel College and of Harvard University, she now teaches in the MFA programs at Eastern Washington University and at Queens University of Charlotte.

One question often debated in the field of literary nonfiction involves how to report those memories of which we don't remember every detail. One school of thought has it that our first concern is to write good literature, and if we are a bit unclear on the minutiae, we should fill in made-up details which make a better essay. (A few writers take this even further, and say that even details we *do* remember can be changed, if they don't change the main "truth" of the piece *and* make a better essay.) If, for instance, you once attended a family picnic during which a long-standing and bitter clan feud was born, and you're *fairly* but not *absolutely* sure the instigating factor was that one uncle spanked another parent's kid for misbehaving, then under these rules you would report the spanking as fact—going so far as to invent a scene to portray it—given that the whole point is the birth of family bitterness.

Other writers feel that nonfiction has a right to be called *nonfic-*

tion only if every fact is precisely accurate. In the clan picnic scenario, then, to report in detail that one character definitely did something to another is potentially false, and therefore potentially misleading, and therefore essentially a lie. Our only real choice, faced with such a memory, is to give a general idea of what we think happened, emphasizing the result (the feud) over what caused it (the possible spanking).

In fact, both of these nonfictive outlooks miss a key truth about this genre, which is that *speculation* is one of the essayist's most useful tools. If we tell a reader what we *do* know for certain—that two branches of the family haven't spoken in years, that they say the feud arises out of a long-ago picnic incident, and that the bitterness is so strong that one cousin's name was changed from "Fred" to "Ted" so as not to have him named after a feuding uncle—then we establish our authority as storytellers. This authority does not diminish if, next, we say forthrightly that we don't remember/know *all* the facts since people are too angry, still, to tell them clearly. The point, remember, is that a family has harbored hatred, and that the form and consequences of this hatred are telling characteristics. Speculation on what *might* have occurred will be based on things we *do* know about our family—which means that, in the course of telling what we *think* happened, we get to reveal ways in which this family characteristically operates. So. A speculative telling of the family feud might begin like this:

The Boatwright branch hasn't spoken to the Capulet branch in years and years, and according to one family legend (there are several versions of "Why We Don't Speak") it all started at the reunion of '83, when Uncle Fred Boatwright caught Tiny Terrence Capulet with a finger in the dump cake, and spanked the rascal soundly. I was at that picnic, and although I don't remember any spanking, or any Crowning Event in particular, I do recall looking up from the sandbox and wondering why Auntie May was throwing dump cake, and whether this would delay the dessert course. I can believe easily, nonetheless, that such a simple thing caused a two-decade rift, first because Tiny Terrence is famous for having barely survived birth; he came out, they say, as just an arm at first, waving a hand as if testing the wind, and when they finally got him born, his neck had been wrenched, his collarbone broken, and he's not been quite "right" ever since. The Capulets call him their "boy miracle" even now, at thirty-three, and he's still permitted to snag, Helen Keller–like, prime morsels from other people's plates.

Most of all, though, I put some stock in the spanking story because of what I know about Uncle Fred . . . [etc., etc., etc.].

EXERCISE

For this exercise, you will select a simple scene from your memory which 1) has significance outside itself [i.e., exemplifies or illustrates a larger issue], and 2) is unclear enough in your mind that you'd have to speculate on the details. Remember that, at your disposal, are useful phrases such as "I'm not sure about _____, but what I do know is _____," "It could be _____, because . . . but is more likely _____, given that . . . ," and so on.

Now write that scene, making sure that its *significance*, and not its mere *occurrence*, is your main point.

HILDA RAZ

"I Can't Go On. I'll Go On":
An Exercise in Bricolage

HILDA RAZ is Luschei professor and editor of *Prairie Schooner* at the University of Nebraska, and founding director of the PS Book Prizes. Her memoir, *What Becomes You*, with Aaron Raz Link, was a finalist for the Lambda Book Award. *All Odd and Splendid* was published this year in the Wesleyan Poetry Series, and *What Happens* (poetry) is in press from Bison Books.

A bricoleur is a person who collects information and things and then puts them together in a new way, a process called bricolage.

Not too long ago I said out loud: I can't go on! But I had to get back to work—to finish a book on sex change, retain my integrity, and honor my collaborator's privacy. What to do? What I did was bricolage.

First I made a trip; stayed in a guest house; and trusted poet Diane Wakoski's advice: what you can't remember, you don't need. Each morning I wrote about the past. At noon I'd stop, meet my collaborator, and gather material from the present. But only details: what he wore, the questions he asked. Where we walked. The names of plants. An azalea flower he put into the palm of a marble bodhisattva. We gardened in his public plot. We went to garage sales. We drove to the beach. We saw elephant seals. I met a woman writing about a mass murderer she'd escaped. I tried to clear my mind of the need for meaning. And I wrote down the details in the order they appeared. Here's a sample:

"Aaron and I look through the newspaper over coffee and find neighborhood garage sales. It's going to be a very hot day. The first house we find is filled with wonders. Aaron opens a paper bag from the stack and collects Swarovski crystal beads in amber and black, a broken necklace of dyed onyx beads with silver charms, and a designer skirt from the seventies in chrome blue Thai silk. The belt loops on the skirt are made of metallic crimson thread. Seven dollars. He'll tear the silk on the bias, string it with vintage beads and charms to sell as treasure necklaces. Gorgeous. I find a dusty rack of clothes on the cracked, hot driveway. An Anne Klein bomber jacket in silk embroidery lined with candlelight chiffon, a browned-butter cashmere jacket with a diagonal placket, a candle-light satin underskirt from the fifties. 'Hooh, boy!' I say. 'Look at this slip.'

"'Why is it a slip, not a skirt?' asks Aaron, who comes over to see. I show him the elastic waistband stitched to the satin and the pliable hoop attached at the hem ruffle. Exquisite.

"'How did you wear it?' he asks, turning up the hem to see the fine stitches. He wants me to tell him a story about my clothes. He knows I'll write down what we say.

"Today Aaron and I are both wearing green shorts and white T-shirts. He has on canvas basketball shoes, one red, one blue, and I'm wearing tattered sandals. We're about the same height and weight but his shoulders and torso are muscular, his chest flat, his waist slender, his hips flat. . . . He's very handsome. The guy with the cash box has been looking and looking. As usual, Aaron is oblivious. The driveway is very hot.

"'How did you get these clothes?' he asks. 'How did you feel wearing them?' Suddenly I know he's working hard. He wants my attention off him. He thinks the book will be better if I write about myself. I want to write about him, the extraordinary story of his sex change. Still, such beautiful clothes. I try to answer."

This text is made of details, a kind of bricolage, a puzzle to show mother and son.

A stalled book, joyless and difficult, was restarted with details. In a world of ironic juxtapositions, how can writers go on when they can't go on? Trust your short-term memory, your senses, and your power to record details as guides to meaning.

EXERCISE

To begin: Take some time off from your writing. Know that you're going on a trip to collect details—the sights, smells, tastes, and talk in the lives of people who are part of your writing project.

First, pack up a notebook or your laptop. Where does your narrative take place? Go there. Get away from your desk.

Second, pay particular attention to your changed surroundings, your conversations. Notice every material detail. Did you go to the farmers' market? What did he buy? Ask why she chose the birdcage and listen to the answer. Invite him to lunch. How did you pick that café? What did she say to the waiter? How did they get to the subject of closed borders? Remember the story of your walk to the park. Why did you pick up a wrecked skateboard? Why did she take home the old telephone? Did you help weed tomatoes? Did you argue? Write down the lines. Stay in the moment. Forget analysis.

Third, open your notebook or your laptop and write down everything you remember each day. Write for as long as you can. Then stop. Know that you're living your life in a place and in company important to your writing.

Finally, after some days away from your desk, pack up and go home.

Read your new text. Choose three places where a series of details seems to stop and another begins. Cut and paste your text into three sections. Give each one a title. Now you're ready to revise and write segues from one section to another. Remember that you're making bricolage, collage, in order to discover meaning. This new material will stand for what's lacking or lost in your writing project. Maybe you'll write four new essays, or maybe one. Maybe you'll see ways to cut and paste new passages of narrative, conversation, and description into texts you've already written.

Remember Samuel Beckett's words "I can't go on. I'll go on" are pure inspiration.

CAROLE MASO

Image Assignment

CAROLE MASO is the author of nine books, including the novels *The Art Lover*, *AVA*, *The American Woman in the Chinese Hat*, and *Defiance*; a book of essays, *Break Every Rule*; poems in prose *Aureole* and *Beauty Is Convulsive: The Passion of Frida Kahlo*; and a memoir, *The Room Lit by Roses*. She teaches at Brown University.

I am always exploring and experimenting with narrative shapes and patterns as I try to get closer to something that seems true to my own experience of story and world. This has often sent me to the other arts as I seek out ways to reflect the more elusive and mysterious universe I experience each day. To find new ways of conceiving and formalizing some of these motions, it has been essential to look to film, the visual arts, critical theory, music, and dance for inspiration. Here is one of many exercises based on film that I have played with. Watch Akira Kurosawa's film *Dreams*, which is in fact five or so discrete films that create a coherent whole through means other than conventional story line. Watch for the dominant images that appear in each film and note the way they reappear either directly or in morphed variations through the films. The recurrent images alone seem to make unconscious links in the mind of the viewer and allow something other than plot to create a kind of "story," more mysterious and elusive and open-ended, but a story nonetheless.

EXERCISE

Now as a writing exercise write five separate prose pieces in which the only thing the pieces share in common is an image. No characters, settings, etc., should be shared. The image may appear as a large emblem in a piece, or in a small and fleeting way—perhaps as part of a simile or in some other more buried way. Keep experimenting with different images and different strategies. Do not force it—allow the image in its integrity to do the work. Be sure to choose an image that resonates and is important or meaningful in some way to you. Trust it, as Kurosawa did in his infinite wisdom at the end of his career.

JOY CASTRO

Seeing Without Judging

Named one of 2009's Best New Latino Authors by LatinoStories .com, Joy Castro is the author of the memoir *The Truth Book*, which was named a Book Sense Notable Book by the American Book-sellers Association. Her fiction, poetry, and creative nonfiction have appeared in anthologies and in journals, including *Fourth Genre* and *The New York Times Magazine*. She teaches English and Ethnic Studies at the University of Nebraska-Lincoln and in the low-residency MFA program in creative writing at Pine Manor College in Boston.

One of the pleasures we leave behind with childhood is the enjoyment of society's permission to stare. Test it: just try staring at another adult for more than a couple of seconds, and things are bound to get uncomfortable. But seeing people and things closely in order to render them as they are is a key skill for the writer of creative nonfiction. One way to practice this is by doing blind contour drawings before freewriting.

While uninhibited looking is a pleasure, the key gift of this exercise is the suspension of the inner critic's judgment. Since it's impossible to be responsible for the drawing's "correctness," there are no worries about whether it's good or bad. The focus shifts entirely to the *experience* of looking and recording. This attentive neutrality is a fine stance for the creative nonfiction writer to cultivate.

Former students report—years later—that blind contour drawing, followed by freewriting, is one of the most powerful exercises we do. Not only does it give us permission to look long and deeply at another human being or at another being from the natural world, but it also, by accessing nonverbal areas of our brains, quiets the chatter of the internal editor. As Dorothea Brande observed long ago in *Becoming a Writer*, our honed inner critic, however valuable during revision, must be hushed long enough for us to generate fresh material freely. Blind contour drawing is a quick, visceral way to access another level of attention, to silence the inner editor and let us say what we have seen. This simple practice of seeing and recording—with judgment of neither the subject described nor the resultant rendering—offers us a way of being fully, quietly present with what's there.

EXERCISE

If you're fortunate to have a writing partner who's interested, you can partner up for this exercise, but it's not necessary. You can select an object that interests you. (A great way to adapt this exercise to nature writing is to select something from outdoors—a pinecone, a piece of wood, a stone, a leaf, an abandoned bird's nest—to use as your subject; I've found that irregular, asymmetrical objects work best.)

On a large sheet of unlined paper, do a blind contour drawing of your object, or of your partner while he or she draws one of you: "blind" in that you don't look down at your paper until you have finished, and "contour" in that you let your writing implement follow (on paper) the edges and textures of your subject as though it were actually touching them, as though you were actually running the tip of your pen or pencil right along the edges of the driftwood, the person's face, hair, glasses, stubble, earrings. . . . You are reproducing on paper, by feel, what your eyes are exploring.

Blind contour drawing requires stillness and attention for a bare minimum of five minutes, a maximum of perhaps twenty: unmiti-gated, uninterrupted staring (and, if with a partner, being stared at) while the hand crawls across the page. Though the situation feels funny and awkward at first, it's best to avoid laughing or talking during this exercise. Silence helps concentration.

At the end of the allotted drawing time, flip the paper over and freewrite for an equivalent period. (I like to share with students beforehand Natalie Goldberg's "Rules for Getting to First Thoughts" from *Writing Down the Bones*; she offers a great primer for freewriting.)

Some writers like to use this period of writing to describe their subject verbally, which is great—they often move to whole new levels of appreciation for detail—while others may need to use the writing to process any awkwardness or frustration they felt. Still others may plunge right into a new piece, exhilarated by the free-dom caused by imposed blindness. If you're pairing up with an-other writer, sharing the pictures with each other after the timed writing always sparks laughter—everyone's a Picasso. This is an exercise to explore and enjoy repeatedly.

DIANNE APRILE

Lost & Found: Uncovering Buried Treasure in Your Stories

DIANNE APRILE, the author of four books of nonfiction, teaches on the faculty of Spalding University's brief-residency Master of Fine Arts in Writing program. Her essay "Count for Me" was nominated for a Pushcart Prize, and she was part of a team of reporters at the Louisville *Courier-Journal* who won a staff Pulitzer Prize. Her essays and reportage appear in literary journals, newspapers, magazines, and anthologies, including *Savory Memories* and *Conversations with Kentucky Authors*.

This is an exercise that demonstrates the importance of conflict in creative nonfiction, particularly personal essays and memoir. In creative nonfiction, you may be tempted to focus on voice, scene-setting, and descriptive detail, while overlooking the fact that without conflict, without friction, without resistance, even the most well-written narrative will fail to sustain a reader's interest.

To highlight the essential role of conflict in nonfiction, I created an exercise called "Lost and Found." The first step in this exercise is to make a list of your experiences that involved losing something important. Next, think about the source of the conflict in those stories (that is, the particular details of the loss). The third step is to identify the energy generated by the conflict, or triggered by the loss, and observe how that energy (the urge to recover or redeem what's been lost) propels the narrative.

Loss is at the heart of much great nonfiction literature, if not all of it, so examples abound. Joan Didion's memoir *The Year of Magical Thinking* is one of my favorite sources for passages that illustrate the kind of conflicts, internal and external, that loss provokes. Other examples of personal nonfiction that I draw into this discussion include Fenton Johnson's memoir *The Geography of the Heart*, and *Meditations from a Movable Chair*, a collection of personal essays by Andre Dubus. These writers create powerful narratives by embracing conflict in their lives, rather than denying or masking it. This exercise almost always taps into fruitful sources of inspiration and often produces surprising results—for writer and reader alike.

The point of the exercise, in simple terms, is to figure out how to get from "lost" to "found," even if "found" is simply a discovery of the depth of the loss. In other words, resolution—as in, a "cure" or a "happy ending"—is not required, nor necessarily desirable. What's important is the process of unfolding the narrative. In the end, the narrator may even discover that the loss wasn't as critical as first thought. The variations on the theme of loss are endless.

As an example of my own creative process, I cite an essay I wrote about my Sicilian grandmother's story of assimilation into American culture at the turn of the twentieth century. At a very young age, soon after coming to the United States with her mother, she was placed in a Catholic orphanage in order to learn English fluently and quickly. However, while there, she lost the ability to communicate with her mother in their native tongue, a tragic and life-altering loss. I learned this story shortly before my grandmother's death but discovered its central meaning in her life a few years after that, while watching, of all things, a documentary about the "Westernization" of American Indians. One of the stories highlighted in the film was that of an old man who had a similar experience in the government-run orphanage where he was forced to give up all the traditional ways of his people and replace them with

American customs and practices, including, most painfully, the English language. Retelling the story, the old man spoke with great sorrow as he remembered how, upon his return home, he faced a terrible conflict: he no longer understood the words spoken by his family and they no longer understood what he said to them. He was caught between two powerful forces: the urge to assimilate with the larger culture, and the urge to remain intimately connected to his family's traditional ways.

My grandmother's loss, oddly enough, became clear to me only after hearing the story of this man's conflict, and his discovery of its deeper meaning. This is a powerful example of how nonfiction literature—memoir, in particular—is able to open the eyes and mind of a reader whose experience, though far different from the writer's on the surface, still resonates at a deeper level.

EXERCISE

Here is a list of specific steps that will prepare you to write this exercise.

- Think of something you once lost that was important to you, and which you later found. Remember: loss comes in many packages. It can be loss of a job, home, or friend; as visceral as a death, as conceptual as a loss of confidence.

- Now recall how you "found" what you lost. Think broadly, imaginatively. Let your mind hover over as many losses and rediscoveries as come to mind, allowing one to gradually emerge as the loss you want to write about.

- Try to remember how it felt when the loss took place (your feelings, as well as the sensual details and memories it calls up).

- Also recall the conflicts generated by this loss—both interior conflicts, in terms of grief or deprivation, and exterior ones, including physical and social challenges along the road to rediscovery.

- Identify what was eventually "found." On the positive side, the discovery that comes out of the conflict of loss is individualized. For some, there may be an epiphany regarding the meaning of a loss. For others, what's found may be a replacement for what was lost. For still others, loss generates a conflict that leads to personal growth. Variations on the lost-found story lie at the heart of many great personal essays and memoirs.

- Finally, when students have selected a story and considered it in terms of loss and rediscovery, I urge them to mine the conflict in their narratives for the treasure buried there. For example, in writing about my grandmother's loss of her native language, and the breach of the mother-child bond it brought about, I probed and explored the long-term consequences of that conflict on her personality, her children, and, indeed, on her pessimistic attitude toward life.

Loss is a universal theme. It was the crux of my first published essay, a meditation on an aborted friendship that appeared in my high-school literary journal. The essay was essentially a remembrance of a friend with whom I had suffered (and survived) a number of conflicts. We were, in fact, proud of our ability to bridge differences and come out stronger on the other side. Yet when she moved away without saying goodbye, I had to face this loss by myself. The struggle was one-sided, at least as far as I knew. And it left me with many questions, some too painful for a child—even for an adolescent looking back—to answer on her own. In retrospect, I see that my high-school essay failed because I did not confront the story's all too obvious conflicts. Instead, I "resolved" the narrative by making what I call "memoir lemonade"—a happy ending contrived by squeezing something cold and achingly sweet out of a bowl of bitterness.

The personal essay and the memoir must be authentic above all else, and authenticity demands an honest grappling with conflict, the buried treasure of all meaningful stories. The "lost and found" exercise is designed to help you do just that.

MARCIE HERSHMAN

Memoir: It's About Time

MARCIE HERSHMAN is the author of the memoir *Speak to Me: Grief, Love and What Endures*, and the novels *Tales of the Master Race* and *Safe in America*. Her essays and reviews have appeared widely: *The New York Times Magazine*, the *Boston Globe*, *Agni*, *Ms.*, *Ploughshares*, *Tikkun*, and *Poets & Writers*. She teaches at Tufts University and leads a private writing group in the Boston area.

Time is short. Time is fleeting. Time is slow. Time is frozen. Time stretches endlessly before us, and behind. We are caught in time's web, so much so that a single moment can hold us fast all of our lives. One hour might haunt us, a night continue to mesmerize.

Many novels and short stories spring from just this dilemma; a good number of nonfiction works do so, too. Yet when it comes to memoir, this central mystery of time, that a minute might muscle aside a decade, and in fact *should* push it from center stage and into the wings, well, in terms of memoir, most new writers go linear. They think it only proper that their own story have a beginning, middle, and end. Fair enough. But they also believe this beginning must itself begin *chronologically* and proceed in ordered lockstep from there. In a misguided fealty to clockhand accuracy, student writers set out to parse every minute. Such memoirs die at their start.

EXERCISE

Here's the exercise. It's always the first one I do, and right on the first day. Since this exercise is meant to sneak up on the class, I enter the room late, so the students' collective energy is high. Then I make a fuss: I comment on the weather, the nervous chatter; I make sure to ask a student to give me his or her chair. The session settles in after that. We have introductions and play what students call "the name game"; we discuss the syllabus, and when the session seems routine, I tell everyone to take out paper and pens. They are to write an accurate account of the first seventeen minutes of class. "No questions. Begin."

Once most students have written about a page, I order all pens down. Some students will have completed their accounts, but the rest are to write the word *TIME*, in capital letters, then and there, and stop.

In the individual readings that follow, the initial discussion question is always: "When did time begin for this writer?" When he stood in the doorway. When she was racing across campus to class. When the teacher entered. Sitting in silence, in a room full of strangers. When the professor told her to give up her chair. With a philosophical question about what it means to want to learn. With the memory of being happy in third grade.

Each account read aloud encourages further questions, among them: Do we, even in a casual exercise, make a conscious decision to override time; do we decide when time (our story) begins? Is time malleable? How do we choose to give time shape?

A couple of observations: the request that students begin writing comes about half an hour into the session. Yet in all the years I've been refining this exercise, maybe ten students have even glanced at their watches to note how much time had elapsed since the formal beginning of class and the moment they're told to start writing. Just as few have ever turned to look for a wall clock. (If there is a clock in the room, position yourself away from it—another reason for cheerily asking a student to give you his or her chair.)

Our discussions reveal that far from being bound to a clock, the students have granted themselves the autonomy to decide what time is for their particular story. They see that some of them define time by physical action, or by thought, or by a "main character" coming onto the stage, or by conflict, and so on and so forth. They see, too, how much, for good or ill, they naturally try to fit inside a given frame ("seventeen minutes"), in ways they often ignore when consciously setting out to write a formal memoir.

Our exercise discussions are full and rich, and they're surprising. By the end of the day, one thing is certain: memoir is about time. How the story moves forward from there, well, truth is, that's up to us.

BRENDA MILLER

The Earliest Memory*

BRENDA MILLER is the author of *Season of the Body* and *Blessing of the Animals*. She coauthored *Tell It Slant: Writing and Shaping Creative Nonfiction*. Her work has received five Pushcart Prizes and she serves as editor in chief of *The Bellingham Review*.

Early memories, those first glimmers of consciousness, provide a starting point for articulating our sense of self. "Our earliest memory is our most important myth," writes John Kotre. "Our first memories are like the creation stories that humans have always told about the origins of the earth . . . In a similar way, the individual self—knowing how the story is coming out—selects its earliest memories to say, 'This is who I am because this is how I began.'"

As writers, we naturally return again and again to these beginnings and scrutinize them. By paying attention to the illogical, unexpected details of these memories, we just might light upon the odd, yet precise, images that help our lives finally make sense, or make sense at least long enough for our purposes as writers. Over and over again, I've done this exercise with undergraduates and graduate students, or with writers in the community, and always some unexpected image or theme arises that spurs new and vigorous writing.

EXERCISE

1. In first-person, present tense, write a scene of a very early, vivid memory. Try to use as many senses as possible—sight, smell, touch, taste, sound—even if you feel like you're making it up. If you get stuck, keep repeating the phrase "I remember" to start off your sentences; allow this rhythm to take you further than you thought you could go.

2. Look through what you wrote and see what calls out for further examination. What are the odd details, the ones that don't seem to fit? Zero in on these details and expand them.

3. Now ask yourself: Why do I remember this? What is the emotional undercurrent of this memory? Write out some speculative answers to this "why" question.

4. Now list other, later memories in your life that might carry this same emotional theme.

5. You now have material for an essay that pinpoints a core theme or idea or emotion that has strong resonance throughout your life.

Variation I: Do you have an ideal "earliest memory"? Write this out and see how your imagination and your memory intersect or diverge. Is there an essay in the process of memory itself?

Variation II: Talk with family members about *their* memories of the time you pinpoint as your first memory. How do they corroborate or deny your own memory? How can you create a "collaborative" memory that includes their versions of the events? How does this memory enact a family "myth"? Is there an essay about the way these divergent accounts work together?

*Adapted from *Tell It Slant: Writing and Shaping Creative Nonfiction,* by Brenda Miller and Suzanne Paola.

CHARACTERIZATION

TILAR J. MAZZEO

Author as Character in Narrative Nonfiction

TILAR J. MAZZEO, a cultural historian and biographer, is the author
of the *New York Times*–bestselling biography *The Widow Clicquot:
The Story of a Champagne Empire and the Woman Who Ruled It*,
which was awarded the Gourmand Award for the Best Work of
Wine Literature in 2008, and of the forthcoming title *The Secret of
Chanel No. 5*. Her work on wine and travel writing has appeared in
venues such as *Food & Wine*, and she is the author of guidebooks
including the *Back-Lane Wineries of Sonoma*, *Back-Lane Wineries
of Napa*. She teaches English at Colby College in Maine, and currently divides her time between New England, the California wine
country, and New York City.

For me, one of the trickiest parts of writing narrative nonfiction, which is generally told from a third-person perspective, is what to do with the problem of turning the first-person
authorial self into a character. Switching between these registers
takes a light touch, and it can sometimes get rhetorically complicated, because it has always been my strong sense that, once you
introduce the authorial persona, you need to follow through on a
commitment to developing that voice as a character—someone in
the text who has motivations, conflicts, and moments of genuine
self-revelation and reflection.

Not all works of narrative nonfiction benefit from the introduction of an authorial character, but in biography, which is my pre-
ferred genre, it can be a powerful and effective tool for making

historically remote people and places relevant and accessible to a reader. One of the masters of this technique, in my mind, is Maxine Hong Kingston, who uses it beautifully in her collection of essays *The Woman Warrior: Memoirs of a Girlhood Among Ghosts*, where she moves effortlessly between telling the story of other women (although it would work just as well for the story of men, of course) and drawing the reader into the narrative with glimpses into her investment in documenting those lives. Used deftly, it has the advantage of bringing some of the intimacy of memoir and the momentum of fiction to the writing of biography, where it is easy to succumb to the relentless petty tyrannies of chronology.

I found this exercise particularly useful when I was working on the manuscript of *The Widow Clicquot: The Story of a Champagne Empire and the Woman Who Ruled It*. Someone afterward described the introduction of the authorial first person in that narrative as a sort of sustained "cameo" appearance, and that idea of the writer as a minor character in the larger narrative trajectory is precisely what I was hoping to craft in that project.

EXERCISE

Begin the exercise by thinking of someone you know and a particular moment in his or her life. Write down on a piece of paper ten facts about your subject and his or her life experience. At this stage, you are documenting just simple facts—some details about where, what, how, and who. The list should be drawn from what you know of someone else and not drawn from your life; part of the point of the exercise is trying to find your own investment in a story that isn't your own.

The second step in the exercise is to write down three details about each of the ten facts on your list. If you are working on a fact about the place where an event occurred, for example, you are looking for details that will help you create a visual picture in your prose. It's okay if the details seem unconnected. This is what biographers deal with all the time. Writing quickly as a simple drafting exercise, take ten or fifteen minutes to write a third-person account of your narrative event, in which you incorporate all the details on your list.

Looking back over your biographical sketch, ask yourself the following questions:

1. What was it about this particular person or event that led me to choose it over others? Be specific in thinking about what grabbed your interest in the story; that's likely to be the same thing that will hold your readers' attention.

2. What seems essential in this narrative and what seems secondary? Notice where those essential elements are located. Do they come at the beginning or ending of paragraphs, or are they buried in the middle? Do they frame the beginning and the ending of the piece you have drafted? If not, this will be something to consider in revising.

3. Why are those things essential? Essential elements of a narrative are pieces that carry some additional weight or serve some additional function apart from the basic documentary telling, i.e., details can reveal character or setting can create narrative tension.

Now that you have identified the central tension of your writing exercise, write it down. It might be a tension between characters. It might be an internal tension in your subject. It might be dramatic narrative. But whatever is compelling, essential, and carries significance beyond the ordinary will be at the heart of your story.

Looking at your description of the central tension, then ask yourself these questions:

1. What piece of missing information or what additional detail or two would make the biggest difference in telling the story of this central narrative tension? What things am I left wondering and wishing for as a reader?

2. Without inventing or adding any additional details about my subject (because this is, after all, a nonfiction exercise), how could I use my personal experience (or lack of personal experience) as a writer or a researcher to supply some of this missing information? How can I answer those questions for my reader by using a first-person strategy?

The final part of the exercise is to revise your piece by incorporating the first-person authorial persona to advance your central narrative tension and to supply details crucial to its development. Take fifteen or twenty minutes to complete the revision.

KATHRYN WATTERSON

Visualizing Your Character

KATHRYN WATTERSON teaches creative writing at the University of Pennsylvania, plays African drums with PLP the Unity, and is author of short stories, essays, and eight books, including her prize-winning explorations of the human condition in *Not by the Sword*; *You Must Be Dreaming*; and *Women in Prison: Inside the Concrete Womb*.

No matter how well I imagine I understand a character I'm writing about, I come up against resistances within myself that require me to open my perspective and deepen my empathy. When I was writing a short story about a recently released prisoner, for instance, I had to sink into the taste of his terror with each small decision required for his surviving the chaos of life outside prison. When I wrote a nonfiction book about a Jewish cantor whose love transformed a white supremacist leader of the KKK, I had to move beyond my rage at the Klansman to hear his story of confused sexual identity, deep anxiety, and suffering as an abused child.

Any character is never simply one thing. We all are illusory, shape-shifting, ever-changing beings. Just like us, our characters have memories, histories, and uncertainties as they create their destinies moment by moment. As authors, we must crawl inside their minds and hearts to know them. Visualization is one way to do this. It is a journey within.

Think of a character, real or imagined, whom you'd like to know better. Think of that character now. Realize that in doing this exercise, you will be entering a dream space that is yours alone. You can read each question by itself, and then shut your eyes to visualize your inner experience. Better yet, make an audio recording of the instructions, leaving about forty to sixty seconds between each question. When you get to the end, keep your eyes closed and notice everything you want to remember. Then, open your eyes and begin to write. Let it happen. Write it down just as you experienced it without trying to organize it or structure it in any other way.

EXERCISE

Prepare your writing materials or computer so you are ready to write when you finish this exercise. Empty your hands. Rest them on your knees. Shut your eyes. Now take in a deep breath. Exhale. Inhale. Relax.

Now you, the author, are taking a walk when you come across your character. Notice where you are. Are you indoors or outdoors? Is it light or dark? What do you hear? What do you smell? Look at your character. What is the expression on your character's face? What is your character's body posture? What impression of your character do you get from looking at him or her?

What feelings rise up in you when you see this person? Why do you feel this way? Look deeper within yourself at that feeling. What strikes you most about your character in this setting? Look at the details. Now, approach your character. Imagine combining with your character.

Now, join with your character. Enter your character's mind. You are becoming one mind. It is your character's mind. Now you *are* this character. Become aware of your feelings as this character. What emotion are you feeling? Feel it strongly. Know why you feel this way. Understand it fully. Do not separate from the character.

As this character, if you could speak the absolute truth about the deepest contradictions in your life, what would you say? Say it now. To whom in your life can you tell these feelings and thoughts? From whom do you want to hide them? Why?

As this character, imagine if you could do anything you want to do, what would it be? Why do you want this? What stands in your way?

Now, as the character, realize that the author's mind has been with you. Is there anything else you want your author to know about you? Later, remember that you can communicate with this author at any time. Just demand the attention that you need.

Now, as the author, you can separate from the character.

You are now only the author. Take a long look at your character. Notice everything you want to remember about this experience. Take your time.

Remember later that you have met this character in a new place. You can return to communicate and observe this character at any time you want.

When you have completed your observations and noticed everything you want to notice, open your eyes and begin to write. Don't speak. Just write what you have experienced during this visit with your character. You'll be amazed at what has happened in such a short time.

To follow up: write an interior, first-, or third-person account from the character's perspective; a first-person account as the author, and/or the story as seen by an all-knowing omnipotent narrator. Pay attention to what's going on beneath surface actions.

SAMANTHA DUNN

The "I Contain Multitudes" Exercise

SAMANTHA DUNN is the author of several books, including *Not by Accident: Reconstructing a Careless Life*, and her work has been featured in *O: The Oprah Magazine*; the *Los Angeles Times*; and many others. She is married and mother to one son.

It's been my experience that people come to memoir writing thinking it's something easy. You know what happens. You don't have to invent characters or places, either. So how hard can talking about your life truly be? The answer is, plenty hard. I always quote Vivian Gornick: "Penetrating the familiar is hard, hard work." Memoir is not merely a recitation of events—no matter how unique, dangerous, inspiring, sexy, or historically significant those events may be. Memoir is not reportage. Memoir is a unique form that demands the writer explore himself as the ultimate subject of his work. Maybe your reaction to reading that is, "I don't want to do that, it makes me uncomfortable." That's fine. Completely understandable, in fact. Write poetry, write fiction, write great reportage in the manner of Tom Wolfe or Capote. But do not write memoir. We are free as artists relative to our medium, and if you chose this medium, you are choosing to enter into a tradition of St. Augustine, of Montaigne, of Rousseau, on down to present masters. These are minds who chose this particular art form to explore The Big Questions, "What meaning do I take from my experiences, and what does that teach me about what it means to be human?" But getting into the nitty-gritty of what makes us tick is not something that comes easily, even for those who are inclined to want to do it. It seems we naturally resist examining why we are the way we are; we want to avoid looking at our contradictions, the places where we don't make sense. That, however, is exactly the place we need to write from in order to arrive at insight.

Every person is a paradox, containing beauty and ugliness, brilliance and stupidity, compassion and cruelty at some measure. I always think of Walt Whitman's line, "Do I contradict myself? I contain multitudes," as a fantastic expression of this. Memoir has to deliver on insight into the human condition or it has not achieved its ultimate purpose. In my experience, you begin a work with a certain amount of insight, but in the process of writing, of exploring, you end with so much more than you could have imagined. This is also just a matter of good storytelling. I learned this from one of my writing teachers, Phillip Lopate: if you stay at the same level of self-understanding throughout the work, you might create a pleasant read, or a funny one, or a mildly interesting one, but the narrative will lack that thrill of discovery, and not give the reader a compelling reason to keep reading. If you yourself are brought into greater understanding in the course of writing, then we, writer and reader, are all elevated in the end.

EXERCISE

To help in the process, I have my students in the UCLA Writers' Program do this as a beginning exercise: As quickly as possible, write fifteen sentences using this construction: "I'm the kind of person who_____ but _____." For example, I'm the kind of person who votes democrat but hates to pay taxes. Think first about actions you take in the world, rather than thoughts or beliefs—the tangible as opposed to the abstract.

After they have done the fifteen, I ask that they observe the list, think hard, then choose one of those sentences to expand upon for a twenty-minute timed writing period. The structure of the sentence usually ends up falling away like old scaffolding, and what emerges instead is a story, an exposition—something that makes their narrative more finely layered, more profound. All this is not to say you have to, or can, have all the answers about who you are and "what's it all about, Alfie"—it's the move toward wisdom that counts.

GWENDOLYN BOUNDS

Character Motivation & "Windows"

GWENDOLYN (WENDY) BOUNDS is a columnist for *The Wall Street Journal* and author of two nonfiction books, including most recently *Little Chapel on the River: A Pub, a Town and the Search for What Matters Most.*

While some memoirs span full lifetimes, others take place within a limited time frame—one dedicated to advancing the primary plot of the story. However, it's tough for readers to fully embrace, understand, or empathize with a character whose past they don't know. Whatever the main story line is, there are inevitably other pieces to a character's life that affect his or her behavior within that primary narrative. Is she in love? Did he come from wealth or poverty? Was she betrayed by a parent or the victim of a crime?

These are "windows" that can help advance your narrative but shouldn't overshadow or distract from it. To create a three-dimensional character, it's critical to figure out which of these details to include, and which ones to leave out in your telling of a tale. When filtered and well-edited, these windows can serve as a spotlight into the protagonist's soul, and those of other characters, illuminating their motivation and behavior.

But how to choose? Such details are like pieces of a puzzle; some fit neatly with each other and the main story and others belong better to another story in another time and place. When you collect enough nuggets of potential windows, and your primary narrative is well fleshed out, it starts to become clear which windows to include and which ones to cast off for your story.

Here's an exercise I used—unwittingly at first, and then later by design—while working on my own memoir to sort through the noise and find windows that fit the puzzle and furthered the main plot.

EXERCISE

Part One. Basic

1. Pick a relatively recent event or turning point in life that consumed your time, energy, and thoughts for a set period of time. If there's conflict involved, that's particularly useful. It should be a period that is memorable—something you would share with others you wanted to know you. This will be your main narrative. Sketch it out in five hundred to a thousand words so you have a road map and this period is fresh in your mind.

2. Then immediately after, for one to two weeks, search your memory for fragments of important moments in your far and recent past that stand out sharply: a funeral, the way fog draped over the hills one summer, the day your grandfather taught you to put bait on a fishing lure, the moment you won a race, the moment you were disappointed by a friend, the way your mother's hair smelled when you were young. E-mail or text these memories to yourself as they come, or scribble them down in a pad. Remember how these memories made you feel. But don't try to make sense of them—yet.

3. After you've collected these moments in one place, begin sorting them looking through the lens of your main narrative. Which of those small moments seem to have some impact, however tangential, on the primary story line and how

you behaved during that period? Can you see threads from these moments that may have motivated you to act a certain way or be drawn to a certain person or place, in your main story line? These threads can help lead you to a "window" worth developing.

4. Pick one of the memories and write it as a full scene that could be attached as a flashback at the end or beginning of your sketched-out main narrative. Now read the entire work. Does this "window" help illuminate your main narrative? Do you see yourself as a character a little more clearly, more completely?

Part Two. Advanced

5. Repeat this exercise, but do it for someone else involved in your main story line. You may have to interview the person depending on how well you know them. The goal is to understand what drives the other people who are part of your story. The more you can flesh out their characters, the richer and more nuanced your entire memoir will become. Life is usually gray, not black and white. And while you might approach a set of circumstances from one point of view and series of windows into your life, the other characters are approaching the same situation from the basis of entirely different experiences and motivations.

There is no single best way to incorporate windows into your story. They can be peppered throughout the narrative arc. Or they can be inserted as interludes. Other characters can offer the details about each other. I wove mine like a subplot as italicized flashbacks at the end of each chapter of my book. However you approach it, the goal is to make your readers' experience with characters richer and more intimate while always propelling the main story forward.

LEAH HAGER COHEN

Humble Pie

LEAH HAGER COHEN is the author of four nonfiction books and three novels. Among the honors her books have received are the *New York Times* Notable Book (four times); American Library Association Ten Best Books of the Year; *Toronto Globe and Mail* Ten Best Books of the Year; and Booksense 76 Pick. She works as a faculty mentor in the Low-Residency MFA Program in Creative Writing at Lesley University, and teaches freshman writing at Boston University.

M y friend Mary says, "People should tell their own stories."

Very sound, that. To be the author of one's own life, the teller of one's own tale, is the basis of selfhood. As writers, as people invested in the act, not to say the sanctity, of creating with words, how could we disagree?

Yet it does put the writer of creative nonfiction in a bit of a bind. Even those who might at first glance seem immune—memoirists—must reckon with the problem. For unless we have been raised by wolves and live as hermits, we cannot tell our own stories without trafficking in the stories of others as well.

Let us presume that part of what has made us writers in the first place is a curiosity about our world and other people in it: how are we to honor these subjects without exploiting them?

When I was in journalism school, we were instructed never to allow subjects to read what we had written about them until publication. There are some practical and even some ethical reasons for this (the latter relating to free speech and the need for journalists to report without bias, without pressure to misrepresent). But there are some problems with the practice as well, from the ubiquitous, near-inevitable occurrence of errors of fact that might have been corrected, to the inflation of a writer's sense of sovereignty over the representation of the story of another.

That's why I call this exercise humble pie.

EXERCISE

Interview a willing collaborator. This might be a fellow writer or classmate, but need not be. After all, storytelling is not the realm or property only of designated "writers." It belongs to everyone. Consider drafting your mother, your neighbor, your barber, your kid. Ask questions and take notes for fifteen minutes. Do not record only your subject's spoken responses, but also what you notice regarding appearance, gesture, pace, vocal quality . . . all the nonverbal cues you are simultaneously receiving. You may wish to use a tape recorder in order to free your receptivity to these many levels of information.

Then switch. Submit to *being* interviewed, by your collaborator, for fifteen minutes, same deal.

Then go away and write. Both of you. Write up your notes as a two-to-three-page character sketch, a mini-profile of the other.

Then trade. Let your "subject" read what you have written about him or her, while you read what has been written about you.

And share your responses. Are there errors of fact? Are there errors of perception? Are there qualities that have been captured just right? What is your experience of seeing yourself rendered in another's prose? How does your collaborator feel, upon reading your words? What, if anything, might you revise, based on hearing his or her responses? How did knowing that your subject would be seeing the piece affect the writing process? Did you feel constrained or limited by it? Were you impelled to work harder to be accurate or compassionate? Do you think this enhanced the literary merit of your piece? Weakened it? What about its social merit? Why do you write?

HOPE EDELMAN

Specificity and Characters

HOPE EDELMAN is the Los Angeles–based author of five nonfiction books, including the best sellers *Motherless Daughters* and *Motherless Mothers*. Her articles, essays, and reviews have appeared in numerous magazines, newspapers, and anthologies, including *The Bitch in the House, Blindsided by a Diaper*, and *Behind the Bedroom Door*. A graduate of the University of Iowa Nonfiction Writing Program, she has been teaching writing workshops since 1995.

I'm a big fan of injecting unique insights and specific detail into writing, particularly with regard to character development. Too many beginning writers interpret the assignment "introduce us to your character" as an invitation to offer bland physical descriptions ("He was six feet tall, with brown hair and deep blue eyes") or lists of vague and uninspiring attributes ("She liked to spend time in the kitchen" or "He could usually be found fishing with his buddies").

It's hard to get a mental picture of a nondescript woman in a kitchen, beyond the generic image of a middle-aged, apron-clad Aunt Bea type standing at the sink. But when we read that it's a young mother sitting at an antique wood table for hours, gazing blankly at the wall clock, while wrapped in her dead husband's hunting shirt for warmth in the middle of July, you've suddenly got what feels like the stuff of story. That's the power of detail.

A few years ago I came up with this exercise to help students add detail and specificity to their characters. We start off by talking about the importance of a "telling detail," a single fact or behavior that offers a window into a character's essence. For example, the sentence "She always gave me the cherry from her Manhattan" from Anna Quindlen's essay "My Grandmother" offers a telling detail that gives readers a sense of the grandmother's generosity and warmth (as well as her drink preference) and—from the way the author writes this statement so simply—of the kind of straightforward relationship they shared.

How can you convey as much information as possible about a character in just a sentence or two? That becomes our goal.

EXERCISE

Part One

Begin with the following sentence:

_____ was the kind of _____ who _____.

Spend ten minutes filling in the blanks. The first space is for identifying the character (e.g., My high school biology teacher, Bonkers Orsini, Miss Mercury). The second line narrows the focus to highlight a single dimension of the character (e.g., "My high school biology teacher was the kind of autocrat," "Bonkers Orsini was the kind of human anachronism," "Miss Mercury was the kind of self-proclaimed clairvoyant"). The third line is for revealing a specific, noteworthy behavior or point of view. For example: "Bonkers Orsini was the kind of human anachronism who spoke and dressed like 1967 in the middle of 2005."

Part Two

General statements about characters reveal even more when they're backed up by specific examples. So now expand your sentence into a paragraph that includes one or more concrete examples. For example: "Bonkers Orsini was the kind of human anachronism who spoke and dressed like 1967 in the middle of 1999. He walked through town with a two-pound peace medallion hanging from a rawhide strap around his neck, and punctuated almost every sentence with murmurs of 'Groovy' and 'Far *out.*'" Ideally, your end result is a two- or three-sentence character sketch that makes a sweeping yet original statement about a person, and then backs it up with specific, vivid examples that prove your point.

For advanced students, this exercise can also be used to help illustrate the importance of balancing narration and reflection in creative nonfiction writing. The best memoir writing results when authors know how to alternate skillfully between story and analysis, dipping in and out of the action.

Good memoir is a function of storytelling skill. Great memoir relies on an author's ability to know when to freeze the action and insert a passage of exposition to explain, describe, or analyze what just happened. That's part of what elevates fact to art.

JOCELYN BARTKEVICIUS

From Life to Narrative: Exploring Character and Story in Third Person

JOCELYN BARTKEVICIUS is the editor of *The Florida Review* and director of the MFA program at the University of Central Florida. Her work has been published in anthologies and such journals as *The Hudson Review*, *The Missouri Review*, *The Bellingham Review*, and *Fourth Genre*. She has received the Annie Dillard Award in the Essay, the Missouri Review Prize, and the Iowa Woman Essay Award. She is completing a memoir, *The Emerald Room*, about growing up in a burlesque nightclub.

Here is a paradox: To write literary nonfiction you must at once know your innermost self, look deep into the past steeped in your own perspective, and also be as clearheaded, distant, and objective about yourself as it is possible to be.

Or, to paraphrase Virginia Woolf on writing the personal essay, the trick is always to be oneself and yet never to be. For literary nonfiction to become artful—more than a blog or diary entry—the self on the page must be rendered as a character. But that is no easy matter.

Let me begin with a confession: for years, I could not write about a pivotal moment in my life with any sense of meaning, story, or character. The moment had become frozen, locked away. Here is the barest outline of the situation:

Brothers, business owners, are six feet underground in a man-hole they have built, drilling the pool filter pipes to remove a block-age. They take turns, electric drill roulette, and halfway into his second turn, one brother, standing in water, electric drill breaking through the water pipe, takes in a jolt of electricity that courses through his body, stops his heart, throws him back into his brother, and leaves him just enough breath to say, softly, "Kurt, this is it." And then he dies.

Kurt, the survivor, is my stepfather. I was nine that day, pacing the pool deck, impatient to get back into the pool. My mother and the brothers' two sisters were lounging under an umbrella, sipping cocktails carried out by the bartender. I heard my stepfather's cry for help, looked down into the hole, saw Uncle Geno (a livid green-ish color—or was it the shadows and reflections of that manhole lit by a single bare bulb?) lying in my stepfather's arms.

My first few drafts of the chapter about that monumental loss that sent our family and the business catapulting toward decline were about as bare as the outlines above. And then, urged by a writ-ing mentor to get around my stale way of telling it, insulating emo-tion, sticking to the family script, I wrote about the moment from multiple points of view: mine, my mother's, my aunts', my stepfa-ther's, my uncle's, even the pipe's.

I started with my mother's, ended with mine. Writing in third person for my mother, aunts, uncle, stepfather, and pipe, I carried third person over to rewriting mine. The distance provided a perspective—and discoveries—that stunned me.

Sketching and drafting with the pronoun "I," the imagination is situated somewhere in the midst of memory, looking back through all the filters and clouds and emotions and grudges and romances the writer may hold unexamined. But exploring in the third person, with the pronoun "she" or "he," many writers are able to transcend that limited self. It is as if one were liberated from the confines of memory, suddenly catapulted outward, looking at the past from somewhere outside.

In my case, I see "her," the nine-year-old girl, pacing the pool deck. I see her as I might see her now—this "I" is an adult, a writer, someone only distantly connected to that little girl. And I tell her story in a harsher light. I don't protect her, shield her, offer her any consolation. I throw off the blinders she wore, that child. And when I look at the others in the story—particularly the young mother, newly married, and with a second daughter—I see her no longer from the point of view of that nine-year-old girl who, though bright and observant, couldn't see far past her own needs and desires. But from the point of view of a woman now decades older than that mother. And I begin to see the story whole.

This is what J. M. Coetzee refers to near the end of his first memoir, *Boyhood*, when he writes of those brief moments of peering at himself and his parents and his homeland as if down from the sky. And it is no coincidence, I think, that he wrote that memoir in third person, using his novelist's eye, his novelist's voice and perspective and remove.

EXERCISE

Choose a key moment from memory, perhaps one that you are having difficulty depicting vividly and with a broad perspective. Write it without looking back at any other drafts in the third person. Write everything you see and feel and hear and smell and think as you look back at the person you were and those people you were with and that place you all inhabited. Write it as you see it now, looking back.

Then write it from the point of view of others in the scene (again using third person). This portion of the exercise is useful in re-seeing other people in terms of situation, story, and even—with a writer's eyes—no longer as you saw them in the moment of the experience.

Keep it in third person if you want to take a risk. But first, "translate" it into first person, just to see what discoveries you might make or incongruities you might encounter.

BRANDON R. SCHRAND

Portrait of the Past as Memory

BRANDON R. SCHRAND is the author of *The Enders Hotel: A Memoir*, the 2007 River Teeth Literary Nonfiction Prize winner, and a 2008 Barnes & Noble Discover Great New Writers selection. His work has appeared in *The Dallas Morning News*, *The Utne Reader*, *Tin House*, *Shenandoah*, *The Missouri Review*, the Pushcart Prize anthology, and other publications. He lives in Moscow, Idaho, with his wife and two children, and he coordinates the MFA Program in Creative Writing at the University of Idaho.

One of my favorite exercises to assign in my creative nonfiction classes is the family photo piece. Typically, I have them read Mary Clearman Blew's stunning essay, "Reading Abraham," from *All But the Waltz*, wherein she interrogates a nineteenth-century photograph of her great-grandparents. She stays with the photograph, and "reads" it again and again, puzzling over where that photograph (and more precisely, her ancestors) left off, and where she began. She poses questions to the photograph. She resists easy answers, and angles, instead, into more complex territory. Blew's essay is largely about the austere, suited man in that photograph, but it is also about her and her own identity. And as readers, we are with her, taking part in that journey of discovery.

When it is time to discuss Blew's essay, I bring to class the only known photograph of my great-grandfather, and when I enlarge it on the screen, the class sees why I brought it in. The photo was taken in the early 1920s and my great-grandfather is crouched on a cobbled plain in the shadow of the Grand Tetons. It is likely lunchtime, because the noon-summer-sun beats down, and his cowboy hat throws his face into total shadow. No trace of his face can be discerned from that blackness. He is there, and he is absent. He is both. It is a photograph that befits his legacy as a vanishing man, and that photograph—coupled with a few unsavory stories—are all my family knows of that man.

Photographs, I tell my students, can be powerful starting places for writing nonfiction. As artifacts, they both certify and elude. They are paradoxical. They defy time. They capture time. They are stuck in time. They are timeless. The discussion goes on like this for several minutes until, inevitably, students start talking about their own family photographs.

EXERCISE

1. Go home and dig up an old family photograph that interests you. You might be attached to it emotionally, or it might be taken of people in your family whom you have never met. But pick one that you find fascinating.

2. Begin describing the basics of the photograph. Set the stage. Where are we? In front of a house on a lawn? In a boat? Hiking? Around a kitchen table? What time period are we in? How many people are in the photograph? Are they looking at the camera or away? Is it a studio portrait or a candid? Who do you suppose is taking the photograph? Does the photographer cast his or her own shadow into the frame of the picture? Also, what kind of photograph is it? A Polaroid? A daguerreotype?

Is it in color? Black and white? Flip it over to see if any text or other clues appear on the back.

3. Next, try to think outside the frame of the picture. What is cropped out of a photograph can be just as telling (or even more telling, perhaps) than the actual subject or subjects. This might require some detective work. In my great-grandfather's photograph, for instance, I learned about Jackson Hole, Wyoming, in the early 1920s. In my great-grandfather's photograph, there aren't any power lines crisscrossing the sky in the background. There is no visible road, no other structures save his small cabin. No airport. It was a different world, in other words. Here, you can experiment with writing in the "negative" as a way to fill in the gaps. "What I can't see in the photograph is . . . ," or, "The person who should be present that day, but isn't is . . ." And then you can pose questions to those absences. "Why wasn't she there that day at the picnic? Where might she have been?"

4. Last, consider what your connection is to the photograph generally, and the subject(s) of the photograph in particular. Why, in other words, did you choose *this* photograph to write about and not any others? What is it about this particular picture that draws you in?

For as long as I have been giving this exercise to students, I have consistently been impressed and often amazed by the kinds of photographs they write about. (I also have them bring their photos into class, if possible, to share.) One student brought a photograph of her family taken one Christmas before her parents separated. The photograph belonged to her grandmother, who also appeared in the picture. Once my student's parents divorced, though, her grandmother took her sewing scissors to the portrait and cut out every last trace of my student's father, and then taped the photo back together as if he had never been there in the first place. It was an unendingly fascinating photograph that made for a powerful and, at times, poignant essay.

PLACE

LIA PURPURA

Walking Through It

LIA PURPURA'S collection of essays, *On Looking*, was nominated for a National Book Critics Circle Award in 2007. Her collection of poems, *King Baby*, won the Beatrice Hawley Award from Alice James Books in 2008. She is writer-in-residence at Loyola College in Baltimore, Maryland.

To introduce this exercise I'd like to extend William Carlos Williams's famous credo about the practice of poetry, "No ideas but in things," and offer this slight variation: "Ideas adhere to things." For some writers, gathering up the stuff of a new essay is the most daunting moment of all. It's a moment that either threatens to overwhelm with its many competing possibilities or one that hoards its goods and offers few satisfying entry points. This exercise, "The Walk Through," has jump-started many dull/ overwhelming moments for students. It is satisfying for list-makers of all kinds—most writers are obsessive list-makers—and, additionally, it helps one enter the past in very concrete ways.

In the world of real estate, the "walk-through" is the time at which the buyers take a last, hard look—room by room, appliance by appliance—at the house they are about to buy. In its intense focus, the walk-through differs from the "showing," that first look a prospective buyer takes at a house; one that shows only the general scheme of things, the layout, the overall floor plan.

Walk-throughs—those bounded and concentrated ways of seeing our environment—are available to us, daily.

EXERCISE

Here's how I've suggested writers take off on a walk-through: Enter, by way of memory, a familiar room from childhood, *from a familiar point of entry*. Often memory, or the act of trying to remember, lands us right in the *center* of a place or a situation and we have to piece the scene together from a hazy, unfixed angle. Enter through the front door, for example, direct yourself through the room and look around as you proceed, controlling the scene, as if from behind a camera. Moving slowly, you'll be able to recall actual objects in your path and you'll rely less on overall "impressions." As you walk through, be sure to turn your head; note various objects to the right, to the left, in front and in back; note objects on top of objects (vases on coffee tables, rings left by errant glasses on coffee tables, things at your child's-eye level). Peer over things. Look down into things. Creep under things. Move pillows and search around in couch cushions (as you used to!). Note the colors of the carpet/wall/curtains.

You'll be stunned, I think, at how many actual objects exist in memory to be recalled and how many *can* be recalled in specificity. It's important not to censor "insignificant" objects out of your scene: each object leads to the next and though they may seem insignificant in the larger scheme, remember that each one serves as a bridge, carrying you forth in your walk.

When you have completed a room (and it may take a few sittings to do this fully) you can go back and include associated sensory information (the *feel* of the dust—or the lack of dust; the quality of light through the blue curtains; how exactly that stubborn ring on the coffee table got there). I have found this exercise to be freeing because it upends the need to "have an idea" at the outset of writing. One is more likely to bump into an idea if s/he can provide little shocks of recognition or memory, or induce a kind of reverie. Walking through, you'll create many instances where you are startled by what you've discovered—sitting there all along somewhere in your memory.

You can vary this exercise in many ways. You might, for example, "walk through" all the literal closets of your past and look at/ note down what you find there. Clothes from different eras, hidden objects—all these *things*, grouped by closet (or room, or car, or whatever organizing principle you employ for the walk-through) will present you with a contained world for exploration. Likely you will want to linger on certain objects, the ones that have a story to tell, that have suffered neglect of some kind. See what happens. I've always found it exciting to know that the objects I'd lived with for so long, and forgotten about consciously, are in some very real way still present and intact, waiting patiently to be found and re- called to mind, so that they might offer their stories.

DAVID GESSNER

Knowing Our Place

DAVID GESSNER is the author of six books of literary nonfiction, including *Sick of Nature, Return of the Osprey,* and *Soaring with Fidel.* His recent essays have appeared in *The New York Times Magazine, Best American Nonrequired Reading,* the Pushcart Prize anthology, and on NPR's "This I Believe." He has taught Environmental Writing as a Briggs-Copeland Lecturer at Harvard, and is currently a professor at the University of North Carolina at Wilmington, where he also edits the literary journal of place *Ecotone.*

For nonfiction writers who are stuck for a subject, writing about place often unlocks other topics and deeper concerns. Places and words have always been intertwined, and for some writers turning their minds to a specific place they care for—a home, a patch of woods, a beach—can prove a reliable muse.

At the same time, writing about deeply knowing a place can make us feel a little mystical, even silly. As the great Alaskan writer John Haines said: "To express a place in art we need to take certain risks . . . we need intimacy of a sort that demands a certain daring and risk: a surrender, an abandonment." Or as Barry Lopez puts it, we need to "become vulnerable to a place."

This exercise hopes to draw on our deep feelings for certain places, and to use those feelings as a base for a longer essay. This, after all, is the template for many essays: writer walks into place, place spurs memory/ideas, writer goes on tangent, writer returns to self/place, writer walks out of place.

Before beginning the exercise, you should choose a place that is important to you. It doesn't have to be a pastoral place, just a place with personal resonance. The only qualifier is that it should also be a place with several memories attached to it.

EXERCISE

1. DETAILS OF PLACE

The first part of the exercise is to conjure up images from your specific place. Dredge up details—the more tangible the better. No need to start with long sentences—single words, caveman-style, will do. In this fashion, you should sketch down concrete details of a place you care about.

2. MEMORY AS SCENE

Next try to write a scene about a memory that is important to you and that is related to that same place. It could be an emotional event in your life or just something that has stuck with you. You should write honestly and simply and try to make it a scene. The only caveat is that you should write it in the past tense. Don't worry so much about getting the memory exactly right. Instead concentrate on making it work as scene. Remember to use so-called fictional techniques in scene-making—sentence variety, dialogue, active, driving verbs.

3. COMBINATION of number 1 and number 2

Now return to the details you've dredged up about a particular place and use those details. Have your first-person narrator—you!—walk into the place from part one and then have that place prompt the memory from part two. It is important to try to use the present tense for the walk into the place before flashing back to the past tense memory. Finally, the piece should end by returning to both the same place and the present tense. This will feel awkward and unnatural at first, and may also come out that way on the page. Try to play with the transitions and see how you can give it a "natural" feel, despite the obvious artificiality.

The first results of the exercise are sometimes awkward, but the potential rewards are twofold. You can begin to see how place can provide material, often unexpected material. And you can also begin to see an essential aspect of structure in the essay, how the concrete world spurs memories, and how that organic reality is mirrored in the form.

NATALIA RACHEL SINGER

Landscape and Memory

NATALIA RACHEL SINGER teaches creative writing and environmental literature at St. Lawrence University. She is the author of the memoir *Scraping by in the Big Eighties*, is coeditor of *Living North Country: Essays on Life and Landscapes in Northern New York*, and is currently completing a novel and a book of travel essays.

I designed this nature-writing exercise for undergraduates, but I have used it with writers of all ages to help them get over the tendency to think of Nature, capitalized, as some lofty abstraction, and to bring their observations down to earth, literally, while employing a voice that is uniquely theirs. Switch the topic from the self to a nonurban landscape and the memoirist who normally crafts prose with grace and wit may, at first, sound stiff or falsely reverent, partly because she feels out of her element, genre-wise, or perhaps because she has been reading deep ecology and has persuaded herself that a human being can only be an intruder on this earth. Even the most accomplished writers can find themselves falling back on stock similes or overly general observations, especially in places they don't know well.

I understand these writers' discomforts because I grew up in Cleveland, Ohio, in the sixties, when our rivers were so polluted that one actually burst into flames; my apprenticeship to the natural world began long after I'd left home. It is helpful sometimes for me to remember that nature writers have to do research like everybody else. They learn as they go. When Annie Dillard was writing *Pilgrim at Tinker Creek* she spent her days outside in rural Virginia—walking, sitting, observing, taking field notes—but she spent her evenings holed up at the library. And whether she is describing an Osage orange tree, a frog, a weasel, or a solar eclipse, she is always mining her own memories for personal stories that make the prose uniquely *hers*.

This exercise allows the writer at any level and of any temperament, inspired or reluctant, focused or distracted, to simply sit in a place, observe it, describe it in detail, and work with the memories that surface, integrating them into the prose rather than resisting them. Don't be surprised if what results is difficult to categorize: Is this a nature essay, a memoir, a personal meditation, or all of the above? The goal is simply to free the writer to be herself on the page, watching and remembering.

EXERCISE

Go walk in a natural setting, find a comfortable spot, and try, weather permitting, to stay at least an hour sitting by yourself. Spend some time taking in your surroundings before you start writing. As you settle in you might, at first, be more aware of the thoughts and worries that followed you onto the trail than what is actually before you. You might want to close your eyes for a minute and listen to the sounds around you while you also pay attention to your breath. Listen to your heart beating; listen to the birdsong, wind, water. Inhale the smells of vegetation and water. Open your eyes and note the palette of colors and textures of the sand, trees, birds, rocks, tracks—animal and human. There is so much life to take in before you even lift your pen!

Now, draw a sketch of what's around you. You may want to try two sketches from two vantage points: the larger scene you are facing, and a small ecosystem near your feet against which you are a giant. Even if drawing is something you never do, making these sketches will give you a sense of your place in the landscape and the relationships between the other elements of the landscape.

When you are ready to write, you may want to begin by simply taking notes on what you see, hear, and smell close at hand. If you know the names of things, write them down. Be specific. Capture what you heard with your eyes closed and what you hear now, waves or birdsong or wind or branches creaking or leaves crunching under other people's boots. Record details that will help you remember the scene later, but don't feel obliged just yet to write in complete sentences. Key words and descriptive phrases will do. What's in the drawing? If the sketch is like a map, what are the landmarks on it?

After you have a page of vivid phrases and key words to work with as a kind of imagery bank, start a new page. Now, as you begin writing your rough draft, try starting with a simple "you are here" map that tells the reader exactly where you are. Think of the reader from outside your world of geographical givens. For example, *I am sitting beneath a willow tree on the banks of the Grass River, in northern New York, watching a great blue heron land across the river.* Look at your imagery bank, your sketches, and work in some of this material. Write for half an hour or more without editing yourself. If memories come, unusual associations, abstract thoughts or personal feelings, feel free to include the ones that seem most compelling. No matter how hard you try to stay in the present moment your mind will wander, so just let it happen and follow the trail. Nudge yourself back to the present now and then, recording what you are seeing now, in the present scene, when you do.

If a number of memories have surfaced, find a trigger from within the scene itself that allows you to explore one of the memories that came up in greater detail. That memory might be something you develop into a short scene in past tense. Example: *As I watch the heron swoop down, I remember the time Loraina tried to teach me to dance the tango. We had just come back from dinner, and* . . . The memory can be a related nature story or something else, a scene from your life.

When you're ready, find a link back to the present scene and end your draft with something that happens now, in today's encounter with the natural world.

When you're ready, find a quiet place indoors to transform your material—sketches, random notes, stream-of-consciousness writing, memories, and what ultimately emerged as a draft—into a short essay. As a first port of call, you may want to consult a nature guide. Look at your sketch of trees and wildflowers and other vegetation or animal prints in the snow and try to match what is unknown to you with what you can find in the guides so that your prose won't be too general. Words like "tree" and "bird" don't create the specific pictures for the reader that "willow" and "blue heron" do. As you retrieve more of these specifics, pay attention as well to the musicality of language. Read what you have written out loud and notice when the voice pleases you, and when it gets in the way of what you're trying to say. Now you're ready to distill, develop, shape. When you were sitting outside writing, a number of disparate sensory impressions and memories may have emerged. As you revise, you will most likely need to cut some and expand others so that the essay coheres into something whole. What did you see today, perhaps for the first time? What hidden kinship did you uncover today between yourself, your past, and what you have just so vividly observed?

ERIC MAISEL

Creating an Intentional World: Using Place in Your Nonfiction

ERIC MAISEL, Ph.D., is the author of more than thirty books, among them *Fearless Creating, Creativity for Life, Coaching the Artist Within*, and *The Van Gogh Blues*. Maisel is a creativity coach who trains creativity coaches worldwide.

I grew up in Brooklyn. I can picture the Brooklyn of my childhood and youth with photographic clarity. I can also picture with great clarity places I have never visited: the Algeria of Albert Camus's childhood, as he described it in *The Last Man*, the pastoral England of Thomas Hardy, the New England whaling world of Herman Melville, the southern small town feel in Harper Lee's *To Kill a Mockingbird*. The richness of these settings is a gift to readers. They allow us not only to travel in imagination, which is no small joy, but they help us fathom what we want our life to mean.

By inhabiting an author's St. Petersburg, Paris, or Savannah for a few hours we rework our understanding of the universe. We augment our understanding of class and privilege as we watch tea served from a silver samovar. We change our mind about how much personal space we need as we live with a character in her under-the-eaves Paris studio. We recalibrate our conception of race relations as we attend an all-white private club luncheon waited on by an all-black waitstaff. We are not in "the real" St. Petersburg, Paris, or Savannah: we are in a place the author has created, learning what the author intends us to learn.

Setting is place and time and much, much more. That "more" includes the author's mind, heart, and intentions. The setting of a piece of writing, whether fiction or nonfiction, poetry or prose, is never some realistic snapshot of a place, as no such realistic snapshot exists. If you were to try to describe with the utmost accuracy every structure in a city—every hovel, every mansion, every church, every shop, every bridge, every government building—and then went on to describe every stitch of clothing, every piece of furniture, every custom, every meal, every parade, you would still not have captured anything essential about life. We would still not know what it felt like to be an abstract painter in Greenwich Village in the forties, for example, or, farther uptown, what life was like for a young girl growing up during the Harlem Renaissance.

As a young reader, place gripped you. You wandered with Huck, Jim, and Mark Twain down an imagined Mississippi through an imagined America. You sat in a dreamy, leafy wood with a sleepy Alice, as shocked as she when the White Rabbit bustled by with no time to spare. Maybe it was the Paris of Madeleine, the Transylvania of Dracula, the Illinois of young Abe Lincoln, the moon of space exploration. You traveled intensely, blissfully, and vicariously— because a writer took you somewhere. Now you, too, can take your readers somewhere. You can take them, young and old, to the worlds you create. And, as you do, you yourself will be transported!— that is the great joy of writing about place. Every world you create is a world that you yourself can inhabit and love.

EXERCISE

Get a place in mind to write about: Paris, San Francisco, Beirut, a Midwest town, a Catskills resort, a desert oasis. Ask yourself the following question: "What is my intention for that place?" You might find yourself answering in one of the following ways:

- I want to communicate something about the way this place has changed and get at something about how the world has changed.

- I want to communicate something about the way this place has remained the same and get at something about how nothing really changes.

- I want to explore why I am (happy, sad, excited, bored, restless, thrilled, despairing, ecstatic, etc.) when I am in this place.

- I want to get at my thoughts about (current politics, culture, spirituality, history, my family, my childhood, etc.) using this place as a backdrop, metaphor, or container for those thoughts.

- I want to (celebrate, excoriate, praise, condemn, etc.) the people who live in this place.

See if you can articulate your intention for your place. It is no problem if you can't, but see if you can. Then write a five-hundred-to fifteen-hundred-word piece that matches your intention. (Note: Maybe you'll only learn your intentions after the piece is done!)

SUZANNE STREMPEK SHEA

Sense of Place

SUZANNE STREMPEK SHEA is the author of five novels and three nonfiction titles, the most recent of which is *Sundays in America: A Yearlong Road Trip in Search of Christian Faith*. Winner of the 2000 New England Book Award, she's a former newspaper reporter who freelances for publications, including *Yankee* magazine, *Bark* magazine, and www.obit.com. Suzanne is a member of the faculty at the University of Southern Maine's Stonecoast MFA program in creative writing and lives in western Massachusetts.

T ake me to Barrytown."

That was the request made by so many Dublin tourists to so many Dublin taxi drivers back in the late eighties and early nineties.

The cabbies happily started their meters and, legend has it, ran up enormous fares while circling the city's ring roads and telling their passengers, "It's here somewhere . . ."

Thing is, Barrytown is nowhere—except in the novels of Irish author Roddy Doyle, who patterned after his childhood Dublin suburb the setting for The Barrytown Trilogy: the novels *The Commitments* (1988), *The Snapper* (1990), and *The Van* (1991).

It should be the goal of every writer to craft a story in such a way that setting becomes yet another character and inspires readers to seek out that place in the real world. In the case of Doyle's trilogy, a working-class neighborhood of row houses and linked back gardens, developments carved from farmland. The language is rough, the people are tough, but dreams of making it big, or simply making do, fuel each home's hearth.

In *The Van*, Jimmy Rabbitte Sr. takes in the state of his front garden, a tired mirror of his life at the start of the story.

"He was tempted to have a bash at the garden but the grass was nearly all gone, he'd been cutting it so often. He'd have looked like a right (idiot) bringing the lawn-mower for a walk around a baldy garden, in the middle of November. There were weeds under the hedge, but they could stay there. Anyway, he liked them; they made the garden look more natural. He'd painted the gate and railings a few months back; red, and a bit of white, the Liverpool colours, but (son) Darren didn't seem to care about that sort of thing any more."

From earliest memory, my favorite stories were those in which I could "see" where a tale was taking place. Writers call that a sense of place, but all I knew was that it meant the Bobbsey Twins weren't just floating in space, they were drifting down a river on a houseboat, and I was next to them on the deck. The mysteries Trixie Belden attempted to solve felt all the more scary because I could stare at the spooky old mansion. I stood awestruck on the vast prairie in Willa Cather's 1918 novel *My Antonia*, wanting, as did the narrator, "to walk straight on through the red grass and over the edge of the world, which could not be very far away."

In more recent reads, I stood at the bedroom window of Henry Perowne's London home, all quiet and just in from the cold in the few hours before the intense drama of Ian McEwan's 2005 novel *Saturday*: "From the second floor he faces the night, the city in its icy white light, the skeletal trees in the square, and thirty feet below, the black arrowhead railings like a row of spears."

Describing the entryway to Linda Manor, the Northampton, Massachusetts, nursing home where Tracy Kidder chronicled the bond between two male residents in his 1993 *Old Friends*, we see and hear the entryway and how it is more than a front door. "Periodically, wheelchair van or ambulances or private cars parked in front of the portico and new residents were escorted in, a few on their own feet, others in wheelchairs, some on gurneys . . . Some arrived directly from their own or their children's homes, and for them the transition tended to be hardest. Some newcomers left their relatives' cars only after coaxing."

When writing *Shelf Life: Romance, Mystery, Drama, and Other Page-Turning Adventures from a Year in a Bookstore*, I wanted to focus on my first year working at Edwards Books in Downtown Springfield, Massachusetts. I knew that the characters would be the staff and customers, but in the process of writing I realized that, like Kidder's Linda Manor, the store itself was another character. The more time I spent there, the more I saw and felt and listened to the space and realized it was a combination of town square, opinion podium, information purveyor, refuge for both employees and shoppers.

Has anyone taken a cab to the store since the book was published? I'm not sure. But we have had a few visitors who sought it out after reading, including a woman who drove the two hours from Boston and before leaving the store asked if there was anything good in the employees' candy drawer, one of the details I'd tucked in to help illustrate what type of store this was.

A reader got a kick out of eating a piece of chocolate from a drawer she'd read about in a place she'd driven two hours to see with her own eyes. An author felt she'd done her job. And all of it tasted pretty sweet.

EXERCISE

Use your senses to clearly form your story's setting. Sit down with your setting for an interview:

What do you look like?—A village of cottages? A concrete city? A Dublin housing estate with a sorry front garden?

Sound like?—Birdsong? Honking horns? Stories recounted by men looking back on their lives?

Smell like?—Fresh-cut meadows? Perfume from the open door of a fancy shop? A thick, muddy riverbank?

Taste like?—Pie right from the oven? Roasted nuts from the corner stand? Successful but hard-earned business survival?

Feel like?—Comfortable and carefree? Exhilarating and never-closing? Silky red grasses of a prairie that seems to have no end?

In the same way that interviewing a character—fictional or not—and doing a few paragraphs of a sketch can give you greater insight into that person, asking these specific questions and writing a paragraph or two to answer each can result in a list of qualities and examples that you can tuck into your work, or riff off, or turn into a continuing theme. Certainly, additional facts will appear as you craft your piece, but there's nothing like having a list of details on hand to inspire you, as well as your story. After all, your place is a character, and deserves to be described as fully as the beings who inhabit it so vividly.

CECILE GODING

Memory Map

CECILE GODING is from South Carolina, where she coordinated community literacy efforts for some years. She teaches writing and literature in colleges and neighborhood centers in the Iowa City area. Her essays, stories, and poems pop up here and there, most recently in *The Georgia Review; The Iowa Review;* and *Creative Writing: Four Genres in Brief.*

Y ou couldn't write a story that happened nowhere," writes Eudora Welty in *One Writer's Beginnings.* Well, it has been done. When we enter the world of literary nonfiction, though, we usually find ourselves grounded in a very particular time and place. A real place, whether the narrator recalls her hometown, or a scene barely glimpsed while traveling.

I am from Florence County, South Carolina. I will always be from Florence County, South Carolina. My childhood rural cross-roads forms a tic-tac-toe of memories. I start with our clapboard house, then move next door to the tiny post office where my mother worked, then cross the blacktop to the farm supply store, facing the abandoned railroad depot and its double set of tracks. Everything radiates from this place. Every few years, I like to get a big sheet of newsprint paper and redraw this map. Every time I do, I add in more and more tracks, invoking more and more memories and moments.

I draw maps of the Saudi Arabian compound where my husband and I once lived, of our Silicon Valley suburb (both before and after earthquakes), and of various wings of the vast hospital that, over the years, we came to know too well. As in the frontispieces of old books, all the people and their stories pop up, filling to overflowing every inch. Each inch has an event, a face, a voice, a temperature, a smell.

EXERCISE

For this exercise, begin by listing five places that surface in your memory. Make one of these your childhood home.

Choosing one of these, begin to sketch a map (a traditional bird's-eye view), encompassing an area of about one or two city blocks. If a scene from childhood, you might start by situating yourself on the map by drawing your house, then spreading out from there. Add favorite trees, your father's workshop, rural outbuildings, then move out to the gas station, the street that led to your school, the nearest neighbor.

For a place you've encountered while traveling, you might start with your port of entry—a bus station in Australia, a truck stop off a Florida interstate, Bombay airport at night—and fill in everything and everyone you remember.

Next, choose one area of your map and focus on one, much smaller, point within. It could be a room, a garden, a person, or an object. Then, write for twenty minutes about that one small item. For example, in a camp while on safari, it might be your backpack. It might be the fire, or the outhouse.

Choosing a small place focuses your memory on what really matters to you, today, about that time. Drawing a map helps you situate yourself. You can write off such a map for months, filling in more and more.

LYNNE BARRETT

Legwork: Exploring Place

LYNNE BARRETT is the author of *The Secret Names of Women* and *The Land of Go* and coeditor of *Birth: A Literary Companion*. Her fiction and nonfiction have appeared most recently in *Delta Blues*, *One Year to a Writing Life*, *A Dixie Christmas*, *Miami Noir*, *Willows Wept Review*, and the *Sun-Sentinel*. She teaches in the MFA program at Florida International University and is editor of *The Florida Book Review*.

When I teach nonfiction writing, I ask my students to explore the world, to learn how to find story and meaning any- and everywhere. I use this legwork exercise to help them practice observation and inquiry, and identify angles that can open up or deepen a project. They learn how to create the vicarious experience that anchors creative nonfiction, whether essay, memoir, narrative nonfiction, or travel writing.

Pieces my students have written show the fascination of what's hiding in plain sight. A day spent with a bridge tender reveals the Intra-Coastal Waterway as boat highway. The local Czech American club offers both the food of nostalgia and stories of displacement and community. The history of a patch of ground where a condo stands half-built holds South Florida crimes and dreams. Often a story can prompt further journeys, research, and longer works. But short place pieces can stand alone, and I've seen many of them published.

EXERCISE

1. Pick a place to visit that you are curious about. It may be nearby, a spot you pass every day, but have not had the time or the nerve to explore. It should not be a location you already know well, unless you have not been there for years. The place should be one that people inhabit, visit, or use in some way. Think about when you'll go; it can be at an odd time, for instance the racetrack early in the morning, or when things are in full swing at the flea market.

2. Before you go, briefly set down your expectations and prejudices, rumors you've heard or images you've had. Jot down your memories if you are going somewhere from your past or to a place equivalent to one you knew. (This can be helpful for memoir writing—if you have been recollecting ninth grade, visit a middle school or the mall when kids are hanging out. If you are writing about your religious upbringing, observe the ceremony of a different faith.)

3. Pack a notebook or pad (preferably small enough to be discreet) and multiple pens or pencils. Camera, optional.

4. Go. For this exercise you are an inquirer, an observer, a spy. Allow yourself to explore. If there's a tour, take it. If there's something to be tasted, sample it. If you need to seek permission to wander about, do so, and ask whoever is in charge how he or she came to be working there. People love to tell their stories.

   Above all, open yourself up, noting anything at all that strikes you, trying not to filter in advance what's important, but instead to see, hear, smell, taste, touch what's there. You want to pursue what strikes and interests you. Be open to surprise and discovery and your own idiosyncratic interests. Pay attention to what memories the place evokes for you.

Observe the people, their dress, talk (get dialogue down if you can), habits, manner, how they interact. Feel free to ask questions; be nosy. Try to learn at least three words that belong to this place, the names of objects, or jargon, or slang. You are licensed as a reporter here to find out whatever you can. Take lots of notes. Do this on the spot, or you can sit down immediately afterward and write down as much as you can recall.

5. Wait till the next day. Then, *without looking at your notes*, see what you remember. Write a few paragraphs that focus on your main impressions, whatever most struck you. You want to synthesize, not to write a blow-by-blow account. Let your memory's filter help you find a theme, subject, or angle.

6. Read what you have written. How good is your recall? What really sticks in your mind? People? Images? A line of dialogue, an incident, a contrast, an oddity? Use these and, drawing on your notes, write a piece of five hundred to seven hundred and fifty words that lets the reader learn about the place and you.

7. What most intrigues you now? Is there another place to visit, a person to talk to, some research that would supplement what you know, telling a larger story or exploring a new fascination? Go out and do some more legwork.

VOICE, DIALOGUE,
AND SOUND

MARILYN ABILDSKOV

All Work and a Little Word Play

MARILYN ABILDSKOV is the author of *The Men in My Country*, a memoir set in Japan. She received her MFA at the University of Iowa and has published fiction, essays, and poetry in such journals as *Southern Review*, *Sonora Review*, *River Teeth*, and *Ascent*. She lives in the San Francisco Bay area and teaches at Saint Mary's College of California.

There's no denying the heat involved in family dramas or the narratives that spring from romantic travails, but work, too, with its petty jealousies and small betrayals and surges of delight so often mixed with despair—this, too, deserves literary space. And whether you're throwing newspapers for a living or calculating odds as an actuary, working as a forest ranger or grading papers as a college professor, whether you're spending your days among redwoods or paper clips, there are stories to be told, scene by scene.

EXERCISE

So try this: Write a workplace drama where the main action takes place in one day. Start with a single scene and then revise that scene in two distinct voices: first the voice of restraint or a voice of abundance; second the voice of stripped-down realism or a voice of subjective romanticism.

The voice of restraint could be described as plain, grounded in realism's charge to depict life as it is experienced for ordinary people. It isn't that the writer of a restrained voice won't use multisyllabic words on occasion, but in general, there is a stripped-down quality to this voice. Consider the opening line of Valerie Martin's story "Love," about a social worker and her client: "The man I am talking to wants to kill me."

Or this, the clear, concise description of the room that comes in Martin's story, absent any metaphorical flourish: "It is hot in the room where we are sitting."

Or a key moment of action that leads to a tender shift in power: "My foot misses a step," the narrator says.

By contrast, the abundant voice favors a romantic style: subjective experience communicated in fresh, spontaneous language. In Dr. Susan Mates's essay "Meningococcus," about doctors trying—and failing—to save a small girl, the writer chooses three or four words where one might do. Where one metaphor might hold, Mates piles them up as if trying to locate language to explain something as inexplicable as a child dying.

"She is a lily among thorns, curls luster like black grapes, lips a scarlet thread." The baby's cheeks in the piece become "flowers of the earth, the singing of birds," her eyes "the eyes of doves by the rivers of water, washed with tears and milk." The mother of the child—a child about to die—becomes a "pillar of salt" and the child's teeth a "flock of sheep."

Once you've experimented by revising your scene in two distinct voices, look back to see what works and why. It's easy to imagine that the voice of realism would be the more reliable of the two, that the romantic voice will be full of flowery nonsense. But reading an essay like the one Mates wrote, where the nearly archaic language of "flowers" and "doves" and a "flock of sheep" stand in contrast to the clinical setting of the hospital, makes me wonder, and sometimes stealing a single line from an exercise will do the trick. After all, a single romantic gesture—ask anyone who has gone without a love note, a bouquet of flowers, or a kiss on the forehead—goes a long, long way, especially after a long dull day of figuring statistics or stealing paper clips.

PHILIP GRAHAM

Can You Hear Me Now?

PHILIP GRAHAM is the author of a collection of essays, *The Moon, Come to Earth: Dispatches from Lisbon*, and coauthor of two memoirs of Africa, *Parallel Worlds* and the forthcoming *Braided Worlds*. He is also the author of two story collections and a novel. Graham teaches at the University of Illinois, Urbana-Champaign, and the Vermont College of Fine Arts, and is a founding editor of the literary/arts journal *Ninth Letter*.

I no longer saw faces, and knew in all probability I should go through life without seeing them." So writes Jacques Lusseyran, in his memoir *And There Was Light*, about the days after he lost his sight at the age of six. Lusseyran's greatest initial challenge wasn't lack of sight, but confounding messages encoded in sound: "People were not at all as they were said to be, and never for more than two minutes at a stretch. Some were, of course, but that was a bad sign, a sign that they did not want to understand or be alive . . . That kind of thing I could [hear] in them right away, because . . . I caught them off guard. People . . . only dress up for those who are looking at them."

Listening deeply, he could hear that the highly praised student had merely memorized the lesson, or that the math teacher's bold voice masked a trouble that turned out to be his wife's desertion. Sound *changed* for Lusseyran, forcing him to reinterpret the world: "Our appetites, our humors, our secret lives, even our best-guarded thoughts [are] translated into the sounds of our voices, into tones, inflections or rhythms."

If you've traveled in a country where you don't understand the language, you've found yourself listening to people speaking in French, Italian, or Yoruba, and gleaning from tone and vocal rhythm someone's emotional state, even a broad sense of what is being said. Being, in a sense, blind to the language, you can concentrate on meaning beyond the actual words, and hear as Lusseyran did.

Why is it so difficult to concentrate on sound's world of meaning? Lusseyran offers this clue: "A very short time after I went blind I forgot the faces of my mother and father and the faces of most of the people I loved . . . Could it be that affection, or love, puts us so close to people that we are no longer able to evoke their image?" Our relationship with the vocal tones of those with whom we are emotionally entangled is indeed complex. People say the opposite of what they mean, or their words contain multiple shades of meaning. How do we separate what we hear from what we wish to hear or what we're told we should be hearing?

Sound reluctantly reveals its mysteries—not only speech, but whatever sets off vibrations in the air. No telephone merely rings. We cocreate the sound that calls to us. Anticipating his lover, a man will approach the ringing phone with pleasure; the ringing during dinner—perhaps a telemarketer's call—sounds abrasive, ugly; and the ringing that wakes us in the night is tinged with our confusion and dread. Each ring sounds different—we provide the emotional notes that create different harmonics.

Often sounds are defined culturally, received wisdom that prevents us from listening. On occasion I've lived in small villages of the Beng people of Ivory Coast, while my wife, Alma Gottlieb, conducts anthropological fieldwork; one day while describing to my friend San Kofi the early morning exchanges of birds as singing, he immediately corrected me: "Birds don't *sing*, they *cry*." Kofi inadvertently taught me that, while music is my culture's metaphor for what birds produce, for the Beng those same sounds are an extended form of weeping. Birds neither sing nor cry unless we say they do.

EXERCISE

There are many ways to hone the skills of listening. Find a street corner or a park; sit, eyes closed, and listen to the passing voices. Form an image of what someone looks like from the sound of his or her voice, and then open your eyes. Did your expectations match what you see?

On a more intimate level, remember a sound that evokes a happy or sorrowful memory and try evoking it so that a reader can feel the emotion that's attached to the sound. I can recall as a child listening to my father's soft steps in the kitchen, the creak of the refrigerator's freezer door, the click of ice cubes in a glass—ordinary sounds, yet my father was filling his glass with ice for another drink of whiskey, easing himself further into a place his family couldn't reach.

Finally, try listening to the emotional topography superimposed over the verbal topography of conversation: look past the people you best know and listen less to their words and more to their delivery. Remember that even a cough, a laugh, or seemingly idle humming can speak, if only we know how to listen.

RICHARD HOFFMAN

Starting from Solitude

RICHARD HOFFMAN is the author of *Half the House: A Memoir*; the poetry collections *Without Paradise* and *Gold Star Road*, winner of the Barrow Street Press Poetry Prize; and *Interference & Other Stories*. His work, both verse and prose, has appeared in *Agni*, *Ascent*, *Harvard Review*, *Hudson Review*, *Poetry*, *Witness*, and other magazines. He teaches at Emerson College and in the Stonecoast MFA Program at the University of Southern Maine.

This exercise is designed to establish an authorial voice and generate the first draft of a one-person scene that will encompass the character I's wishes, fears, worries, regrets, hopes.

You will see that, in addition to creating a sense of your character's interiority, you are being directed to entertain the counterfactual, the conditional, what did not happen but could have under other circumstances. (A cautionary note: This interior point of view, coupled with the sense of "what might have been," can be a powerful experience. Grief is not an uncommon response while doing this exercise.) You are also being prompted to present the space itself and the objects in it as sensory experience for the reader.

EXERCISE

First write each of the following directions on a single index card. Number each card on the back. (Note: All directions refer to "you" in the scene you're creating, not you the writer doing this exercise. Likewise, "here" means the space in which the scene occurs, not the space where you are doing this exercise.)

1. Enter the space. Be sure to use an action verb.

2. Where is the source of light?

3. What special or important object is there with you?

4. Notice what you are wearing.

5. Why are you wearing these clothes?

6. What can you hear from here?

7. What can you hear if you listen very carefully?

8. Mention the position of your body.

9. Where were you before you arrived here?

10. Who was there?

11. Describe your interaction with that person or persons.

12. Was that interaction the one you would have wanted?

13. What do you wish had happened?

14. Change the position of your body.

15. Reach out and touch or handle an object in this space.

16. What is your biggest fear?

17. When you leave this space, where will you go?

18. Is there someplace where you would rather be going?

19. Why?

20. Shift the position of your body again.

21. When was the last time you ate?

22. What did you eat?

23. Are you hungry?

24. What do you know now, at this writing, at the age you are now, that it would have been useful to know then?

25. Take a deep breath. What do you smell?

26. How will you know it's time to leave this space?

27. How will you prepare yourself to leave?

28. What did you know then, what were you sure of, that you see now, at this writing, at the age you are now, to be false?

29. Can you still hear what you heard before? Any new sounds?

30. What has changed since you entered the space?

31. Prepare to leave. Begin by moving your body.

32. And, finally, exit the space.

Arrange the cards facedown, in order, with the number one card on top.

Now, think of a crucial moment of solitude in the story you wish to tell. Or choose a place where you were often alone, perhaps a place you retreated to for solitude: a bedroom, up a tree, by a creek, under the porch. When you have chosen the place, turn over the first card and follow the directions. Continue through all thirty-two cards. Do not skip ahead.

Of course, once you are finished, and after a suitable "cooling off" period, you are free to depart from the instructions by deleting what doesn't serve the scene that's emerged, adding detail, moving things around. Often the resulting scene, even if it turns out to be a minor one, works as a kind of keynote since it sets a precedent for the portrayal of a multidimensional self-aware first-person protagonist, the strength of any good memoir.

CARL H. KLAUS

The Artful "I": Exercises in Style and Voice

CARL H. KLAUS, professor emeritus at the University of Iowa and founder of Iowa's Nonfiction Writing Program, currently serves as coeditor (with Patricia Hampl) of Sightline Books: the University of Iowa Press Series in Literary Nonfiction. He is the author of *My Vegetable Love: A Journal of a Growing Season; Weathering Winter: A Gardener's Daybook; Taking Retirement: A Beginner's Diary;* and *Letters to Kate: Life after Life.* His forthcoming book is *The Chameleon "I": Personae in the Personal Essay.*

Voice—such a revered thing in nonfiction writing that it's often invoked in worshipful phrases like "finding one's voice" or "having a pitch-perfect voice," as if having found it or perfected it, one will never lose it or change it. But the nature of experience suggests otherwise, as Montaigne makes clear in his Heraclitean assertion that "I may presently change, not only by chance, but also by intention," and as Nancy Mairs reveals in her declaration that "I have indeed always had *a* voice, but it wasn't *this* voice." Or as Edward Hoagland affirms in declaring that "the artful 'I' of an essay can be as chameleon as any narrator in fiction."

So it might be useful to think of trying out several voices and not only to suit the changing circumstances of one's life, but also to become as flexible in writing as most of us are in the give-and-take of our daily lives, moving back and forth between such a variety of public and private roles that we often modulate our style and voice without even thinking about it. The changes might be as wide-ranging as E. B. White's exuberant list [in the foreword to his *Essays*] of roles an essayist can play—"philosopher, scold, jester, raconteur, confidante, pundit, devil's advocate, enthusiast"—shape-shifting roles that can tell us things we might not have realized without seeing things through the lens of different styles and voices.

Once upon a time, for example, I asked my students to write three or four different versions of an opening autobiographical paragraph—using the same facts but a different style and voice in each version. So it was that I felt obliged to produce some autobiographical openings of my own, which led me to realize that I had a much more complicated set of feelings about the basic circumstances of my early life—being orphaned before the age of six—than I had previously imagined. When I started writing my first piece, it never occurred to me that I might be as tough, or seemingly calloused, as I sounded in that version. I had wanted just to produce something in as direct a style as possible, using plain language in straightforward declarative sentences, and suddenly I found myself claiming to have been untouched by the premature deaths of my parents: "I didn't let it get to me, otherwise I would have been dead like the rest of them." Likewise, in my second version, I didn't set out to play the role of a tender, self-pitying fellow, but that's the voice that emerged when I tried to craft something in a more artfully balanced syntax: "When I was very young, both of my parents passed away—my father when I was only two, my mother just before I was six." So too, in the third version, I began with the intent to produce a piece in lengthy, periodic structures, withholding the main clause of each until the very end of each sentence, and those elaborately structured sentences led me into a much more contemplative voice than before. In each case, a deliberate stylistic choice to write this way or that led to a distinctly different voice, different point of view, and different way of thinking and feeling about those basic facts of my life. That exercise turned out to be so instructive for my students and for me that I invite you to try it yourself.

EXERCISE

Imagine that you're about to write the opening paragraph of your autobiography, or of a memoir about an especially important period in your life. What are the basic facts that you want to establish in that paragraph? Once you've settled upon the facts, then write them up in three or four distinctly different styles—one in simple sentences and plain language, restricting yourself as much as possible to words of no more than two syllables; another in lengthy periodic structures, using diction of your own choice; a third featuring an extended metaphor, using syntax and diction of your own choice; and a fourth involving yet a different stylistic prescription of your own choice.

Once you've produced each version, then consider the different voices you've created as well as the different perceptions you've had as a result of each style, and how they might lead you and your readers to an engaging and thoughtfully developed portrait of yourself. For it's well to remember that the way we come across in writing is not just the result of what we say about ourselves, but the way(s) in which we say it. Or as Scott Russell Sanders once said, "What we meet on the page is not the flesh and blood author, but a simulacrum, a character who wears the label I"—a thing made of carefully and artfully chosen words.

REBECCA McCLANAHAN

The Music of Sentences

REBECCA McCLANAHAN has published nine books, most recently *Deep Light: New and Selected Poems 1987–2007* and *The Riddle Song and Other Rememberings*, which won the 2005 Glasgow Award for nonfiction. Her work has appeared in *The Best American Essays*, the Pushcart anthology, and *The Best American Poetry* series, among other publications. She lives in New York and teaches in the low-residency MFA programs of Queens University of Charlotte and Pacific Lutheran University.

The ear writes my poems, not the mind," said Stanley Kunitz in a PBS interview. "The ear is the infallible test." Nonfiction writers, too, often speak of the important role the ear plays in the writing and revision process. When our writing is going well, we don't worry about sentences. Guided by natural rhythms, one sentence appears, then another and another, and before we know it, we've reached the end of the paragraph. If we're lucky, the sentences will hold, the paragraph will retain its beauty and poise, and the essay will snap into place.

Then, there are those other times.

We reread our essay and despair. There is no music in our language. The prose is stilted. Chopped into fragments. Then in the next breath hurtling like this sentence at unsafe speeds taking every shortcut possible, every hairpin curve, shrieking and squealing and threatening to collide with the next sentence unless it can find, and fast, a safe exit. At these times, it's helpful to know what our sentences are doing and how we can nudge them in the right direction.

One way to musically tune our sentences is to listen carefully to the sounds of individual words. When possible, these sounds should reinforce the imagistic and emotional content of our sentence. For instance, *ripple* is probably not the best word to use in a sentence about the weight of loneliness. Not only does *ripple* mean something slight; it sounds slight. The short *i* is a bantam-weight vowel, the lightest, most childlike sound in our language. A more weighty choice would be a word like *stone* or *root* or *nobody*. Is there a vowel more heavy or sad than the long *o*? It hollows out the mouth, intones the deepest sorrow. And it isn't merely the long vowel that makes *stone* and *root* weigh more than *ripple*. Because they are one-syllable words, their individual heft is felt as we place them on the page. And their ending sounds make strong final impressions. The *t* of *root* supplies an abrupt ending, while the *n* of *stone* remains deep in our throats, providing weight and texture to reinforce the feeling of heaviness.

But individual words alone, however musically apt, cannot make our sentences sing. We also need an underlying rhythm, a musical line playing beneath our words. Just as singers vary the tone of a musical phrase by prolonging it, shortening it, pitching it higher or lower, or changing its sound color (breathy, harsh, resonant, liquid), writers vary the tone of passages by the sounds they choose and by the way they "sing" these sounds. A nonfiction narrator who speaks in carefully balanced, grammatically correct sentences will lead readers on a different route from, say, a narrator who speaks in jagged, streetwise slang. No sentence style is inherently superior to another, but each style makes a different contract with the reader. For instance, the energetic prose style of a writer like Eldridge Cleaver slaps us awake. In *Soul on Ice*, the rollicking, rolling syntax catches our attention and we grab on, riding its rhythm. We're heading somewhere, we're not sure where, but we feel the power snowballing, gathering weight as it tumbles toward its end. We revel in Cleaver's prose, his brilliantly tuned sentences. And some new journalists, such as Melissa Faye Greene, carefully modulate the cadences, syntax, and diction of their sentences to suggest the emotional landscape of their informants. In *Praying for Sheetrock*, Greene takes us inside Fanny's mind as Fanny recalls a difficult childhood filled with monotonous toil:

> Sleep, pick, eat, pick, pray . . .
> Bed, field, table, field, church. Bed. Field. Table: a hollow gallop of wooden bowls on a wooden table. Field. Church: a chase through dark woods and climbing vines, barefoot behind her grandmother . . . Bed. Field. Table. Field . . .

By cycling and recycling the same words through recurring staccato rhythms, Greene mimics the rhythms of Fanny's thoughts, revealing the weight of weariness and the monotony of Fanny's days.

As you review your drafts, don't just *look* at the words. *Listen* to their musical pitch, color, and volume. Did you use soft, soothing consonants in one description and harsh, cacophonous consonants in another? Did you use deep-toned, solemn vowels in one section of dialogue and high-pitched vowels in another? What about the lengths and rhythms of your phrases? Did one paragraph gallop while the other minced, step by step, toward its end? In return for your attention to their needs, your sentences will reward you by helping to tune your essay to its most effective musical key.

EXERCISE

1. As an exercise in varying the sound qualities of your sentences, write three different descriptions of the same character or setting. In the first version, use lots of deep vowel tones

(long *o*, long *u*) and liquid or resonant consonants (*r, l, w, y, m, n, ng, z*). Then rewrite the description changing the deep vowels to light vowels (short *i*, short *a*). Finally, rewrite it using harsh consonants (*k*, hard *g*, hard *c, t, p*) or sibilants (*s, sh, ch*). Notice how the musical tone of the description changes depending on the sound qualities of your language.

2. Write two or three different versions of the same scene. Don't change the basic facts of the scene; change only the sounds of the words and the lengths and rhythms of your sentences. Here are examples of the same scene—a woman washing dishes while her children play outside—written in two different musical keys with two different rhythms:

> *She watches through the kitchen window the comings and goings of her children as one by one the dinner dishes slide from her hands and into the steaming dishwater, one plate still holding the memory of potatoes and gravy.*

> *Saucers clatter. Cups clank. Platters rattle. She grabs a plate, scrubs its crusted skin. Dried potato. Gravy. Outside the window her kids scream and scatter.*

3. Practice new syntactic rhythms by copying out whole passages by an author whose sentences you admire. Then, if you're eager for a challenge, write a "grammatical rhyme" modeled on that author's words. In a grammatical rhyme, you imitate the rhythmic and syntactic structures of a piece while using your own words. Don't worry about reproducing the sense of the passage; pay attention only to the structure of the sentences. Here's a brief passage from Richard Selzer's essay "Four Appointments with the Discus Thrower," followed by my grammatical rhyme, my imitation of Selzer's syntactic structures:

> *In the evening, I go once more to that ward to make my rounds. The head nurse reports to me that Room 542 is deceased. She has*

discovered this quite by accident, she says. No, there had been no sound. Nothing. It's a blessing, she says.

In my dream, I stumble yet again over the weeds to get to him. The doggy moon barks to me that my boy is gone. "I have sniffed it through my nose," it says. "Yes, there will be no boy. Never. That's the end," it barks.

MICHAEL McGREGOR

Hanging Around Time

MICHAEL McGREGOR is an associate professor of nonfiction (and fiction) writing in the MFA program at Portland State University. He has written about people for *Poets & Writers*, *The Writer's Chronicle*, *American Theatre*, *The Seattle Review*, *Weber: The Contemporary West*, *Portland*, *Portland Monthly*, *The Oregonian*, and the Oregon Historical Society. His writing awards include an Illinois Arts Council literary grant and the Daniel Curley Award for Best Short Fiction.

E ffective writing about another person always involves an encounter between writer and subject. The story that ends up being told is about the subject but it belongs to the writer and is based primarily on the writer's perceptions and evaluations of the information she has gathered. The writer isn't a mouthpiece for the subject but rather a stand-in for the reader, conveying what an actual encounter with the subject is like.

The temptation in writing a profile is to limit your research to interviewing your subject and maybe reading what has been written about him or by him. Some more-adventurous writers might talk to people who know him or have worked with him. The best way to give a strong sense of a person, however, is to show him living his life, using as many of your senses as you can to collect information not only about your subject but also about his surroundings and his actions. One of the masters of this approach is Susan Orlean, who puts her "hanging around time" with a subject at the center of most of her profiles, using her observations to construct not just ideas about a subject but scenes in which we see the subject as a character.

Gathering the information necessary to construct a full scene and thereby give a full picture of a subject is difficult, especially when you're concentrating on recording what the subject is saying while keeping him engaged with you in a meaningful conversation. Add to this the emotional difficulty of asking someone about his personal life—in effect, eavesdropping on conversations he usually has only with family or friends, if he has them at all—and it's easy to come away from time with your subject, even a formal interview, with little that is useful or interesting.

EXERCISE

To practice tackling several of these matters at once, go to a public place like a park, café, or dining hall where people are talking freely and sit down near a group in conversation—at least two but not more than four people, so the logistics of the interaction don't become too difficult. Using paper and pen, record the conversation in as much detail as you can, noting how the people are dressed, their relative ages, what kinds of gestures they make, and what their interactions are like. For example, do they seem to have the same socioeconomic background? Do they have equal power in the relationship? Are they comfortable with one another? Does one of them dominate? Do they talk about intimate subjects or keep their conversation light? Are they serious and earnest or breezy and sarcastic? Are there contradictions between how they look and how they act?

Observe for as long as you can—at least half an hour, if possible—and note how the conversation and the dynamics of the interaction change. At the same time, jot down as much of the actual conversation as you can. When you're done recording or, better yet, while you're still recording, note as many details of the setting as possible—not only visual details but also sounds and smells and even how the air feels. Describe the mood of the place you're in, the weather, the time of day, and the level of energy. Think of comparisons and metaphors, too—what are all of these things like?

You might balk at first at recording someone else's conversation, but remember that this is just an exercise, one that will help you transcend the emotional barriers that keep a writer from asking her subject probing questions or noting potentially unflattering details.

Above all, this exercise will show you:

1. how much information is available to you when you observe a subject in context rather than just recording a voice answering questions.

2. the rewards of forcing yourself beyond your own emotional hesitancies.

Once you've collected your information, write a scene based on some part of the conversation you recorded—with a vivid setting, rounded characters, and a clear emotional arc—just as you would in working on a profile for publication.

CHRISTOPHER MERRILL

He Said *What?*

CHRISTOPHER MERRILL'S books include *Things of the Hidden God: Journey to the Holy Mountain; Only the Nails Remain: Scenes from the Balkan Wars*; and *The Tree of the Doves*. He directs the International Writing Program at the University of Iowa.

J ust as writers must interrogate their materials, their notes and impressions, their research and revelations, and their shifting relationship to the language, so from time to time they might examine their working methods in order to maintain the rigor of their craft. The poet Louise Glück has described the culmination of each of her books as "a conscious diagnostic act, a swearing off" of a certain approach to writing poems, now forgoing Latinate suspended sentences, now dispensing with certain nouns. Nonfiction writers might make a similar inventory of what has become habitual in their practice—the tools used without thinking—and discard or modify them in favor of discovering what may in the end prove to be a better means of expression—that is, adequate to the subject at hand, not to an earlier conception of what good writing entails.

Writing dialogue is surely one of the more difficult aspects of the craft to master, more so for a nonfiction writer obliged to report faithfully what was said. The interview, of course, remains dialogue's staple, and while there is no right or wrong way to conduct an interview, certain rules obtain: to ask questions that will elicit meaningful responses; to accurately chronicle the conversation—on tape, in a notebook, on a computer; and then to frame it in a revelatory manner. John McPhee once noted that the tape recorder "does not select," and indeed the interviewer who takes notes has already begun to write the piece, choosing this inflection, tone, or turn of phrase over that. Not that I am arguing for one method or another: each writer discovers for him- or herself what works best. But I do want to suggest that every method of recording an interview has limitations, which the writer should acknowledge not just for honesty's sake but for the possibility of learning something essential about his or her own process of selection: the key to writing.

In the game of telephone a whispered word or phrase is passed from one person to another until it is unrecognizable: the hallmark of the dialogue composed by a writer who does not listen very well. And we all know how our words can be misconstrued or taken out of context—which is why hearsay is not allowed in a court of law. We expect a fair hearing in a work of literary nonfiction: the writer must fashion dialogue that represents what was actually said, not what he or she wishes was said.

EXERCISE

Here, then, is a three-part exercise designed to reveal to you something about your listening abilities. Conduct an interview in the following manner: tape and transcribe it; take contemporaneous notes, assuming that the tape recorder may not work (and who has not lost an interview to a depleted battery, background noise, or the gods of misrule?); and then, after the conversation, write down what you can remember about it—every question and answer, every detail of the setting. Then compare the three versions of the interview, which will probably differ one from another. In those differences lie the keys to what you hear, and perhaps even why— keys that may open doors to rooms in which you may listen more closely to the conversations integral to your next piece of writing.

MALINA SAVAL

Permission to Eavesdrop

MALINA SAVAL is a journalist, writer, and the author of the nonfiction book *The Secret Lives of Boys*, which was inspired by a single line of dialogue uttered by one of her male teenage students. She lives with her husband, son, and daughter, and their two dogs, in Los Angeles, California.

I'm a natural born snoop, so it's lucky that I make my living as a journalist. Wherever I am, I am armed and dangerous, my weapons of choice alternating between a Power Book g-4, a mini microcassette recorder, or, when I'm feeling old-fashioned, a notepad and pen. I have a gift for deciphering dialogue between perfect strangers seated six rows in front of me; I can read lips. In Los Angeles, where I live, I am often found at little outdoor cafés, sipping a vanilla soy latte while simultaneously angling my Dictaphone surreptitiously (it's tucked underneath a napkin) in the direction of a delicious conversation held, for example, by two snooty intellectual types draped all in black at the next table over: "It's like explaining fire to a fish," says one. Responds the other, "It's true. Once you have found God, God ceases to be that which you were searching for. By definition you can't possibly conceptualize Him." A short essay that I had due for a required graduate-level philosophy course about man's quest for God was thus hatched.

Other eavesdropping opportunities have borne far fluffier fare. I was once in an airport on an extended layover from Los Angeles to Boston, stuck in Dallas. In the bathroom I overheard two women—

both with matching Texan beehives and valises the size of longhorn bulls—complaining about the direction in which bathroom stalls opened. "Why do airport bathrooms open from the outside in?" inquired one of the women. "I can barely fit myself in here without brushing my ass against the toilet, never mind my Louis Vuitton carry-on." I thought about it; the woman was right. Shortly after, I penned a whimsical, short article on the subject of airport bathrooms for a leading travel magazine.

Capturing the essence of natural-sounding dialogue is one of the most crucial elements for stringing together a refined piece of nonfiction featuring human conversation. The words must sing to the writer and reader alike. Possessing a keen ear for dialogue can function as the essential technical tool when aiming to convey realism in a work of nonfiction. Snippets of conversation can often become the jumping-off point for an essay, an editorial, perhaps an entire memoir.

EXERCISE

Venture out in public. Maybe it's your favorite park. Or a local café in your neighborhood. Maybe the beach. Or a dog run. Or a run-down, smoky watering hole serving two-dollar beers from the tap. Anywhere where there are sure to be people milling about and chatting.

Park yourself in the midst of your surroundings. To start, commit to at least an hour. Once you get comfortable, this time frame can be extended.

Listen. Don' be discouraged if on your first outing nothing more titillating than someone asking the time is overheard. Many a morning I have dragged my fluffy mutts to the dog park in the hopes of creative inspiration and the only living, breathing being mouthing anything of any interest is I to my dogs (Fenway and Coco, by the way, are superb conversationalists—Woof! Woof!). Conversely, the next time I venture out, I'll eavesdrop on some disgruntled owner lecturing his stubborn dog that he needs a shrink. I've overheard posh Beverly Hills poodle owners compare the perks and pitfalls of veterinary health insurance. Poop is a popular conversation starter. "Look at its size and color!" I once heard a proud dog owner exclaim, beaming over her puppy's poop as if it were the meconium diaper of a newborn baby. It prompted me to submit a little ditty about the joys of dog defecation to *The Bark*. (Hmmm . . . they still haven't gotten back to me; maybe poop is passé?)

Bottom line: Be patient. Much of the creative process does involve letting the muses come to you.

Write down conversation bites of any sort of appeal. It may be an entire paragraph, or a sentence, or a single word. Or a sound—a gesture.

Free-associate. Does the paragraph, sentence, words, sounds, and gestures inspire you to think of a particular subject? Is the conversation, perhaps, reminiscent of one you yourself have had? Did it make you laugh? Did it make you cry? Did it make you angry? Did you want to smack the characters engaged in the conversation because they sounded so utterly stupid? Did you want to contribute in any way your own opinion? Jot down words, sentences, syllables—anything that comes to mind having to do with the conversation bites you have scribbled. You're likely sitting on a wonderful slice of your own work of nonfiction—a scene, a chapter, the beginning of an essay or memoir.

SUE WILLIAM SILVERMAN

Innocence & Experience:
Voice in Creative Nonfiction

SUE WILLIAM SILVERMAN is the author of the memoirs *Because I Remember Terror, Father, I Remember You* and *Love Sick: One Woman's Journey Through Sexual Addiction*. She teaches in the low-residency MFA in Writing Program at Vermont College and is associate editor of *Fourth Genre: Explorations in Nonfiction*. Her poetry collection is *Hieroglyphics in Neon*.

When I studied fiction writing, one of my teachers told me that "voice is everything." As true as this is in fiction, it's equally true in nonfiction. For even though I'm telling my personal story, the voice I use isn't my everyday speaking voice. In fact, my observation both from writing and reading creative nonfiction is that most writers, in order to fully develop their stories, employ two major voices. I've defined these voices by re-imagining phrases originated by the poet William Blake, labeling one a Song (or Voice) of Innocence, the other a Song (or Voice) of Experience.

The Voice of Innocence relates the facts of the experience, the surface subject. It's the voice that says, in effect, "first this happened to me, then this next thing happened." It reveals the sequence of events, the particulars of your experience, the relatively "innocent," unaware persona in the immediacy of the moment, describing events as if *they are happening now.*

This Voice of Innocence is then twined to what I dub the Voice of Experience, thus adding a more mature author-persona. This second narrator establishes the progression of thought in creative nonfiction, allowing the reader to know what the Voice of Innocence, what the facts, mean. By use of irony, reflection, and metaphor, it interprets the surface subject. It reflects upon the story, thus exploring the complexity of any given experience.

For example, in *Love Sick: One Woman's Journey Through Sexual Addiction,* I implement an addict voice (the Song of Innocence) as well as a sober voice (the Song of Experience). Here is a paragraph that utilizes both voices, where I, a college freshman, describe my feelings toward a scarf given to me by my older, married lover: "I press the scarf against my nose and mouth. I take a deep breath. The scent is of him—leaves smoldering in autumn dusk—and I believe it is a scent I have always craved, one I will always want. **I don't understand why the scent of the scarf . . . seems more knowable, more tangible than the rest of him.**"

Here, I begin in the addict persona where the Voice of Innocence romanticizes the man and the maroon-scarf scent (just as I actually did in college), before moving into a more sober persona, the Voice of Experience (in **bold**), which then reveals that the scarf is actually a metaphor for loneliness. Since at the time of any given event we're usually not aware of meaning and metaphor, we need this more experienced voice, reflecting back, to guide the reader deeper into the moment—whatever the theme (sadness, loss, trauma, illness, childhood, etc.).

In sum, these two voices interact throughout an essay or memoir to create a relationship between the story itself and the more mature insights you want the story to convey.

EXERCISE

Step 1: Recall a room from a house in which you lived as a child. Using the voice of the younger you (Innocence), describe the room (couch, television, vase, curtains, bookcase, etc.) relying on sensory details. What did the room sound like, smell like, feel like, taste like, look like (be imaginative). As you write, be sure to place yourself in the scene, in the room. *I brush my fingers across the green velvety couch.*

Step 2: In a separate paragraph choose one particular detail from the room (couch, lamp) and, using the Voice of Experience persona (who you are now), describe it in such a way that it conveys how you feel about the room *now*, reflecting back (knowledge you lacked in the past). Was the room "safe"? Scary? Was it a room in which you experienced love? Anger? In effect, you'll use words that give this specific detail an "attitude" or a slant. Remember, depending upon how a thing (or person) is described, you reveal your attitude toward it. *This attitude toward an object will likewise reflect a deeper attitude (Voice of Experience) toward your life.*

Here's an example. Suppose a detail in this room is a vase with a hairline crack from when it was dropped (or thrown?). Now, if you have sad or "negative" feelings toward the room (i.e., *life*) in which the vase is displayed, you can describe how the crack ruins it, mars the beauty of the glaze. In this description, therefore, the vase becomes a metaphor for the idea of loss.

If, on the other hand, you want the vase to represent how this room (or life) is full of safety and companionship, you might describe how the long-lasting glue safely holds the vase together. In other words, depending upon the *attitude* you wish to convey, you can describe the same image quite differently. Thus, the images in the Voice of Experience are slanted to reveal this attitude, metaphor, or theme.

Let's look at another example or detail in the room: curtains. They can be described to reveal a metaphor for safety. Their thick, velvety texture protects windows; therefore, they likewise protect you. Or, on the other hand, these same curtains can be described as a metaphor for entrapment: they're *blocking* the windows, no way out. In short, when your descriptions are slanted, you are developing the Voice of Experience.

Result

By combining your sensory description of the room with the more fully developed detail, the voices of Innocence and Experience seamlessly merge together into a cohesive whole, thus examining the totality of an experience. In short, you're exploring both the event itself (the past) as well as your present interpretation of it, reflecting back on it as an author, writing. (*One summer day when my family lives on Southern Avenue, I sit on the couch gazing toward the window. But the thick textured curtains prevent me from seeing outside. The air in the room feels static, unmoving. Soon, I'm too exhausted to run into the yard to play. Silence wells up around me as if I'll never play outside again. . . .)*

Example

In the first three sentences of the following paragraph, from my essay "Tiles for a Mosaic," I present a straightforward, Voice of Innocence account of what I observe while sitting on a terrace in Portugal: the scent of trees, fluttering paper, sun and shade. Back then, I wasn't aware of any significance of that moment. It is only *now* that the Voice of Experience examines the meaning of these sensory images. Only at my desk, writing, am I able to add the last sentence, which reveals the theme of the essay: that the potency of sensory experience evokes memory.

From the valley rises the warm, spicy scent of eucalyptus and olive, lupine and poppy. Cerise bougainvilleas etch whitewashed walls. I drift in sun, in shade from cork trees, sun and shade, pages of the book, the aerogramme, fluttering against my fingertips. The day is transparent, I see straight through it, as if I'm watching time itself alchemize the sun, the book, the aerogramme into images freighted with memory.

NED STUCKEY-FRENCH

Starting with Dialogue

NED STUCKEY-FRENCH'S work has appeared in journals and maga-
zines such as *In These Times, The Missouri Review, The Iowa Review,
Walking Magazine, culturefront, Fourth Genre, Pinch,* and *American
Literature,* and has twice been listed among the notable essays in
Best American Essays. He is an assistant professor at Florida State
University and book review editor of *Fourth Genre.*

A recurring problem in writing creative nonfiction is the
problem of truth. How creative can I be? Where is the line
between fiction and nonfiction? It's a hard tightrope to
walk: we have to call on our imagination to supplement our memory, but when have we gone too far and turned our essay into story?
If you worry about this problem too little, you can hurt people's
feelings or even find yourself apologizing on *Oprah.* But, if you
worry about it too much, you never get started, and what we're
about right now is getting started.

Often this problem first raises its ugly head when we have to
write dialogue. How can I put words in my dear, departed grandmother's mouth?

We know dramatized scenes are the building blocks of personal
essays and that scenes require dialogue, but as essayists we usually
rely on our memories, not interviews or transcripts. True, we may
be able to ask others if they remember what they said, but their
memories, if they are able and willing to share them, are as selective
as our own.

I think the best way to solve the dialogue problem is to begin with the dialogue itself. We all remember some remark that stung, a comeback that was perfect, or, perhaps more suggestively, some sentence that seemed out of character or otherwise puzzling. For years I remembered a remark my father made, but until I finally wrote an essay about it, I wasn't sure what it meant.

When I was twelve or so, my dad, my younger brother, and I spent most of August building a tree house. One afternoon, during which we had been back and forth between the table saw in the basement and the biggest maple in our backyard several times, my dad was hanging upside down twelve feet off the ground in ninety-degree heat trying to bang yet another 20-penny nail through a two-by-four into the trunk of the tree. I was struggling to hold the board in place, when we were caught off guard by a voice from below. It was our neighbor Virgil Anderson calling up to my dad: "Charlie, what you doing up there?" I still remember the surprise in my dad's eyes as he wiped his brow and struggled to get upright, before finally saying, "Oh, I'm just trying to get this damn thing up."

Damn thing?! This was a temple to fathers and sons, the best tree house in town, *our* tree house, but I felt as shocked as I did betrayed. My dad was a devout Methodist and this was the first time I'd heard him swear. In a few years I came to see that he had needed to separate himself from his boyish predicament and that a cuss word can be a shortcut to manhood, but it was not until much later, when I wrote the essay, that it dawned on me that there was more at stake. Virgil Anderson was a country club Republican and drove an Oldsmobile; my dad was a farm boy from Missouri who had worked his way up. He drove a Chevy. Our backyard already had a Tarzan swing and a pigeon cage; the Andersons' had a putting green.

An essay about adulthood and shame, about family history and the politics of class grew out of one snippet of dialogue.

EXERCISE

Begin by making a list of some similar remarks that have stayed with you. Then, pick one and write a scene. Keep it simple at first. Don't crowd the stage. Stick to two characters, one of which is you. Write the first draft as if it were a play or film script. Put the characters' names to the left and their talk to the right. Later on, you can fill it in with taglines, description, significant details, and even your own retrospective point of view in which you analyze what was really happening, but this first time through, just try to get the conversation down.

When picking from your list of recollected dialogue, try to choose a comment or exchange that is puzzling and inherently dramatic. Here are a few possibilities (besides the first time you heard your dad swear):

1. **A situation in which one person is trying to teach someone else how to do something.** Maybe the student is not a very good one—clumsy or resistant, afraid to admit that he doesn't already know how to do this task. Maybe the teacher is actually teaching a lesson that goes beyond the technicalities of the task at hand (e.g., not just how to play pool, but how to be cool).

2. **A near or suppressed argument.** Perhaps the tension has to do with something bigger than the trivial issue at hand (e.g., it's not just about the remote control but about being remote and in control, about who has the power in the relationship).

3. **Someone is conveying some news to someone else that is hard to convey.** This news might be bad, even tragic, or just difficult in some other way (e.g., "I want to break up, but I hope we can still be friends.").

4. **Two people find themselves at a crossroads.** You got a promotion; I got fired. Now what?

5. **Someone says something that reveals them in a new light.** Maybe it's explicit: "You're having an affair with your dentist!" Maybe it's unwitting and inadvertent: "Wait a minute, hold it, you did what?!"

6. **Flirtation.** Two people are feeling each other out, not sure how far to go in revealing their feelings, not sure if the other person is just being friendly or is really interested, not sure whether to play hard to get, not sure . . . not sure.

When turning your exercise into an essay, you might look at some oft anthologized essays that make good use of dialogue, such as George Orwell's "A Hanging" or Richard Wright's "The Ethics of Living Jim Crow: An Autobiographical Sketch."

IRA SUKRUNGRUANG

Can You Smell What [Your Name Here]
Is Cooking?

IRA SUKRUNGRUANG is a Thai-American. His essays have been published in many journals, including *Isotope, Post Road*, and *The Bellingham Review*. He is the coeditor of two anthologies about obesity: *What Are You Looking At?; The First Fat Fiction Anthology*; and *Scoot Over, Skinny: The Fat Nonfiction Anthology*. He teaches creative writing at the University of South Florida.

I'm about to reveal a deep, dark secret. I watch wrestling. Not the Olympic, Greco-Roman kind, but the kind with beer can–crushing Texans, Samoan beasts, and men who have ominous names like The Undertaker. I've been following wrestling off and on since I was eight. Backbreakers and pile drivers and figure four leg locks don't quite thrill me like they used to, though I did practice all those moves on a body pillow my mother made with leftover carpet padding. Now, what I enjoy about wrestling are the mini story lines that carry on from week to week, the off-the-wall, off-beat, off-their-rockers wrestlers, characters that have made me laugh, got my heart going with adrenaline, and once, when the great Hulk Hogan lost his title to the Ultimate Warrior, made me cry.

Believe it or not, watching wrestling has helped shape my own work. No, I am not a wrestler. And no, I haven't written about wrestling. I am, in fact, an overweight pacifist Buddhist. When I started writing creative nonfiction, however, the biggest problem I faced was seeing myself—the "I" of the piece—as a character. The "I" was

240

me after all; there was no separation. I knew my past. I knew my stories. In my mind, all I had to do was simply retell them. What became of my early narratives, however, was something I saw more and more of as a teacher in my beginning creative nonfiction students' work. They wrote essays with characters that went through the motions, characters that simply acted. Yes, the "I" did do things of significance. Yes, the "I" was part of the conflict. But the important part of the "I" was missing.

When interviewed before matches, many wrestlers slip into the third person, notably former WWE wrestler The Rock, who used to bellow into the microphone: "Can you smell what The Rock is cooking?" Speaking in the third person separates and highlights the character from the person. In The Rock's case, there is the charismatic, one-eyebrow-raising wrestling maniac, and then there is Dwayne Johnson, the man who plays The Rock. This separation is similar in nonfiction writing. There is the character and there is the writer; the two are linked, but the writer has additional responsibilities—to portray and to explore the character, to make sense of the character's experiences, to make meaning out of them. In my early nonfiction, Ira Sukrungruang wasn't there. The shell of him was present, the "I" that did this and that, but *he* was absent, like a daydreaming student looking out the window, one who is there in body but absent in mind. Because of this, my early essays failed to be anything more than interesting but simple stories. I needed Ira Sukrungruang to come alive. I needed him to be more than an "I," to be a character with thoughts and analytical skills, to elevate the story to another level. I needed the other half of him to surface.

EXERCISE

1. Take a tip from wrestling interviews. Write a nonfiction narrative in the third person. Discard the "I" and allow the "he/

she" to take over. By doing this, you might be able to separate yourself from the narrative. The trick to this exercise is to detach from the character. The writer becomes an omniscient overseer of his or her actions. In many ways, you become Ebenezer Scrooge, revisiting the past with a different set of eyes, making sense of the things the character in the moment could not.

2. After completing the draft, change all "he's or she's" to "I." Some sentences may have to be rewritten, but you may find that the "I" is now not just a skinny pronoun. The "I" has biceps like mountains.

THRITY UMRIGAR

Whose Voice Is Telling the Story?

THRITY UMRIGAR is the author of the novels *Bombay Time*, *The Space Between Us*, *If Today Be Sweet*, and *The Weight of Heaven* and the memoir *First Darling of the Morning*. She is an associate professor of English at Case Western Reserve University.

Before I began writing my memoir, *First Darling of the Morning*, the question of voice was one that I grappled with continually. In whose voice would I tell the story of my childhood? In the voice of the adult narrator looking back on the first twenty-one years of her life? Or should I let the child—and later, the teenager—speak for herself?

The problem was, both approaches could be effective. I'd read enough memoirs to know that. For instance, I loved the passages in Tobias Wolff's *This Boy's Life* when he foreshadows his adult self, makes that leap across the decades to tell us who that young boy becomes. The introduction of the adult Tobias gives the story a breadth, an expansiveness that feels right.

But I also loved the tightness of Frank McCourt's *Angela's Ashes*. I loved the claustrophobic, insular quality of that book, how the focus is always on little Frank and his thoughts and inner life. I love that Frank's perspective—as narrow and misguided as it sometimes is—is never trodden upon by a knowing, adult perspective.

In the end, I resolved my dilemma by telling my story in the present tense and in the voice of the young narrator. There were occasional lapses when the book lurched into the future but for the most part, the voice of the memoir was urgent and rooted in present time. And somehow that felt right for this particular book.

I was lucky that the story came to me in the voice of the child narrator. But sometimes, our choices are not that clear and our narrators don't announce themselves as clearly and insistently. Here is an exercise in points of view and in objective versus subjective writing that may help clarify the issue.

EXERCISE

Think of an incident from your childhood. Preferably, an incident that was meaningful to you, one that provoked some strong emotion and feeling. The feeling could be positive or negative—you could've felt abandoned, isolated, scared, or you might've felt safe, euphoric, powerful. Imagine yourself as a child; try to remember, in as much detail as you can, how it felt to experience that event. Allow yourself to feel all the feelings that you felt at that time. You should be able to "remember" the event not just in your mind but in your body.

Next, write a narrative of that event. But write it from an adult point of view. And write it in the third person. Try to capture the same emotions and feelings that you were able to conjure up but filter those feelings through the lens of adulthood. The adult narrator can be sympathetic to what the child felt but make sure that yours is an adult perspective on the incident. The purpose of this exercise is to let time and distance (and adult cognition) change the experience of that childhood event, to play around with shifting perceptions and different points of view.

Now, go back to how you felt as a child when you experienced that event. Write a description of the event from a child's point of view. Use the first person; make it as subjective a narrative as you can. Enter the child's mind and heart. The purpose of this exercise is to write from as closed, intimate, narrow, and self-centered a perspective as you can.

The adult narrative is like an aerial view—it can encompass different perspectives and interpretations, it can see the larger picture and the larger implications, it can symbolically and metaphorically interpret the events.

The child's perspective will be that of a close-up photograph—it will go deep rather than wide; it will interpret the events through a subjective frame. It will be more preoccupied with the inner life than the outer one.

You can do this with several episodes in your life until it becomes clear to you which voice the story demands to be told in.

CRAFT

GAY TALESE

Outlining: The Writer's Road Map

GAY TALESE is the bestselling author of eleven books, including *Thy Neighbor's Wife, A Writer's Life*, and *Honor Thy Father*. He was a reporter for *The New York Times* from 1956 to 1965, and since then he has written for the *Times, Esquire, The New Yorker, Harper's Magazine*, and other national publications. His groundbreaking article "Frank Sinatra Has a Cold" was named the "best story *Esquire* ever published," and he was credited by Tom Wolfe with the creation of an inventive form of nonfiction writing called "The New Journalism."

Whether I'm working on a short article or a full-length book, having an outline helps me navigate when I sit down to write. The shape this outline takes is instinctual and varies in length and complexity from project to project. The directional path I chose for my 1981 book *Thy Neighbor's Wife*, for instance, was straightforward enough to be captured on a single sheet of paper, despite the fact that the book was nearly five hundred pages long (Figure A). The fourteen-thousand-word *Esquire* article "Frank Sinatra Has a Cold," by contrast, required two elaborately annotated pages (Figures B and C).

The way you choose to present information in outline form should depend entirely on how your mind works. I write visually. I think in terms of scenes, like a movie director.

As an author, I want to know (even before I begin writing) who I'll first introduce to the reader, and then who's next, and then next.

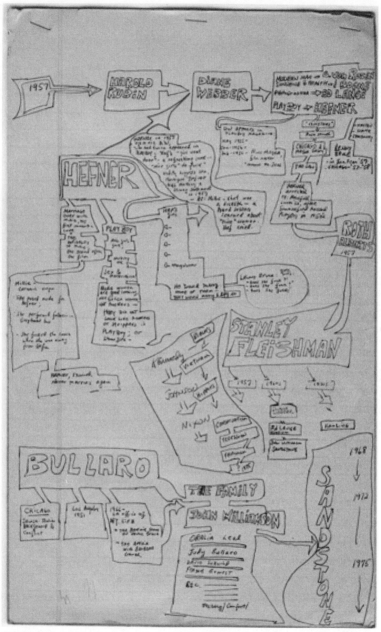

Figure A

Before I sit down at my typewriter, I have charted a course from scene to scene, character to character, and chapter to chapter. The end result is an outline that looks a lot like a director's storyboard. It's my mental road map—my reminder of what I have in store for the reader, and who stands where in my scripted receiving line.

Take Figure A, for example. This is the outline I put together for *Thy Neighbor's Wife*. You'll notice on the upper left-hand corner of the page the words "Harold Rubin."

He is the teenager described in the opening chapter of *Thy Neighbor's Wife*. By writing the name "Harold Rubin" at the beginning of the outline, I placed him in the overall context of my book: he is the first person the reader will meet. You'll note that to the right of "Harold Rubin" is "Diane Webber." She is the nude woman who obsessed young Harold Rubin. In Chapter II, I deal with her. Next to her (to the right) you'll see these words: "Modern Man— G. Von Rosen . . . Playboy > Hefner." These men (Van Rosen and Hefner) were in the "men's magazine world" that published pin-ups, and Diane Webber was one of their favorite models.

This isn't just a random assortment of characters. The characters that inhabit the first three chapters of *Thy Neighbor's Wife* help me create a world for the reader. First there is Rubin, the young magazine reader clandestinely enjoying nude photos of his fantasy woman, Diane Webber. He is a stand-in for millions of American boys. Then there is Diane Webber, the woman behind the fantasy, the archetype come to life. Then there are Van Rosen and Hefner, two magazine editors who trade on the obsessions of such readers as Rubin and such un-shy models as Diane Webber. These are the men who first figured out how to turn America's appetite for porn into a multimillion-dollar industry. I use these four characters as an entrée into the world of American sexuality; they are the foundation from which the rest of the story branches off.

At its best, outlining is an organic process, but there is one hard-and-fast rule when it comes to outlining a work of nonfiction:

Scene I ----- "THE DAISY" DISCOTHEQUE
[NOV 4th]

FRANK Sinatra standing at the bar, late at night, pals and two blondes nearby; he is tense, tired — Hey are aware of this, Do not risk irritating him. The stereo, which had been playing rock'n'roll music before, now is playing a Sinatra song, "In the Wee Small Hours of the Morning," but F.S. does not seem to be listening; he talks instead to a blonde, a girl who sits on stool looking at his hands; she looks like a manicurist, a little make-up, which F.S. doesn't like — but nothing will really please him anyway tonight; He HAS a COLD!

When F.S. has a cold...his whole world plunges in gloom... maybe that is why his music at this moment seemed to displease him — but it was pleasing the young people who were dancing... I was moved by it — felt that all over America, in discotheques or taverns or roadsides, people were dancing to this, slow and sexy, and later, all over America, they would go to bed, make love — Thanks, in no small part, to the mood, the mellow mood of F.S. — I myself for years had benefited by his ballads; my whole generation, I thought — owed this man much... Tipped the scales with some girl (in a parked car; in a penthouse; in a usaae apartment; in an Army town near Fort Knox) These girls, with songs such as these, here in The mood for love. F.S. had done our wooing —

Yet here, in this Los Angeles tavern, here was the man himself standing looking bored, bothered. (HE HAD TOLD them before he didn't want to hear his own records!)

Frank WAS irritated by many things — The CBS show, coming up Nov. 16; by NBC "Special"; by the Film "Assault"; Also, He did not, I presume, welcome me at This time. He had so much publicity — Life; Look; Magazine — They'd already been there — "be talked out." Also, suspicious...

The sort of piece I wanted to do required cooperation — and I had great ambitions. I had read almost every article written about him — and they read with one exception, like slicked copy on his record albums — all the words and pictures, I felt, were embellishments of the cliché — F.S. The swinger; the lover; the Tough guy. At 50, battling the Beatles — matching his pitch to a new generation —

I am a great admirer of F.S. and wished to do an article about — This man who, at 50, has done it all — can do whatever he wants. He has money; power; talent. I felt that there was a kind of male love — The barracks — the locker room — a non-homosexual but indefinable male love... The Mafia... the "Slum Kid".
[*34 is not our world; it is his — he just lets us look in*]
I had seen him, before this night at "The Daisy" I had seen him in person once at Forest Hills; Also at Jilly's.

¶ At Jilly's saloon — Il Padrone — He was the Boss — a glimpse at him in the back... he was not a kid from the neighborhood, I thought; he brings his neighborhood with him.
— FRANK'S MOTHER — BLUE-EYED WOP

¶ The Italian. I, an Italian-American from New Jersey — would do THE Italian-American from New Jersey.

¶ JANE HOAG STORY. THE ALABASTER BIRD story — ⊘⊘⊘

¶. Magazines: "Life", "Newsweek", "Look" and I felt "Hell with T.J."

"... I felt much was left to be said if I could get to him — but now, anger — His feeling of mistrust (CBS show); The pressures — I did not want it here. But the magazine 'Esquire' had for years wanted a cover of Sinatra — and I was unable to talk Harold Hayes out of it... not fully trust — but if I failed, he would not be interested in such excuse about FS's cold — fuck Hayes...

S. — arrive Beverly. Wilshire Hotel
    a) sexy chambermaids ; TWA Stewardess when flying in...
    b) full of hopes - (ride with Sinatra — broads; sex; blasts)
    c) Article would be an opportunity to 'swing' - have fun.

- here Mahoney was saying be careful... don't talk to him ---
I saw the situation exactly what I wanted — bar; informal; no Al Farrell to make Frank nervous... but FRANK Sinatra had a cold

is restless... he wandered into the "Pool Room" of "The Daisy"

— Pool Room Scene

Scene II ---

→ NBC Studio (rehearsal)

FEAR

Nov 8 | How's Frank? How's Frank?
FRANK? Anxiety: apprehension...
night Frank worries about CBS getting publicity ; ("It's a promo" - JM)
Igato arrives — people wandered out
with - "his hope!" "How is he?"
the lean figure arrived - all expectation
- it FS - it was his double - Dalgato
(Dalgato)

(Tue Nov 9) ⟹ back to Palm Springs
¶ The long wait in Arrangements
¶ JM anxious — want to see piece
but can't - JM now wants to
see the piece - CBS Money Room
get G.T. out — magic piece -
"gotta protect my client - JM, you're
... yourself — FEAR —
... fuckups (Yes, blame it
... on FS.

arrives — and there was no
this time. Sore throat... it was
... at orchestra stage — it was
... he'd gardened.
Died (sore)

NBC rehearsal begins
...; Devton; Al Silvani; Dalgato;
Mahoney; Hair Lady;
Dialogue — ange-
...ows — FS stands out...
follows with rest. "Couldn't..."

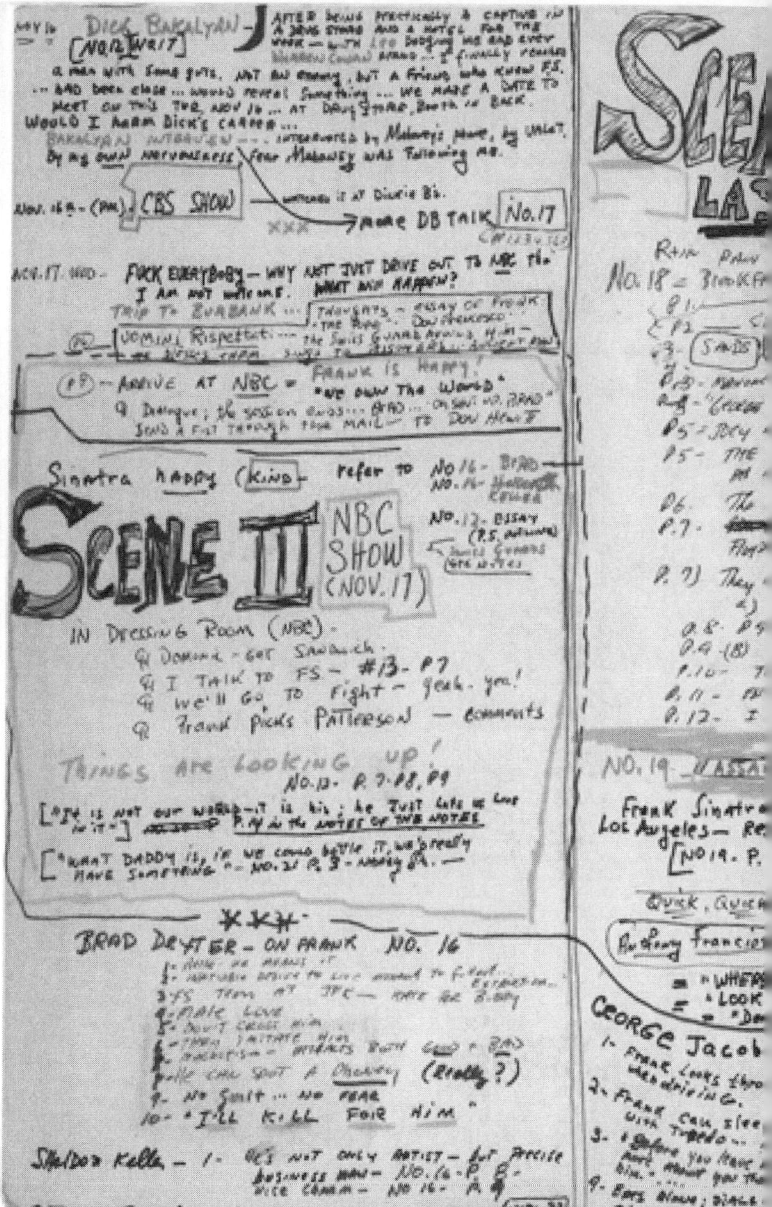
DICK BAKALYAN
CBS SHOW
SCENE III
NBC SHOW (NOV. 17)
IN DRESSING ROOM (NBC).
THINGS ARE LOOKING UP!
BRAD DEXTER - ON FRANK NO. 16
GEORGE Jacobs

Figure C

IV THE FIGHT

NOV 22

...gas

L. SIVANI — His Thing —
(He Training Frank S. Songs)...
no Thing Thing Mister
on Haven. Go Play for; grand
— Ugly People —

Lady Drunk Trying to get FS
Sex..
"I Sit Next to FS."
Gather (Frank stays up
to get them all Down!)

The Comment; flood · Mood.?

FITE —
— is me ---

AP — Ran off to other arts.
Don Rickles —

"S)
Audio grabbing at [SANDS]
The entertain —
Frank Pushes Hand to Face?
is on — They all leave;
man — I Work Martin like
[QUEEN]

[SCENE 5]

, a Day Late, To
ming "Assault on A Queen"
fight with them Like!
of Press!
my Fag" - 31 · P.1
. Fucking Picture over with

23 P. 2 (His Views)

Fat Director's [24-16]
ne " — Likes it —
y Bird!" —
-. = The Long Kiss
cy = Cagney Imitation
P. 13

My only TALK
with Him [24·9]
[Got him a Chair]

SCENE 6

[No 24]
Recording Session
(No Choire · Singers · Ital)
[Moynihan]
— TALK with Nancy Junior I
[Cyrano Restaurant]
= TALK with ~~Buddy Bird~~ — Sanicola - 25-1
"   "   Kenny - 25-1
"   "   (Tour) 3rd Dexter 25-3
(Fine List)

[No.25]
Recording "Moon Light Sinatra" [25.]

1) Quote Robins Douglas—Home
(See Magazine Notes)

2) Advice Was great—

3) TALK Vicenzo - [25=5]

4) TALK Dan Lillie 26-1
5) " Patty D'Amore 26- 5
6) " Sanicola - 26. 7
7) " Lazar (Curse The Bastard)
26-9

No.27. + TALK - Nancy 27·4
(Hang-ups — Also See 24-9)
→ He's Just Like Anybody Else

No.28 - Parking Lot Essay
(He Connelly -) - 28- C
Recollections of Brief FS TALK
28-2

No.29 - Nancy - "He's Better Than
Anybody Else - or Any."
29-4 - Repeat Harlan Ellison

No. 30 = Return to New York
Recollections - Thoughts - No. 30

No. 31 - Jilly - FR Jr.

No. 32 - Parents + Fr. Junior
• Slum Kid?
• Mother Goodworks
• Frank Takes After Me"
= Frank Junior - Dad Steers Normal

complete your research before you plot your story. It's important to note that while Harold Rubin functions as a stand-in for millions of boys just like him, he is not a cardboard cutout. The reason Harold Rubin's experience of mooning over pictures of Diane Webber rings true for so many readers is because the description is so specific, so tangible. Before I'd written the words "Harold Rubin" on the outline, I'd spent days and days with Rubin in Chicago, in 1957, interviewing him again and again, until I thought I knew him as a "character" as well as if I'd created him for a novel. I took the same pains with all of the other characters in *Thy Neighbor's Wife*. I interviewed Diane Webber in Los Angeles many times prior to writing about her, and spent months submerging myself in the world of Hugh Hefner.

Why do this? Why draw an outline? There is real value in creating a visual concept of what you're writing. When done well, it can help you conceive of where to begin, how to proceed, and when to stop. For writers, like myself, who organize information visually, an outline can help impose a narrative order. For less visually minded writers, an outline can encourage a more scenic approach to storytelling. In both cases, an outline can provide a framework for the story—a structure that can keep nonfiction writers, in particular, from veering too far off.

If you're lucky, an outline can do more than that: it can help you uncork words that have already been forming in the back of your mind. When I sat down to plot out "Frank Sinatra Has a Cold," for instance, I knew I had a firm idea of the scenes I wanted to include. But in this case, I got more than I'd hoped for. The simple act of organizing my thoughts helped me start composing the piece. The first paragraph of the outline (shown in Figure B) matches the opening of the published piece almost word for word.

EXERCISE

The next time you're trying to develop a story, write or draw an outline including the names of the major characters, the characters you will introduce, and the scenes that they will be in. Whether you write or draw the outline should be a function of what you are most comfortable with. Don't forget to complete your research before you plot your story.

PATRICIA FOSTER

Creating Shape in Scene:
Image as Strategic Bookend

PATRICIA FOSTER is the author of the memoir *All the Lost Girls*; a collection of essays, *Just Beneath My Skin*; and editor of *Minding the Body* and *Sister to Sister*. She is a professor in the MFA Program in Nonfiction at the University of Iowa and has taught in France, Spain, Italy, and the Czech Republic.

Nonfiction is as engaged in dramatic storytelling as it is in reflection, meditation, and exposition. When writers approach emblematic moments, they often write easily, quickly, getting to what we often think of as "the good part" of a story. In other words, they quickly focus on a conflict that has emotional weight, a moment rich in sensory details and intuitive perception. And yet getting into a scene requires subtlety and insight. Too often beginning writers depend exclusively on the "drama" of the moment and don't know how to ease into the moment, using *image, action, description,* and *dialogue* to effectively flesh out the emblematic moment.

This exercise encourages the writer to consider sequence in scene, to see how image, description, action and dialogue–even imagined dialogue–can evoke a specific moment that allows the writer to circle back to the original image (slightly revised).

Let me give you an example of a scene from my life that uses this strategy:

"CIRCLING"

My mother's small hands clench the steering wheel, her diamond wedding ring blinking in the harsh summer light. We're driving past Piggly Wiggly, past Willie's Tavern, past the sign that says CAT XING. I don't see any cats, but maybe they're hiding in the bushes, staying cool beneath the trees. The day is hot, thick with humidity, dense with insects swirling in galaxies. My mother is fretting about my August wedding, about who we can and can't invite because of who won't come if so-and-so is there. I'm nodding, staring out at the dogwood trees just coming into bloom. I know we're circling the issue of feuds and jealousies in our family and of which one of us gets final dibs on the guest list. If one of my best friends is invited, my brother's wife won't come. If Aunt Jenny is invited, Aunt Doris won't show. This wedding business suddenly seems so freighted with worry, I feel like one of those cats hiding in the bushes, waiting for darkness to arrive. I need to get the upper hand, but I don't know how.

"Don't you think women should masturbate?" I ask suddenly as if this non sequitur makes sense. But of course, I'm just trying to goad my mother, distracting her from talk about the wedding.

"Oh, for goodness sakes," she says, turning to me. Her hands look prim, the nails a soft polished pink. "Women don't need that. Whoever gave you such an idea?"

"Nobody *gave* me the idea. It's what women do. They use their hands. Just like men. Don't you *know* that?"

"I certainly don't."

"You mean you haven't ever—"

She looks straight ahead, her eyebrows lifted. "I would never—" she says, one hand pushing back a stray bit of hair, "—*never* do it. And not only that, I don't need to—"

And that's when I laugh. "Well, well, lucky you!"

She smiles at me, surprised, I think, and secretly pleased at my response.

"Let's ask Aunt Jenny and Aunt Doris both," I say quickly. "Let's let the wedding be the event and not worry about the watchers."

Mother starts to speak, but then stops. Instead, she reaches over and touches my thigh, her hand light, caressing. I stare at her hand, the one that has never stroked her own body. "Of course," she says as we cross the Fish River Bridge. "We'll just tell them they have to behave."

EXERCISE

Choose a person you know well, someone with whom you have had intense engagement (pleasure/disagreements/issues) in the past. Let yourself drift back to a particular moment with this person.

1. Start with an image. For example, describe this person's hands (one or two sentences).

2. Narrate an action. Describe something she is doing with her hands (this may be only a small task, your grandmother wiping her hands with a dish towel).

3. Describe something about the surroundings, giving the reader a sense of where you are and what the situation is (in the kitchen with your grandmother while she peels carrots and you sulk at the table because your boyfriend didn't call).

4. Ask this person a question you've always wanted to ask or begin a dialogue about the problem or issue. (Did your grandfather ever ignore her this way?)

5. Let the question be a catalyst for a scene. If in real life you didn't ask a question directly, but always wanted to, you can push the scene by imagining the other person's response and telling the reader that this is a dialogue in your head. Imagining the response is not cheating. It's a legitimate way to let the reader see more deeply into your character and into your perception of the other person.

6. Come back to the image of the person's hands. The image will be slightly different because the narrator's perception has been aroused by the exchange.

The important thing in this exercise is progression from image to action to setting to conflict and back to image. I've used this strategy as an in-class exercise many times, and always to good result. Often students like the initial prompt of the in-class writing so much that they want to revise the scene, developing it into a short-short that can stand alone or fleshing out the scene into a larger essay.

IRA WOOD

On Achieving Distance—
The Parallel Universe

IRA WOOD is the author of three novels, *The Kitchen Man, Going Public,* and *Storm Tide* (with Marge Piercy). He is the coauthor (with Marge Piercy) of *So You Want to Write: How to Master the Craft of Writing Fiction and Memoir.* Together they run Leapfrog Press, an independent literary publishing company, and teach workshops across the country that address writers' feelings of hopelessness and defeating the inner censor.

Any fiction writer who has ever tried to write his or her own life story knows it is far more difficult to write a memoir than a novel. It would seem easy at the outset: you've lived the experience so the research is already done. You've interacted with the people so the characters will just begin speaking to you, as they did in real life. Descriptions will flow from your fingers to the keyboard. Why wouldn't they, you've already been there. If memoir writing was that easy, however, my workshops wouldn't be packed with people who have lived incredibly interesting lives but are stopped short when trying to write about themselves.

I sympathize with them. I've grappled with that nasty inner censor that folds its arms like a border guard and will not let you pass. I've attempted to satisfy its request for a passport, which is in reality the answer to the question, What makes you think your life is interesting enough to write about? I've stared bleary-eyed at my computer screen, waiting for a story that I've lived through once to make a repeat appearance on the page. Most days it doesn't show up.

Other days the characters show up, all right, but what they have to say is not what you want to hear. *It didn't happen that way at all,* they wail. Or, *You're not being fair to me.* Or, *You write one more word and I'll sue!* And they're not the only voices in your head. Suddenly your parents and/or children show up: *You did that? You should be ashamed of yourself! If you put that down on paper, you'll embarrass us all.* There are often a whole lot of other voices up there, too, all shouting, *Loser!*

Hey. One of the reasons I teach this stuff is because I've been there, done that, heard the voices, fought them off . . . some days successfully, some days not. What I've learned to do is to distance myself. For one thing, I call what I write (and teach) *personal narrative,* not memoir, not autobiography, not nonfiction. What I aim for is *emotional truth.* If I feel the finished product adequately describes events as they actually occurred, I may then label it memoir. If I feel that there was a deviation from events that somewhat contradicted fact, I might label it a memoir-novel. (In my role as publisher of Leapfrog Press, I made this distinction with a book we published in which an author felt that her handling of the material of her life might hurt people that she loved, but that the events in the book were mostly true. We agreed to label the book a memoir-novel. The reviews were fantastic.) If, as in my own life story, *The Kitchen Man,* I allowed my imagination to take command, rather than the strict mapping of chronological fact, I labeled the result an autobiographical novel. In all cases it was the *emotional truth* that was of primary importance, because I believe that what is of ultimate importance to a reader is a good read, and this is the direct result of the emotional impact of your story. If you have written a good book, a gripping read, an experience that moves the reader, it doesn't matter what label you give it. That's a marketing decision. First you have to write the book.

To reach this emotional truth it is sometimes necessary to distance yourself from the experience. To tell that former lover you're writing about: *It's not you, so shut up!* To stand up to your mother (in your head, of course) and say, *This is not my first sexual experience, it's somebody else's.* Or to your cousins who insist that Grandma was a lily white virgin before she met Grandpa, the love of her life, *Don't be ridiculous, how can this be our family, the story takes place in Oahu in 1946.* Much historical and speculative fiction—writings that take place in the past or the future—deal with events and situations that are emotionally true to a writer. After all, it is naïve to imagine that people in the past were free of the complications we suffer through today and overly optimistic to think that people in the future will have rid themselves of the most basic human emotions.

The exercise that follows is a little trick that I use when the material or the characters that I am writing about feel too emotionally close to allow me to tell the story.

EXERCISE

The Parallel Universe

Think of an incident in your own life. It can be an argument, or an erotic experience, or your first music recital; some memorable incident. The best incidents for this exercise carry some emotional weight: happiness or misery, fear, nervousness, embarrassment. (If it's been an incident you've been reluctant to tackle in your writing, so much the better.)

You are going to write about that incident. You are the main character in that story. But . . . you are going to disguise things in a big way.

Here are some suggestions (choose one or more):

- —Write in the third person.

- —Pick a main character that is not you.

- —Change the place the incident occurred.

- —Change the time period (make it happen in the past or the future).

- —Change the sex of the character.

Naturally, you'll have to make adjustments. If your incident concerns a crush you had on the captain of the ice hockey team and you decide to set your piece in Barcelona instead of Minnesota, the object of your affections will also have to change to accommodate the new surroundings (maybe captain of the soccer team? maybe a matador?).

Your aim is to be true to your emotions and your version of the incident but to distance yourself from it, disguise it so that:

1. the average reader of the piece would not see you in it but feel what you felt, and,

2. perhaps more important, you can write your story without worrying about whether someone will see you in it or whether you are betraying other people.

BARBARA HURD

Zigzags and Leaps: Ways of Locating Our Real Subjects

BARBARA HURD is the author of *Walking the Wrack Line: On Tidal Shifts and What Remains*; *Entering the Stone: On Caves and Feeling Through the Dark*, a Library Journal Best Natural History Book of the Year; *The Singer's Temple*; *Stirring the Mud: On Swamps, Bogs, and Human Imagination*, a *Los Angeles Times* Best Book of 2001; and *Objects in This Mirror*. Her essays have appeared in numerous journals, including *Best American Essays 1999*, *Best American Essays 2001*, *The Yale Review*, *The Georgia Review*, *Orion*, *Audubon*, and others. She teaches creative writing at Frostburg State University in Frostburg, Maryland, and in the Stonecoast MFA program at the University of Southern Maine.

Whether we write poems, stories, or essays, we might sometimes suspect that the apparent subject of the work is not the real subject that interests us. We might even realize that our involvement with that apparent subject could be keeping our attention diverted from the subject that more powerfully compels.

The question is, then, how do we uncover that real subject? How do we find the thing we're not even sure we're looking for? Think of a bloodhound following a fugitive's scent out in the field. His head is low; he's moving quickly, darting from side to side, circling, or his head is high; he's sniffing the air. He's trained to detect red herrings and not to follow distractions that will lead him away from his target. When he loses the scent, he doubles back until he finds it and can begin tracking it again.

Sometimes writers need similar tactics, only we're not out there in the field, noses to the ground. Instead, we're at our desks, minds on the page. So the question becomes: how to make the mind move, how to make our thinking zigzag and swerve, plunge and leap as we search for the right direction? I often propose that students with listless drafts make a series of mental moves that might open up things a bit, allow a little more in, including, we hope, the discovery that's been eluding them. The point of this exercise isn't a finished draft; the point is an unexpected realization that can get them on the right track.

EXERCISE

Directions: Take a piece of writing that seems flat, static, stiff. Circle a few ideas/scenes/moments in the piece that seem to suggest something significant but haven't yet deepened. For each of these moments, try the suggestions below. Write quickly, loosely. Don't worry at this point about consistency or logic. Think of these little jottings as ways of flexing the mind, increasing the range of your thinking.

1. *Zigzag between physical and imaginative places.* Start with a specific place (the north bank of the Potomac River, for example, ten miles from its headwaters) and shift to the speaker's own imaginings about that place (source waters, wellsprings, the place where water surfaces, etc.).

2. *Alternate between fact and myth.* Research, research. Mythologies often contain some fundamental truths about human phenomena. Is there anything in the story of, say, the Midas

touch that might open up your information on self-defeating behaviors?

3. *Leap around in time.* From the present story, swerve backward to the past and then forward into the imagined or predicted future.

4. *Move back and forth between self and abstractions.* Use some personal experience of your character/self to make a generalization about human behavior, and then hypothesize some theory about that behavior. How do your subject's actions/ characteristics resonate with other human tendencies? What might, at least theoretically, explain that resonance?

5. *Switch back and forth between expansive and intensive.* Think telescopic, wide-angle lens vs. microscope. Extend the senses first: think about things wider and farther away in both place and time; imagine yourself beyond the boundaries even of your own biology. Then reverse direction: zero in and examine your subject minutely, every tic and square inch.

6. *Replace stasis with dynamism and vice versa.* How is your subject changing? What will he/she/it be like in ten years? A hundred? Under high heat? Intense cold, pressure, earthquakes? (Think both literally and metaphorically.) Then write about what *won't* change. What's at the core that endures?

The purpose of this exercise isn't to yield finished paragraphs but to get the mind to move more nimbly, to practice quick swerves in various directions so that we don't get stuck in writing ruts or stopped on dead-end ideas. To return to the metaphor of the bloodhound, the idea is to practice the kind of wide, experimental sweeping that often uncovers the trail that matters, the one that might lead to the more urgent, often buried story.

MARY KAY SHANLEY

The WHY of Taking Smaller Pictures

MARY KAY SHANLEY is the author of eight books, with the ninth—a memoir—due for completion before the end of the twenty-first century. She teaches at the University of Iowa's Summer Writing Festival and offers the annual Women and Memoir four-day writing retreat. She's also a public speaker.

If I could post one road sign at the beginning of any writing journey, it would warn, "Slow Down." It's not that your fingers are flying across the keyboard too quickly, but rather that you're so anxious to share your story, you commit it to paper (okay, to the monitor) too quickly. What results tends to be the Big Picture. True, the whole story—beginning, middle, end—is present. Even so, the Big Picture is weak.

Why? Because when you tell the whole story all at once, you only skim the surface. Readers get a panoramic overview, but the nuggets buried beneath that overview—rich details that make your story memorable—don't get a chance to surface and shine. They only emerge when you break the Big Picture down into smaller pictures, and that takes time and patience. Once those smaller pictures are complete and strung together, you have the fully developed story that was in your writerly mind all along.

I see this skimming the surface especially with beginning writers who are bursting with stories and all they want is to just get writing. They end up providing the story's skeleton, but the details are left somewhere along the side of the road.

I'll show you about the richness of smaller pictures by telling you a story about my summer visits to Aunt Frances's farm when I was growing up. The family lived in a big, square, 1920s house, the kind with a porch that wrapped itself around two sides.

The story starts in my aunt's big square—always hot—kitchen. My aunt is stirring a pot on the stove. A golden, boxy fan on the floor rattles endlessly, but instead of pulling in cool air (from where, I wouldn't know), it spews hot air in spasmodic blasts.

Aunt Frances does not notice. Wearing an apron that you put your arms through, button at the nape, and tie at the waist, she stirs with a wooden spoon slanted on one side from decades of use. A little girl is standing next to her on a kitchen chair, waiting to do her job. That would be to taste. I am that little girl, and I do a very good job of tasting.

Every year, my farm responsibilities increase. In the summer of my tenth year, Aunt Frances announces that I am to gather eggs from the chicken coop. No news can be more devastating. Chicken coops are dank, dark, loud (hens cackle a lot) with air so heavy it defies the physics of circulation. Not to mention the hen poop everywhere.

But in the fifties, if your aunt tells you to gather the eggs, you gather the eggs.

I pick up the galvanized egg pail that, in many respects, mimics the chicken coop. Holding it at arm's length, I trudge across the farmyard, wondering how my life has come to this. Just before opening the coop door, I inhale to the bottom of my feet, believing that God lets good little girls hold their breath for five minutes.

First, I gather all the eggs from the empty nests. That done, I walk back to the first nest where a hen still sits on her yet-unborn family. I look the hen squarely in the eye. She returns my glare. I lean forward, trying hard to snarl. Magically, her neck becomes very long, placing her beady eyes uncomfortably close to my face.

I snap my fingers at her. She snips her beak at me. We repeat this three times, until I announce, "Okay. You win. Hatch those eggs. Raise those chicks. I don't care." And with that, I flee the henhouse, breathing heavily but not deeply, and begin the long walk back to the kitchen, carrying a half-full bucket of eggs.

Aunt Frances looks into the bucket, then at me. "The bucket's only half-full."

"Yes," I say, affirming the obvious.

"Well," she says finally, "it's really hot out. Maybe the hens aren't laying today."

To which I respond, "Well, it really is hot out."

That night—every night, actually—I sleep upstairs in the spare bedroom. The quiet of night on the farm is broken by the occasional clank of the metal feeder lids out in the hog lot, and by the hum of the telephone lines along the gravel road. I miss my parents now, and begin to trace the phone line east through Luvern, then south through Renwick, Goldfield, and Eagle Grove, then east again, passing the "Welcome to Webster City" sign, rounding the curve by the bowling alley and heading down Main Street. At the corner of Main and Willson, I turn south and, five blocks later, I'm home. Then, connected to my parents, I fall asleep.

At this point, I ask my class how many stories I just shared. They realize I shared three stories—of the kitchen, the chicken coop, and bedtime, all strung together into one big picture. (Some think I shared five or six stories.)

If I had hurried to get it all told, I would only have provided a skimming-the-surface Big Picture of summer on the farm. But by breaking the experience down into smaller pictures and carefully developing each one, the rich details emerged—the golden, boxy fan that rattled endlessly, the slanted wooden spoon, holding the galvanized egg pail at arm's length, the hen and I snapping at each other, the clank of the metal feeder lids in the hog lot, the telephone line snaking its way through Iowa villages.

It is details that connect the reader with your story, emotionally and through the senses. And it is connections that cause the reader to remember.

Don't tell me there was a bowl of fruit on the table. Tell me there was a bowl of pomegranates, apples, and one banana.

Don't tell me there was a tree outside your kitchen window. Tell me it was a maple. Or a locust. There's a difference, you know.

Consider this: the Vietnam War Memorial in Washington, D.C., lists each fallen soldier by first, middle, and last name. If you know one of those soldiers, if you read his or her first, middle, and last names, you will remember that detail for the rest of your life.

Pay attention to your experiences, always identifying and examining the details. And try this exercise: think of one experience—one story—you want to share.

EXERCISE

1. In one paragraph, describe that story. Ask yourself: Is it only one story or can it be broken into several smaller stories? Thinking about the rich details within the Big Picture leads writers to conclude that, indeed, several small stories are there.

2. Pick one of those smaller stories and repeat the steps listed above.

3. When you're satisfied that you are down to the nitty-gritty, develop one of your smaller pictures in two hundred words, *maximum*, sharing those rich details.

4. Write other small stories, too, then string all together into a seamless tale.

ISHMAEL BEAH

The Relationship of Words to
Characters and Landscapes

ISHMAEL BEAH is the *New York Times*–bestselling author of *A Long Way Gone: Memoirs of a Boy Soldier*. He lives in Brooklyn, New York.

There is no doubt that contact with reality can be invigorating.
I hope that firm and prolonged intercourse with reality, if I can
manage it, will have a good effect on my character as well as my
health, and perhaps even improve my writing.
                                        —*DUSKLANDS*, J. M. COETZEE

E very writer must have a "firm and prolonged intercourse with reality." It is only through this involvement that he or she will be able to genuinely observe human interactions and behavior and write about them with the same intensity, sensitivity, confusion, or whatever the condition might be. When you observe without an understanding of some realities, particularly as a nonfiction writer, all you see are the visible acts of people or your characters. You miss the nuances of people's manners, their speech—the words they use, their gestures and what is not said. These characteristics add depth to the most simple sentences about characters, when you describe them or write a dialogue. Through descriptions and dialogue you can either capture your characters very well or lose their authenticity and place in the narrative. In short, there is a remarkable relationship between words, characters, and landscapes or where the characters inhabit. If the words you choose to use do not fit the character or the landscape, there will undoubtedly be a disjoint in the narrative. In Chinua Achebe's essay entitled "English and the African Writer," in *Transitions* 18 (1965), the author provides an excellent example from one of his works, *The Arrow of God*, that will shed further light on the usage of words and their relationship to characters and landscapes.

"The Chief Priest is telling one of his sons why it is necessary to send him to church: 'I want one of my sons to join these people and be my eyes. If there is nothing in it you will come back. But if there is something there you will bring home my share. The world is like a Mask, dancing. If you want to see it well you do not stand in one place. My spirit tells me that those who do not befriend the white man today will be saying, 'Had we known . . . tomorrow.'

"Now supposing I had put it another way. Like this, for instance: 'I am sending you as my representative among those people—just to be on the safe side in case the new religion develops. One has to move with the times or else one is left behind. I have a hunch that those who fail to come to terms with the white man's way may well regret their lack of foresight.'

"The material is the same. But the first one is in character and the other is not." The language of the first speech from the Chief Priest has an identity that is grounded to the place, tradition, and elocution. "The world is like a Mask, dancing" shows the usage of an object within the environment of the Priest to illustrate the constant changes in the world and simultaneously remaining in the context of the Priest's world. If you carefully read on, "my spirit tells me . . ." you are well aware without being told directly that this person speaking is not European or Western. For the second part of the same speech, the opening sentence, "I am sending you as my representative . . ." evokes something entirely different in the mind of the reader, the environment changes, the context has altered in comparison to the first form of the same sentence.

If Achebe did not have an informed, realistic view of where he was writing about, and the people, his dialogue would have been the latter, which doesn't fit the landscape and the character at all, and therefore the story becomes less of a visual journey, a disjoint between the character and the landscape occurs and brings about confusion in the mind of the reader. In my writing, I try to apply this rule and will give you a very simple example.

Adults in my culture, when they speak to young people, do not refer to them as "kids." They would either say "children" or "boys and girls." The word "kids" is an American usage of the English language to refer to children. So I will not use that word if my story is situated on the West African Landscape of Sierra Leone. Here are some exercises that will help to make sure your narrative, its words, characters, and landscapes, stay in focus and harmony.

EXERCISE

1. Using your procrastination time to observe

Procrastination is very much a process of writing as long as it isn't overdone. It is an essential process to rest and rejuvenate the creative and critical cells of the mind to prepare it for writing. However, you have to make sure that after the time of procrastinating comes to a conclusion, you have ample time to write. In addition, use that time to observe people, the environment, and for eavesdropping. Make sure you do not make anyone uncomfortable!

Find a public place and sit down quietly. In the winter I prefer a café that has a mirror and allows me to see what is going on outside, and also who comes in and out of the café.

If you have trouble remembering things then get a notepad. Refrain from writing full sentences, just words, phrases, ideas, feelings, images, just the raw reactions. Enjoy the observation and internalize what you see. Do not look only at what people are doing but also at what is around them, the sounds that may or may not complement their actions and speech, the interruptions, the sky, the sun, the clouds, gestures, and so forth. At the end of these observations, try to write what you remember. Use these observation techniques when you are on your way to interview someone, doing research for a nonfiction piece. Through these exercises, you learn not only to listen to what people are saying, but to notice where they are, their manner of speech, gestures, etc. This allows you to choose the appropriate words to describe your characters, their actions, the places they function, and their relationship to elements around them.

2. **Pre-event occurrences**

A good number of people always think that their lives are boring to write about. The reason for such conclusions is that they are only thinking about the facts of things that have occurred in their lives. They do not think about the events that led to that fact, signs along the way, and how that event shaped the individual. This exercise requires you to go back a few hours before, three days before, a week before, months before, a main event happened in your life. You will be surprised to learn things that actually connect to that event, how daily energies and activities shift and are affected in preparation for momentous events.

Think about where you were before a historical event occurred, before you heard about it, and what you were doing when you heard the news. For example, 9/11, the assassination of John F. Kennedy, Nelson Mandela's release from prison in South Africa. Don't write about the event; rather write about what was happening in your life, what was interrupted for you to receive that news, and how that interruption affected you and others around you. Use exercise 1 to re-observe and write about your own life.

DAVID VANN

Every Good Story Is At Least Two Stories

DAVID VANN'S story collection, *Legend of a Suicide*, is the winner of the Grace Paley Prize and was named a Notable Book of 2008 by *The New York Times*, *San Francisco Chronicle*, *Kansas City Star*, and the Story Prize. A contributor to *Esquire*, *The Atlantic Monthly*, *Men's Journal*, *Outside*, and *National Geographic Adventure*, Vann is also author of the bestselling memoir *A Mile Down: The True Story of a Disastrous Career at Sea*, and a forthcoming novel, *Caribou Island*. He's been a National Endowment for the Arts Fellow and a Wallace Stegner and John L'Heureux Fellow. He taught at Stanford and Cornell, where he received his degrees, and is currently a professor at Florida State University.

E very good story is at least two stories," Grace Paley told us in a workshop when I was an undergrad at Stanford. I write memoirs now rather than short stories, but I keep remembering what she said, partly because she refused to explain what she meant. Everything about her workshop was different from the others I had taken. We read our manuscripts aloud, for instance, instead of handing them out in the previous class, and this meant we had to learn to hear a story once and hold all of it in our heads to discuss it. Her suggestions for revision were different, too. Instead of telling us a scene or character needed development, she'd tell us that a story is shaped almost like a circle, but at the last moment, instead of closing that circle, the story turns the other way and opens out. "Everyone, real or invented, deserves the open destiny of life," she writes in her story "A Conversation with My Father."

As I write memoir now, I think of stories and novels because I believe that's what readers expect from a memoir. They're expecting a story as cohesive as fiction, without an unimportant sibling or any of the other random details that clutter up daily existence. The fact that something happened or existed is not enough. And the story, finally, should be about more than it at first seemed to be about. The author tells one story as a way of telling another, and there's a process of discovery, for both the author and the reader. In my memoir, *A Mile Down*, for instance, I tell the story of building a boat in Turkey and sinking in a freak storm in the Caribbean on my honeymoon, but this is only the apparent story, the adventure on the surface. The book is really about getting over the last parts of the legacy of my father's suicide, including facing the fear of some-day ending my own life the same way.

In Grace Paley's very brief story "Wants," the surface story is her trip to the library to finally return some books after eighteen years. This is the occasion, the event. She's taking care of something long overdue. But then she happens to run into her ex-husband. They talk, and in his bitterness he accuses her of never having wanted anything. He wanted things—specifically a sailboat—and he's getting them now, but she never wanted anything.

This is the dramatic story, a conflict between the main character and an antagonist, who is not a bad person but simply someone close who wanted something else, something in competition. Drama (the conflict between two characters, shown to us in particular time and place, in scenes) is as essential to memoir as it is to fiction: we won't read several hundred pages of a character we can't watch struggling with others. But we can't stop here. There's another layer still, which we might call vision.

In "Wants," after the upsetting encounter with the ex-husband and his "narrow remark" that she never wanted anything, our hero thinks of all the things she did in fact want. She promised her children "to end the war before they grew up," for instance, and she "wanted to have been married forever to one person." She offers this as a mini essay, listing and describing the things she wanted, and we come to understand her vision, how she sees herself and others and the world. We have a sense, also, of a shift that has occurred. She's been affected by her run-in with her ex.

"Wants" offers, in less than four pages, an exceptionally clear look into the layers of a good story. Vision, and a shift in the protagonist's vision, can be hidden away in landscape description, or in the subtext of dialogue or gesture, etc., but here Paley has brought it to the surface. How the occasion and the dramatic story work is also clear.

EXERCISE

So the exercise for writing memoir is this: in just three or four pages, describe an occasion or event. It can be something small or seemingly unimportant, but let a dramatic conflict emerge within it, something unexpected, something that caught you off guard. You may want to think of this in the reverse: remember an important, disturbing conflict with someone close to you, someone you love or loved, and then try to find the other story, the smaller thing you can write about as a way of telling your conflict indirectly. It might be you were caught up in this other thing and so didn't quite notice the conflict brewing.

Once you've described the occasion and finally the conflict (in a scene with dialogue and gesture), step back from it. Let your character (it's you, but remember it's really only a version of you) mull things over a bit, either through direct assertion, as in Paley's story, or through observation of landscape or a shift to a memory or observations about the other characters. There are many ways to do this, but what you're hoping for is the truth. The truth about this person (you) at this time, about who she is and how she views herself and others and the world. Ideally, your scene of conflict brings you to this moment of recognition. Remember, also, that your memoir may take years and many different versions, but none of the work is wasted. All your work and focus and even failures are how you earn the moment, finally, when what emerges from your writing is true and feels like a gift.

BRUCE DOBLER

Don't Just Describe It . . .
Evoke It . . . Make It Real!

BRUCE DOBLER is the author of two novels, *Icepick* and *The Last Rush North*, and an "as-told-to" memoir of a counterfeiter, *I Made It Myself*. Retired in 2008, Dobler is now an associate professor emeritus from the University of Pittsburgh. Currently he's working on a textbook for Palgave Macmillan, *Writing Creative Nonfiction: Creative and Critical Approaches*, to be published in the fall of 2010.

The best advice I ever got on describing "place" came to me from a New York printer turned counterfeiter, Mike Landress, the man whose story I told in my first book, *I Made It Myself*. Mike's advice came after his friends, learning that I'd grown up in Chicago and had never lived in New York, begged him to find someone else to write the book. "He's from Chicago!" they'd shout. "C'mon! He'll never get it right."

Mike, who had read some of my early, unpublished work, pondered this for a while and finally told me what we'd do. "I'm taking you to every spot where the 'setup' happened . . . the night all those Secret Service guys were waiting for me to meet up with another counterfeiter. Taking you there at the same time, right to the exact same spot where I stood that night, waiting with a Secret Service agent dressed like he was some kind of mobster. And I'm leaving you there for . . . maybe half an hour or so. And you'll write down everything you see and hear and smell, every impression you get. And don't move. You stay there until I come back for you."

I knew the story of that night, Secret Service agents pretending to be bums, or hiding around a corner or drunk and ambling along, and knew it would be the opening chapter of our book. But standing there, just paying close attention for a long time and having no place else to go, that was something new.

So Mike left me. And I stood there. Seventh Avenue in the garment district. Gas station, run-down store-apartment building, a couple of print shops, alleys on both sides, just like Mike told me. Even a panhandler, but this time not a Secret Service agent, just a guy with a plastic shopping bag over one shoulder and his hand out. I gave him a buck and he left. I looked around. I waited on the curb. But I didn't know for what . . . and then the ground under my feet began to tremble slightly and I heard a noise from the barred grating along the curbside, an opening about two feet long or so, and recognized the sound, a subway train, and then, unexpected, a whiff of warm, slightly acrid air, a soft breeze rose from the tunnel below. And it was gone, and I thought of what it might have been like to stand there, waiting, tense, nervous, waiting for the shoot-out to come, and trying to remember where to duck for cover, knowing things could go wrong, knowing you could get shot, too. I was relieved when Mike finally came to get me. He took one look at my expression and nodded, satisfied. "Good," he said. "It works."

Mike Landress took me to other locations, too. The small lot where the kidnappers dumped him and told him that if he talked he'd end up "in a heap with his tongue on the ground." He drove me to that small lot and took me right to the spot where he got dumped, and told me to spend about half an hour there, then walk up the street about five blocks toward his old home, and he'd meet me there. *And to pay attention.*

You could do this, too. We, all of us, tend, in moments of stress, fear, sadness, even outright violence, to notice things around us that we might not normally pay attention to. And sometimes, falling in love, or happy about some surprising turn in our lives, we regard an object once familiar, and see it in a wholly new way. Even though this is really a double-task, noting what *you* experience and hoping that it can make some event more meaningful to a reader, it requires that you also consider the emotional state of *the person you are writing about*. Or, if you want to push the edge, to imagine how people would have perceived it then, and how differently you see it now. But, in either case, the magic is in eliciting a compelling description, rich in *details that matter*, in *sensory impressions* that put us in your skin (or that of the person you're writing about) and that allow you to describe the events with such authority that the readers (and you!) feel they are there!

EXERCISE

Want to get started? Go to a place that matters to you, a place you react to—whether with pleasure or calm or excitement and energy or fear and . . . loathing. Take the reader there (yes, put us in your skin). In your description/narration don't just tell us what it means. Tell the reader what you are looking at, touching, tasting, smelling, feeling—first tactile, then, if needed, emotionally. There are few "tricks" in writing that you can rely on and that don't seem mere artifice . . . and one of the most powerful is to mix two or three sensations in a single sentence. The evocation of place and situation through a combination of sensory details can be quite compelling, can really make readers feel as though they are there. Keep your "telling" to a minimum. Trust the reader to "get it."

Then, when you feel you've done that successfully, take this even deeper by going to a place that is new to you—a new neighborhood, maybe a small town you've only driven through, some sports venue that you haven't really seen (*experienced!*), or, better still, a location where you know something important, something newsworthy or otherwise memorable, even historic, has taken place . . . and think about what happened there as you linger and "soak up" the details, and either write about the memory, or, if you know of the event, try re-creating it.

Put yourself in such a situation if you can. Where someone perhaps helped another, or saved a life, or saw some accident, witnessed or was part of something heroic or sad or painful or even funny or sweet . . . a moment that you'd like to recapture and put on the page—and put yourself and the reader *right there*, the night, the morning, the afternoon, when it happened. That's all Mike Landress needed from me. He had a story to tell, but he needed to make place, with all of its intrinsic and unique characteristics, come alive, so that readers who knew the place would recognize it in a heartbeat, and readers who had never been there would inevitably "get it."

Are We There Yet? How to Create
a Structural Road Map

LESLIE LEHR is an award-winning novelist, nonfiction author, and screenwriter. Her novels include *Wife Goes On* and *66 Laps*; her essays have been featured in *Mommy Wars* and lauded by Katie Couric and Ariana Huffington; and her romantic thriller *Heartless* is playing for the sixth year in theaters across Europe. Lehr lives in Southern California, where she consults and teaches in the Writers Program at UCLA.

Everything has a beginning, middle, and end: in every sentence, every paragraph, every chapter—as well as every day, every year, every life. It's just as important in every piece of writing. From birth, we are plied with fairy tales. "Once upon a time" builds to "happily ever after" in a way that helps organize our thoughts and gives a causal effect to the events. Yet while the concept is ingrained in our unconscious, it can be easy to forget in our zeal to put our prose on paper.

Many people scoff at the word "outline" and insist that they can write a story by doing just that: writing and writing and writing. Many writers find their story buried in these pages. Yet once they find the story, they must begin it, pursue it, and end it. Think of it as a road map, where you know you want to travel from Los Angeles to New York, but you haven't decided what route to take. In creative nonfiction, you have already taken this trip and have so many side trips to talk about, the challenge is in choosing the route that includes the best cities. In writing terms, that means deciding what plot points will best serve your theme.

Organizing your events into a Beginning, Middle, and End can save you time and heartache. If you are telling a true story, there will be a very clear order to use. If you alter the structure or use a parallel narrative, you still must know how it fits together. When exploring a subject without a specific chronology, these decisions are even more crucial. Once you have a clear order, it will be easier to make other important decisions. How long should you spend on certain parts? How many incidents should you relate? Which events or ideas will make it the most compelling?

Your biggest challenge may be in deciding what to omit. The main things to avoid are parts that don't offer new information, parts that repeat earlier ideas or those that distract the reader from the main concept. In terms of our map metaphor, this means you want to avoid driving in circles, seeing too many similar sights, and wasting too much time in bars. If you want to describe every national park, so be it. If you want to show the diversity of our nation, that's an entirely different trip. Since you've chosen to be creative in the telling, you can drive wherever you want as long as you don't run out of gas before you get to the end. That kind of planning provides freedom within structure.

EXERCISE

1. Make a list of the three main events that take place in your story. Not just three random events, but the three things you are most likely to tell your best friend when describing what happens. If you are writing about a subject rather than a story, then write down three main things you want to talk about: 1, 2, and 3. Aha! You have an outline. Label #1, Beginning; #2, Middle; and #3, End.

2. Make a list of five other things that happen, or that you want to mention, in your piece. You may use full sentences or simple phrases, but do not go into detail.

3. Add these to the first three parts and put them all in order. If history doesn't require a strict chronology, play around with the order. You can always revise it later. Once you do commit, each event must build to the next. What happens in number 7 could not possibly have happened at number 4. Or, the point you are making will make the most sense and sound stronger because of the ideas that built up to it.

4. Draw two horizontal lines separating the middle of the story from the beginning and the end. Now your eight events or ideas are in three sections.

   • According to the laws of the universe—or the basic three-act structure—you will end up with more in the middle than on either end. Many writers start out with more writing in the beginning section, but since we often develop the setup before the rest of the story, much of what appears at the beginning can be crossed off or combined as backstory. If you truly have more events in the beginning, determine where the jumping-off point is to the journey of Act Two.

   • Think of more things that happen, be they obstacles or examples, that must occur before the turning point that leads to the end. These belong in the middle.

   • Even if the end seems obvious, i.e., they get to New York, write it down. You can flesh it out later. Keeping the goal in mind can help keep you excited about the trip.

5. Feel free to go into more detail now. Some people expand each plot point into a paragraph or even a whole scene, making the first draft even easier to write. Others add more events or ideas until they have a full list. From there it might

be helpful to put each event or idea on a separate note card. Remember to be flexible—if you take a wrong turn to the Grand Canyon, you might want to check out the view.

Now you have a simple outline to use as a road map while you write. Whether you like to drive aimlessly to see what you discover or you like a full itinerary, you can't get across the country without some idea of where you're going. Bon voyage!

NEAL BOWERS

Make It Brief

NEAL BOWERS is the author of eight books, including the novel *Loose Ends* and the memoir *Words for the Taking*. He is a poet as well and the recipient of various literary awards, including a National Endowment for the Arts Fellowship. His short nonfiction has appeared as a weekly newspaper column for several years and was nominated for a Pulitzer Prize in the category of feature writing. He recently retired after thirty-one years of teaching at Iowa State University.

Nonfiction is the province of memoir, biography, and history—all suitable for book-length presentation. Shorter nonfiction exists in essay-sized pieces of three thousand to five thousand words, but few writers other than journalists have explored the possibilities of short, short nonfiction.

EXERCISE

My own definition of this minimalist category of literary nonfiction is fairly simple. The piece must be no shorter than five hundred words and no longer than six hundred (the size of a standard newspaper column). It must present factual information but do so in a way that distinguishes the writing from straightforward journalism. While the compressed space may seem restrictive, it can actually liberate the writer, allowing him to explore the possibilities of figurative language within the confines of factual material.

In addition to figurative language, the writer of short, short nonfiction can also make good use of point of view and organization of the facts. The goal is to invest prose with lyrical power while stopping short of prose poetry or some kind of loose-lined free verse.

The place to look for material is in the ordinary world. Short, short nonfiction is best when it illuminates the mundane, causing the reader to stop and think for at least a moment or two about the extraordinary moments that comprise his routine days. The following excerpt from one of my own brief essays came from the experience of getting the wrong carryout order:

> *Sincere apologies to the couple whose carryout order we were accidentally given one night last week at the Chinese restaurant. The bag seemed too bulky for our simple soup noodles, but we took it home without looking inside and then were too embarrassed to return it. Anyhow, the dinner seemed more a gift than a mistake—each little box tucked shut on its surprise.*
>
> *Inside were only a few things we recognized: sweet and sour soup, egg rolls, rice. The rest was fragrant mystery, hints of seasoning, wisps of combinations we had never tried. Like finicky kids resisting anything new, we sniffed each carton, took a balky bite. Miraculous! Our homely order had been conjured into an exotic dinner for two.*
>
> *As we ate, we thought of you, the strangers who understood our tastes so thoroughly. Such incandescence of ginger, subtlety of sesame. Half-a-dozen times we toasted you with our hot tea and wished you well, wondering if you had packed off our two waxed cups of noodle soup, wishing you could be here to see how much we appreciated your choices.*

While this passage is more lyrical than narrative, it still tells a story, though its components are more implied than directly expressed. The limited space makes digression impossible and keeps the writer focused on the material at hand. His challenge is to speak volumes in the span of about two typewritten pages.

Here's another excerpt from a 522 word piece about people singing along with their radios, CDs, and IPods while driving:

> What a chorus we must be on the interstate, going 65 or 70, the wind's falsetto, the tires doing do-wop on the pavement joints. Everything from Cole Porter to Pearl Jam, Billie Holiday to Jewel. Pick a decade and someone is in the money, waiting for the lights to go on again all over the world, crossing Moon River in style, walking the floor over you, remembering the crocodile rock. Call us the traveling troubadours, the freeway minstrels. What a group we'd make, if everyone didn't want to sing lead, if everyone didn't go dry-mouth-shy at the slightest glance.

What intrigues me about this kind of writing is how it transgresses genres. Think of it as poetic prose occupying a journalistic space. Though writers have long experimented with the short, short story, nonfiction of comparable brevity remains wide-open territory for exploration.

Because this type of nonfiction hasn't been exploited, it affords great opportunities for students to do something truly fresh and engaging within the context of a classroom assignment. Simple facts of daily life—getting up when the clock goes off (or not getting up), sitting through a boring lecture, eating cafeteria food, talking on the cell phone—can be invigorated through the figurative compression of short, short nonfiction.

JANET BURROWAY

The True Disclaimer

JANET BURROWAY is the author of seven novels, including the 2009 *Bridge of Sand*, and the texts *Writing Fiction* and *Imaginative Writing*. Recent works include the play *Parts of Speech* and a collection of essays, *Embalming Mom*. She is Robert O. Lawton Distinguished Professor Emerita at the Florida State University.

There will always be a conflict between "creative" and "nonfiction." In that paradox lies the richness of the form. The question is, at what point does *creative* embellish itself into *fiction*? On the other hand, at what point does *truth* squat on the page as inert and unedifying *data*?

Writers of creative nonfiction make decisions in this arena with virtually every sentence, but are often unsure or uneasy about their choices, and the tension has been exacerbated in the early years of the new century by newspaper scandals and the very public dressing-down (nothing more public than the *Oprah* hour) of James Frey and his sham memoir.

Yet I think it's easy to be truthful with the reader if you're honest with yourself, and that there's a clear and simple touchstone of nonfiction truth: absence of the intent to deceive.

Most of the time this means that you bring all your writerly skills to bear on capturing the truth as you perceive it. But it also means that you have very wide latitude in invention as long as you let the reader know you are inventing. *I imagine, I see, it seemed to me, I thought, I suppose, I don't remember exactly, but*—such phrases describe mental activities that we engage in every day, and that we use along with the data to arrive at our perception of the truth.

As long as you clearly signal to the reader the nature of your speculation, speculation can be a path to vivid accuracy. "I spent three months in jail" when you only spent one night there is a lie. "That one night in jail seemed to last three months" could well be a truth, though it's a cliché, and you can do better, *creatively*.

Here is Fred D'Aguilar at the opening of his essay "A Son in Shadow:"

> *I know nothing about how they meet. She is a schoolgirl. He is at work, probably a government clerk in a building near her school. At the hour when the school and the office are out for lunch their lives intersect at sandwich counters, soft drink stands, traffic lights, market squares . . .*

The disclaimers "I know nothing" and "probably" clearly say that this is invention, and allow D'Aguilar to bring very specifically to mind the events and atmosphere of his parents' meeting, which he could not know. We don't feel cheated, but allowed access to his thoughts and feelings.

Here is a more elaborate disclaimer from my own "I Didn't Know Sylvia Plath":

> *The evening was pleasant, staccato, strained, as such evenings tend to be. I didn't know Sylvia Plath. I remember nothing vivid except that moment and don't know what the situation was between them. I'm a novelist. I make things up—not "out of whole cloth," but out of scraps and ravelings, the motives, tensions, failures, dinners, guests, guilt, babies, bitterness, and blame of lived and watched experience. Oh, yes, with a little license, out of my own quarrel-stunned later years, if I wanted to write a fiction of*

that evening such as to charge it with everything to come, I could
assemble a marital scenario . . .

And then, of course, I am free to do so.

As in these instances, a fantasy-within-the-facts usually tells us more about the writer than about the person, place, event, or thing described, but the mind of the writer is after all an important part of what we want from creative nonfiction. As Phillip Lopate says, " . . . if the essayist can delve further underneath, until we feel the topic has been handled as honestly, as *fairly* as possible," then the piece has a chance of awakening "that shiver of self-recognition . . . which all lovers of the personal essay await as a reward."

EXERCISE

Begin with one or two (no more) paragraphs about a real event, autobiographical or otherwise. Then, with a clear disclaimer to signal that you are heading into the imaginative realm, fantasize about what might have happened, characterize by invention, or re-create a scene you don't remember. Your goals should be: (a) that the reader is never in doubt about what's fact and what's invented, and (b) that the "made-up" part does, in *fact*, bring you closer to the truth.

SANDRA SCOFIELD

Crafting Truthful Scenes in Memoir

SANDRA SCOFIELD is the author of seven novels, a memoir, and a craft book, *The Scene Book: A Primer for the Fiction Writer.* She teaches in the Solstice MFA Creative Writing Program at Pine Manor College, and she paints.

Surely nobody needs to hear again why it isn't okay to make things up in memoir. Yet inevitably the memoirist faces points in a manuscript when the question is: Do I have enough to write a scene? How do I fill in the blanks?

First of all, let me say straight up: I don't believe in compressing characters, chronology, or settings. I think a scene should represent something in memory that is clear enough (and urgent enough) to merit the close view of the scene. You always have the alternative of talking "about" an event, citing what you do remember, as you also discuss your doubts about your recollections. This sort of discursiveness is interesting and revealing to readers. On the other hand, a scene has the special quality of immediacy and intimacy, so go for it when you have what you need.

EXERCISE

So what do you need? I'd say, start with a fast account of the event and then inventory your material. You should have certain things that ring true to you: objects, scraps of dialogue, time of day, elements of place. List these and write descriptive phrases.

More importantly, ask yourself what the scene is really about. What key feeling do you have about it? What was happening for you at the time? Why do you want to take the reader there? This helps you to analyze the purpose of your scene, such as capturing an aspect of a relationship or the ambience of a place or time.

Now you have a reason for the scene, and you have key facts. What next? Cull images from your memory of "how things were at the time." Think conditional sense: "We always used to make peach ice cream and then light the sparklers." "My mother could never give me advice without making me sit down, as if I needed to take notes."

The background of a scene is often made up of these things, along with your vestigial emotions about the event. You won't remember everything exactly, but you won't be winging it, either.

With these things in mind and with the initial work, described above, done:

1. Identify the heart or "pulse" of the scene: the source of its tension and energy. Is it yearning? Fear? Anger? Let it beat in your scene!

2. List the beats of the scene, i.e., the steps of action you will elucidate. This helps you keep from going off on imaginative tangents.

3. Write the scene slowly and with images that anchor it, attention to beats, and a careful weaving of facts and "conditional circumstances" discussed above.

4. Combine elements of summary and reflection to provide exposition and insight. Often, this is where you account for whatever slipperiness you may feel about the scene; for sure it's where you account for your sense of its meaning. Remember that in the memoir, "tell" is a rich part of the narrator's gift to the reader.

MIMI SCHWARTZ

The Power of Present Tense

MIMI SCHWARTZ'S most recent book is *Good Neighbors, Bad Times—Echoes of My Father's German Village*. Others include *Thoughts from a Queen-Sized Bed* and *Writing True: The Art and Craft of Creative Nonfiction* (with Sondra Perl). She is professor emerita at Richard Stockton College of New Jersey and lives in Princeton, New Jersey.

Writing in the present tense helps to transport us back in time and relive a moment with more immediacy. Writing "I am" rather than "I was" often releases more of the sensory details we need, particularly for memoir and personal essay. There's also another perk: the double perspective of then and now. The old "I" and the current "I" work as a team; the first reacts to the immediacy of the moment; the second knows the consequences of that moment. The tensions between the two selves energize the narrative and lead to epiphanies.

Of course, writing in present tense is technically a fiction; we are using "I am" for something that happened six or twenty years ago—or last week. But readers know that. They accept that "I scream as the roller coaster dives yet again!" is a literary conceit for what *was*, not what *is*.

Another literary conceit is the author's innocence. The author *was* innocent at the time, but now knows what will happen on that roller coaster, even as the "I" plunges downward. But *why* does this memory matter? *Why* did the author need to return to ride, yet again? That's what the act of writing and revising uncovers.

Sometimes the answers come in present tense; sometimes we need to switch to past tense for less immediacy and more reflection. I discovered that in my essay "My Father Always Said." I began it, in present tense, as the bratty American teenager on a family trip to my father's German village seven years after World War II:

> *I am being dragged through Europe by a father who is intent on convincing me that Forest Hills, Queens, is not the world. He hates that his Yankee-born daughter—ME!—wants to be exactly like my best friend Arlene, whose mother has bleached blond hair and serves Campbell Soup for dinner. "In Benheim, you didn't do such things!" he'll say, 100 times a day—especially when I want to hang out at Penn Drug on Friday night after the basketball games. Or when I want to go to a party where they "don't know the family."*

But halfway through the essay, I got stuck. This child was unable to narrate my father's grief over the life he lost fleeing Hitler fifteen years before—and that, I was discovering, was key to this essay. Only after I switched to my adult perspective, in past tense, did everything come together. There is still the echo of the bratty kid, but the main narrator is me now, remembering that girl.

> *For years I heard the same line: "In Benheim, you didn't do such things!" It was repeated whenever the American world of his daughters took my father by surprise. Sometimes it came out softly, in amusement, as when I was a Pilgrim turkey in the P.S. 3 Thanksgiving play. But usually, it was a red-faced, high-blood-pressure shout, especially when my sister, Ruth, became pinned to Mel from Brooklyn or I wanted to go with friends whose families he didn't know. . . .*

Sometimes the present tense keeps on working, particularly if you are on a journey of discovery to capture, in real time, how things are changing, particularly for the innocent and often naïve "I." A sense of Immediacy is essential for that, and when you want a longer view, phrases such as "Later I will find out . . ." or "It will be forty years until I . . ." allow you to move out of present tense and reflect as needed.

To explore how the power of present tense can trigger and inform memory, try this three-part exercise. Part I involves reliving the past in first person, present tense; Part II encourages reflection on this same event in past tense; Part III explores the tensions and synergy of putting the perspectives together.

EXERCISE

- Think of a "first" from your childhood—first kiss, first defeat, first Big Mac, whatever, and write as if you were again in that moment. Use present tense and capture the voice of the point of view you had *at that time.*

- Now write as the adult looking back. Use past tense and say different things, using the language and perspective of who you have become.

- Reread both versions and do one of the following: (1) go with the voice that seems most powerful; or (2) combine the two voices into one piece.

XU XI

Playing the Changes

XU XI is author of seven books of fiction and essays; recent titles are *Evanescent Isles*, *Overleaf Hong Kong*, and *The Unwalled City*. She is a member of the MFA writing prose faculty at Vermont College of Fine Arts. A native of Hong Kong, she splits her time between New York, Hong Kong, and the South Island of New Zealand.

How do we improvise on the stuff of our lives? Let us say we meet a new person—at work, in the neighborhood, through a friend—and immediately sense a connection we recognize must be pursued. It may be straightforward: a common passion for hybrid roses; children of the same age; the possibility of carpooling. Or it may be complex: the spouse is someone to whom we've long wanted an introduction for professional reasons; an uncanny resemblance to a former lover where the relationship ended abruptly, without explanation. In that moment of recognition, we go into connect mode, and find words to say or *not* say, as the case may be, drawing on all our "how to connect" experience to date, and hope that when we speak, we will say or not say the right thing.

In jazz improvisation, musicians do more or less the same thing onstage. They learn the jazz repertoire of standards until the music is second nature; each piece has a set of "changes," a chord progression that is the harmonic basis on which improvisation occurs. Unless they know or can hear the changes, which the rest of the band will play, they cannot hope to improvise successfully when the turn to do so arrives.

In writing creative nonfiction, we are essentially finding words that mark an improvisatory turn in the study of our lives. Unlike the writing of fiction, in which the chronology, backstory, setting, plot, even the characteristics of the protagonist are all open to the author to invent as needed for the narrative, the *facts* of our lives are incontestable. Those facts are in effect our "changes" on which we improvise. Whether we execute this through choice of perspective or by laying a path across memory, the raison d'être of what we write is founded on a set of immovable, unchangeable facts. For instance, if a certain incident calls upon us to shape words around it, a starting point might be a statement of that incident, what in jazz parlance would be comparable to playing the changes (which usually includes the "head" or melody), in other words, the song as it was originally written, before beginning the improvisation.

EXERCISE

As a longtime, die-hard jazz head, the literary equivalent of playing the changes has proven one of my best techniques for starting any new piece of creative nonfiction. The very act of writing CNF is a form of improvising on our lives. A beautiful narrative illustration of this principle is in Delmore Schwartz's short story "In Dreams Begin Responsibilities," which opens: "I think it is the year 1909." The narrator then describes the sensation of being in a theater and watching a silent picture, one that flashes inconsistently as an old print will, where "the shots are full of rays and dots." The paragraph concludes: "The light is bad." And then in the second paragraph, the story begins: "It is Sunday afternoon, June 12th, 1909, and my father is walking down the quiet streets of Brooklyn on his way to visit my mother." From the seeming uncertainty of "I think"—an improvisatory perspective—Schwartz returns to a "time fact" to guide the narrative, this specific day on which the protagonist's father comes to court the woman who is not yet his wife. Although Schwartz's story was ostensibly a piece of fiction, the narrative principle employed can and does apply to the writing of CNF.

Play your "changes" as a way of finding the right opening for a piece.

The easiest approach is to isolate a chronological fact associated with the material in question, for example, the day of the week an incident occurs, the season in which you first felt relief after the passing of a loved one, the time of day you met the person about whom you wish to write. Write a sentence that is an *incontestable statement* of the factual element of chronology.

Factual Statement

On Thursday, the school called to say my son had punched a girl in the face.

Then, improvise on that sentence by playing around with the chronological element.

Improvisations

Thursday's child, they say, is fair of face.

It is Thursdays I crave because the week is almost but not quite over and I still have the luxury of a quiet, child-free house for one more day.

Do this to try to decide whether or not chronology is the "change" that needs to lead the narrative, and if not, move on to another factual element.

Doing this exercise around the central facts that are fundamental to your material will help you improvise around the shape of the facts for your narrative. Here are examples of "changes" a narrative might include with sample sentences that could embody incontestable statements of fact for the hypothetical material of a writer's life:

303

Specific details of place or setting: San Francisco, the city where my husband was born, is not the state's capital.

Sequence of events: My mother died on June first and her lawyer, the appointed executor of her will, died the following day.

Biographical facts of person(s) described: Carter Wallace joined our company after his divorce was final.

Details of weather or environment at a specific moment: According to the archives of the Weather Channel, the temperature in Maine was unseasonably cool the week my cousin eloped there with her fourth husband.

Nomenclature: Our dog's name was Stalker until my brother re-named him Muttonhead.

The purpose of the exercise is not necessarily to write sentences that will end up in your final version, but to provide *a framework for the facts upon which to improvise.* As is evident from the sample sentences above, implicit in each is the thread of a possible narrative someone might want to write. In jazz, the purpose of improvisation is manifold: to offer a new musical perspective on a familiar tune; to test a musician's harmonic and technical prowess; to speak emotion through music; to coax out what might be the hidden or underlying feelings in a song; to emulate the masters and extend the tradition of the music, and so forth. We could speak similarly of the writing of CNF that is, in its fashion, an improvisation on the stuff that is our lives.

REVISION

LEE GUTKIND

The Yellow Test

LEE GUTKIND is the founding editor of *Creative Nonfiction* and prizewinning author or editor of more than a dozen books, including his most recent work, *Keeping It Real: Everything You Need to Know About Researching and Writing Creative Nonfiction*. Another recent book, *Almost Human: Making Robots Think*, was featured on *The Daily Show* with Jon Stewart.

Vignettes, episodes, slices of reality—all narrative or scenes—are the building blocks of creative nonfiction, the primary distinguishing factor between traditional reportage/journalism and "literary" and/or creative nonfiction and between good, evocative writing and ordinary prose. The uninspired writer will tell the reader about a subject, place, or personality, but the creative nonfiction writer will show that subject, place, or personality in action. Before discussing the actual content or construction of a scene, I ask my students to perform what I like to call the "yellow test."

"Take a yellow Hi-Liter or Magic Marker and leaf through your favorite magazines," I tell them. *Esquire, The New Yorker,* or *Creative Nonfiction*—any publication you respect. Or return to favorite chapters in books you really appreciate from Annie Dillard, Diane Ackerman, Hemingway, James Baldwin, John McPhee, or Gay Talese—on and on. Then simply yellow-in the scenes, just the scenes, large and small. Return to the beginning and review your handiwork. Chances are, anywhere from 40 to 60 percent of each essay or article or chapter selected will be yellow.

EXERCISE

Before submitting your work to your professor or your editor, do the yellow test. If it turns out that you are mostly telling and not showing, if not a lot happens in your manuscript, as evidenced by the yellow test, then it may not mean that your work is ineffective. But it is a definite warning flag—an aspect to be pondered and understand. Ask yourself, "Why aren't my pages yellow? How might I make my work more action-oriented and evocative?" There's no rule that mandates that you have to write in scenes, but since narrative is a basic anchor of most of the best work in the genre, then you should know, at the very least, the reasons why your prose is not as yellow as—or is different from—that of some of the masters of the genre.

ROBERT LELEUX

Abracadabra! The Art Is in the Editing

ROBERT LELEUX is the author of *The Memoirs of a Beautiful Boy*. His writings have appeared in such publications as *The New York Times Magazine* and *The Texas Observer*, to which he is a regular contributor. He lives in New York City.

Okay, so don't tell anybody I said this, because it sounds hippy-dippy and woo-woo New Age-y, and I'm really not like that, I promise. But I've come to believe that whatever you sit down to write already exists outside of you—it's standing right there like *Topper*, or *Blithe Spirit*, or any of those old TV shows where a perfectly normal human (the writer) is run ragged by the Great Beyond. (I mean, how Shirley MacLaine can you get, right? How *Tonight Show* mystic?) But the reason I've come to believe something so dumb-sounding is because a great writing teacher once told me, "There's only one right word." There's only one right word, and it's only spoken to you, and your job is to listen so dearly you don't miss it. The good news is you don't have to worry about giving life to your writing, and the bad news is that you're completely responsible, with the burden of precision, for conveying the message exactly.

Now, you're probably thinking that I'm downplaying the role of the writer; that I'm reducing an artist to a Western Union operator relaying transmissions. Maybe you're thinking that when you sit down at that desk, you're infuriatingly alone, with no spectral hand to guide you. That writing is hard work, and the very notion of some pithy ghost feeding you lines is nothing more than a charming fantasy. Well, if that *is* what you're thinking, then you'll be thrilled to know I don't believe in ghosts, and the exercise I prescribe may or may not be magical, but certainly involves lots of grueling hard work. And since the best place to look for anything grueling is poetry, it's appropriate that I stole this exercise from a poetry workshop, and adapted it to prose.

So, let's say you're writing a memoir. Let's say you've finished the first draft of a chapter, and it's all about Cynthia, your mother's best girlfriend, who used to introduce herself by saying, "Hello, my name is Cynthia, and I'm sorry my nose is so big." Well, you read it, and it's all wrong. In fact, it's heinous. Even though while you were writing it every line seemed like genius. And you see just where the problem lies. It's in the scene about how Cynthia's mother, Mary Lou, who only wore navy blue clothing, used to say during the commercials of *The Dean Martin Show*, "I love Dean Martin more than anybody in the whole world, 'cept Tommy." And since Tommy, her husband, would eventually leave her for the secretary he was schtupping while she was watching *Dean Martin*, this scene is supposed to convey a romantic tragedy that it lacks. So, you start picking it apart, line by line, and, as if to spite you, it only gets worse, and you start wishing for the good old heinous days. Which brings me to . . .

EXERCISE

Here's what I suggest: retype the whole chapter. And, I mean, start with the title. Retype every word, and while you do, listen up. Forget about that gruesome *Dean Martin* scene. Humor me, and pretend the writing is alive, and that it wants to use you as its medium. Listen so respectfully that you allow it to tell a different story than you'd intended. Retype every word, but allow the characters to say unexpected things. Maybe that's what they were really trying to say all along, only you didn't hear them. Listen so that you allow even the things you still think are brilliant to change themselves completely. Who knows, you might find that the real problem occurs much earlier in the chapter, in the scene where Jack Leech, the only boy in your mother's high school who drove a Cadillac convertible, asks Cynthia about the color of her pubic hair. You adored that scene, but as you retype it, you listen as it becomes something strange and different, which changes, forever, the way we think about Dean Martin.

By the time you get to Mary Lou and Tommy, they're unrecognizable. You look at Jack Leech, and you're almost wistful, because you know he's not your Jack Leech anymore. You reread your new draft, and it makes you positively weep, it's so poignant and hilarious and agonizing. And, to be honest, you're a little nervous. Because you've signed your name to something you're convinced you didn't write. But that's crazy, because if you didn't write it, well then, who did? Which is a question that makes you really nervous. I should know. It's happened to me a million times. Only, please, don't tell anybody.

FRITZ McDONALD

Finding the Center

FRITZ McDONALD contributed to *The Workshop: Seven Decades of the Iowa Writers' Workshop.* His fiction recently appeared in *Confrontation*; his script *North Carolina* is an upcoming PBS production; and he writes the blog Create2o. He is VP for Creative Strategy for Stamats, Inc., where his creative work has been recognized by the Council for Advancement and Support of Education.

Structure, that necessary demon, usually eludes our first drafts. Its lack keeps many writers trapped at the starting gate, blinkered by the empty page or the blank screen before them. Structure is further complicated by its relation to "plot" and "story," terms bandied about in workshops so often they've become indistinguishable from each other. Out of the fear that attends the act of writing, we scramble for a solution like a drowning man flailing for a rope. If we can just find that single thing—that hook, gimmick, or formula—we'll be saved. Of course, the rope we grab might be wet, disintegrate in our hands, or worse, not be attached to anything. Gimmicks and formulas regularly fail because they lock us into narrative patterns that leech the life out of the story or turn it into a cliché.

Experienced writers know there is no surefire way to map a plot ahead of time. At its best, writing a book is a process of discovery. E. L. Doctorow once likened the experience to driving across the country in a fog with only fog lamps on—we can't discern the final destination, but we can see well enough to make progress. Yet even if we agree with this metaphor, we still need a direction to move in, a place to start—how do we find the highway?

The goal of this exercise is to help memoirists ferret out the tension that will drive their stories. Unlike novelists, who are constrained only by the limits of their imagination, a memoir writer confronts the amorphous mass of his or her life. What to include or leave out is a major challenge—life as we live it is clearly not a novel.

Yet a little fiction can help. A good novelist has a nose for finding those uncomfortable moments that give birth to an interesting narrative. The tension that arises from this discovery drives any good narrative no matter what story shape it assumes. In *Aspects of the Novel*, E. M. Forster tells us that a writer should decide "what his major event is to be." What he means by this is something I call the "central event," the one event the book cannot do without—it is central to and creates the story; without it, the book collapses like a house of cards. Nearly every work of fiction has one. The central event can occur at any time before, during, or after the story, and can perform any function—it can generate the narrative, serve as a key point of exposition, build to a climax, or even be the climax; what's important is that without a central event, there is no story.

For example, in *The Scarlet Letter*, the birth of Pearl is the central event; if she had not been born, Hester could have kept her affair with Dimmesdale hidden, would not have been branded with the scarlet "A," and would have led a very different life. In *The Great Gatsby*, the central event is the first time Jimmy Gatz sees Daisy Buchanan, a scene Nick Carraway describes late in the novel, but one that is crucial to understanding Gatsby. In this case, the central event describes the unifying action of the novel—Gatsby looking at Daisy, from his dock, from Tom Buchanan's porch, from outside Nick's living room. In these examples, the central event is expositional. When Huck Finn fakes his own murder to escape his drunken father—the central event of *Huckleberry Finn*—it plays an active role in the narrative. Think of the central event as a stone thrown into a pond; the story lies in ripples that reverberate out from its splash.

EXERCISE

This exercise, then, should help you find your central event. It works through the process of elimination, discovery, and construction. You start by making a series of lists, a common activity whose usefulness we often underestimate. The lists follow a pattern:

1. First, write a list of all the events in your memoir. Don't worry about what order they fall in, whether they are important or not important, or even if they are central to the story. Write quickly and list everything you can think of on a few sheets of paper. Keep the language simple—remember, these are only lists.

2. Choose the twenty most important events from this list and write them on one side of a fresh piece of paper. Ask yourself why you chose them.

3. Examine this list carefully. Circle the events that describe actions (hint: look for verbs). Actions not only lead to scenes but help focus you away from generalities.

4. Create a new list on a new piece of paper from the circled entries above, skipping a few lines after each entry on your list. These are your key events.

5. Determine which of these events could be deleted from your story without eliminating the entire story. The one that remains is your central event.

Think of this event as the center of your narrative. In one way or another, everything connects to it, leads away from it, or moves toward it. What you are looking for is the most critical thing that needs to happen either inside or outside your story. And dramatizing what is critical is at the heart of every good book. Just as Fitzgerald wrote about longing and loss and Hawthorne the complicated nature of love, the central event is the story you most want to tell. There is no question that your central event will be intimately connected to your central character. Discovering it may not make writing it any easier. It will, however, give you some sense of the territory you need to discover. From here, you can at least find Doctorow's highway.

ASHLEY SHELBY

Revision for the Obsessive Writer

ASHLEY SHELBY is an author and editor, whose first book, *Red River Rising: The Anatomy of a Flood and the Survival of an American City*, was praised by publications ranging from *Salon* to the Associated Press. She is currently director of Mill City Writers' Workshop in the Twin Cities.

I 've always loved those old photographs of the great writers of fiction sitting at their desks. Nabokov with his index cards. Fitzgerald at his typewriter. Flannery O'Connor in bed with a lap desk on her knees. But I've always wondered where The Piles were: the unscalable mountains of interview transcripts, articles torn from magazines and newspapers, the notes jotted on napkins, the first, second, third, and fifteenth drafts. Maybe I've never seen The Piles in the photographs of the great fiction writers because the sort of dross found on, in, and around the desks of nonfiction writers is the exclusive detritus of their genre. It is the residue, the inevitable footprint of the writer who aims to tell a true story. Even if we are as spare as mendicant monks in our personal lives, most of us nonfiction writers are, in our writing lives at least, pack rats.

It's not just our desks that are prone to hoarding. In the course of all that research or all that self-examination, many of us become besotted with our material. We've all read those works of history, narrative journalism, and memoir that say too much. They go off on uninteresting tangents. They slip in impressive but irrelevant statistics. They take us through an old curiosity shop of whimsical asides. The only remedy for this kind of literary caching is revision. Ruthless and methodical revision. In fact, revision is really the only effective self-help for a nonfiction writer.

EXERCISE

Before beginning, choose a topic, using an existing scrap or sketch that you've saved, or open up a piece you've already been working on.

1. Get it all down. All of it. Quality is not the utmost concern here. Hemingway said: "The first draft of anything is shit." Embrace this sentiment. Don't self-censor, don't worry about going off on tangents. There will be time to fix things later, but you can't fix what is not there. This stage could take days or weeks.

2. Let the piece **cool off**. Unless you are on deadline, leave it alone for at least two weeks. *This is essential.* Don't even peek. If ideas, words, thoughts, possible angles come to you in the interim, write them down in a journal, but avoid the temptation to integrate these into your existing manuscript.

3. Revisit your piece. After two weeks away, you will see your work with fresh eyes. Now is the time for **Big Revision**. This round of revision addresses major issues. Leave the line editing and word editing for the next stage. Of course, if you see grammatical mistakes and a misused word—or a place where a better word could be used—change them. But don't concentrate on these sorts of edits at this stage. Look at the Big Picture. Do I have an angle? Do I have too many? Which one is the most compelling? Is the structure clear and does it serve my material well? The answer to this latter question is

likely a big no. You wrote with abandon. You indulged. Your structure probably doesn't exist yet. So now is the time to begin ordering your material. Do you have enough background material? Do you have too much? Is there enough human interest in the story—i.e., are there enough people? Are there too many? Is there anything you need to expand, to deepen with more research?

Give yourself at least two days between steps 3 and 4 in which you do not look at the material.

4. Now is the time to begin **The Cuts**. Armed with a better perspective on the work, thanks to your earlier revisions, you will be well prepared to identify "extraneous material." Cuts are so important in streamlining a piece of writing. We writers are undeniably self-indulgent in our work: we ramble, we follow uninteresting tangents and expect our readers to follow. That's part of our charm. But at the end of the day, revision requires the excruciating process of cutting chunks of good writing, of pet topics. Ask yourself here: Am I telling a good story? Have I in mind a specific point? Begin making decisions on these key points and implement them.

5. Now comes **The Middle Draft**. Examine the smaller things, like your opening. Do you have the best possible opening? As an editor, I invariably found that the true beginnings of my writers' work was found in the third, fourth, or fifth paragraph. Never the first. I called this the "clearing the throat" effect. Search your manuscript for a better opening. A stark line. A poetic sentence. Even a quote from one of your "characters." How are the transitions? Are there paragraphs that seem unlinked or tenuously linked? Are there non sequiturs

(this is extremely common in early drafts)? Do your points and paragraphs build on one another? How is your pacing? Are you moving too fast in some parts, sluggish in others? Is there too much research integrated into the piece? Is there more research needed to solidify a point?

Note: While working, keep in mind that while this exercise outlines revision in a series of steps, drafts are not static stages, they are elements of a work in progress. They are fluid documents. So if you have to go back and rework the structure even though you have reached the Middle Draft step, do it with no hesitation.

6. Print out your work for **The Line Edit**. Treat the manuscript like an editor would. Look for grammatical mistakes and misspellings. *Do not rely on your Word program's spell-check.* While it will catch egregious misspellings, it will not correct "diving" if you meant to write "divining." After checking for grammar, begin editing line by line. How can you improve each sentence? Are you writing in passive voice too often? Are your sentences convoluted? Have you mixed any metaphors? If you are on assignment, watch word count. Don't leave it to your editor to trim for you.

7. Finally, **read your work aloud**. At this point, a strange thing happens. After having worked with the material for so long, you become blind to errors on the page. This is a phenomenon I've seen in myself, as well as in the authors I've edited. A trick I've learned for combating this Revision Blindness is to read the piece aloud. It is remarkable how many mistakes your ear will catch that your eyes did not. Typos that you missed on the page will be obvious when you hear the words aloud. Clumsy or dull sections will become glaringly obvious.

Should you seek outside advice during revision? It depends on the way you work. As a rule, I do not show my work to others until I've completed my Middle Draft. Other writers have a reader for every draft. This is a personal decision. However, be aware that an extra set of eyes and the advice that goes along with it can complicate matters during the early stages of revision. You may be unduly influenced by one person's opinion early in your revision process. Also, be careful about who you ask to read your work. Friends and family will rarely give you an honest opinion—not because they're bad people, but because they're good people. They don't want to hurt your feelings. Overly polite people are useless to a writer. Overly negative people are similarly useless. The best arrangement is usually a swap with a fellow writer: you read her work and she reads yours.

And then, finally, how do I know when I'm done? It's a tough question, perhaps the ultimate question for a writer. In truth, we are never done; the pieces we write never leave us entirely. But there is a point in the revision process when the changes become minor, almost fussy. Stop short of fussy. Don't tinker (tinkering is the act of changing things for the hell of it). Trust your judgment as a writer. When the work has reached the point of clarity, of transparency, then chances are you have completed your work. Now, step away from the keyboard.

ROBERT ATWAN

Writing the Memoir: "Suddenly I Realized . . . My Prose Need Editing!"

ROBERT ATWAN is the series editor of *The Best American Essays*, which he founded in 1985. He has written extensively on the essay genre, literary nonfiction, and composition, and is the director of the Blue Hills Writing Institute at Curry College, where he helped develop its ongoing "Nine Month Memoir Project."

This is an exercise I use in my Curry College memoir workshop. The exercise is intended to make memoirists more sensitive to the quality of their prose and to the absolute necessity of self-editing.

When a poet works on a poem, he or she invariably struggles with word selection, sound, rhythm, and overall construction. In other words, all the stringent demands of creative language come into play. So why is it that when someone decides to write a memoir the first words that enter one's head apparently seem to suffice? As I read hundreds of memoir-essays each year for the annual *Best American Essays* series, I continually wonder why a writer's self-imposed literary standards would be so acceptably lower for one genre than the other. No matter what the genre, shouldn't writers try to write as well as they can?

Truman Capote once said during a television interview that Jack Kerouac's *On the Road* wasn't writing but merely *typing*. Too often I see memoirs that I imagine are the result of mere "keyboarding." The memoir is deceptively easy: you tell what happened in your life word by word, sentence by sentence. It's all there just waiting for transcription. You try to sound sincere, honest, and conversational—a tone of voice you think depends on simple, straightforward, declarative sentences, the ones that come spontaneously off the top of your head.

That's fine for a first draft; strong memorable writing, however, requires a process of rigorous self-editing. As encouragingly critical as your friends may be, they will most likely not subject your writing to line editing. You will need to do that yourself. Go back to basics. Are your sentences slack? Tighten them. Do you use the verb "to be" over and over again in sentence after sentence? Eliminate it and stretch your vocabulary to come up with real verbs. The heart and soul of a sentence is its main verb—not the adjectives and adverbs that seem to write themselves. And your diction. Do you try to think of the best word, or do you just keyboard the first word that comes to mind? And the phrasing. Do you lean too heavily on off-the-rack idioms?

EXERCISE

What follows is a typical portion of memoir, a composite of perhaps hundreds. The situation is psychologically dramatic and of course crucial to the writer. But the writing—though serviceable and salvageable—clearly lacks the level of editing that a powerful autobiographical moment deserves. Your task: read the passage carefully a few times and then go at it. Without changing any of the episode's substance, edit the passage so that the moment shines as it should. Feel free to rearrange sequence, add specific details, and make whatever word changes you believe necessary. And one other thing—see if you can reduce the number of verbs "to be" to two or three.

"It was very late at night when I drove up to my parents' home.

There were no lights on in the house and I wasn't sure whether I should ring the bell or drive off and find a motel for the night. They were probably both sound asleep and the doorbell would surely alarm them. I realized I should have called earlier but unfortunately given my state of mind I hadn't considered it. I was acting on automatic pilot.

"Just as I decided to pull away, I realized that there was no turning back. Besides, there was no motel or hotel anywhere near. I had nowhere else to go. I was frightened, totally exhausted, and terribly upset. I turned off the car, sat there for a moment, and then got out. I shut the car door quietly. I thought that I must look like hell and that my sudden appearance would frighten them. How would I explain what I had just done—suddenly jumped in the car with no suitcase or destination? How would I explain leaving Pat and the kids at home? How would I explain that I wasn't sure whether I ever wanted to return to them? They loved Pat and the kids with all their heart. I was sure that they were going to see me as a horrible person. I knew that they were going to talk me into going back. Trembling with angst, I rang the doorbell and waited.

"It seemed like an eternity before I heard my father ask, 'Who is it?' I was hoping my mother would be the one to respond. It was always more difficult for me to communicate with Dad. I hesitated before answering, 'It's just me.' When the door opened, I felt relieved and suddenly realized that I was home again."

CONTRIBUTORS' WEBSITES

Reza Aslan www.rezaaslan.com

Lynne Barrett http://lynne.barrett.googlepages.com

Ishmael Beah www.alongwaygone.com

Barrie Jean Borich www.barriejeanborich.net

Jenny Boully http://jennyboully.blogspot.com

Neal Bowers www.nealbowers.com

Janet Burroway http://janetburroway.com

Joy Castro www.joycastro.com

Samantha Dunn www.samanthadunn.biz

Hope Edelman www.hopeedelman.com

Celeste Fremon www.witnessla.com

Philip Gerard www.philipgerard.com

David Gessner www.davidgessner.com

Philip Graham http://creativewriting.english.uiuc.edu/faculty/philip_graham

Robin Hemley www.robinhemley.com

Christine Hemp www.christinehemp.com

Richard Hoffman www.abbington.com/hoffman

Barbara Hurd www.barbarahurd.com

Judith Kitchen www.judithkitchen.com

Carl Klaus www.carlklaus.com

Sydney Lea www.sydneylea.net

Gretchen Legler http://faculty.umf.maine.edu/~legler

Leslie Lehr www.leslielehr.com

Robert Leleux www.robertleleux.com/home2009.html

Paul Lisicky http://paullisicky.blogspot.com

Eric Maisel www.ericmaisel.com

Tilar Mazzeo www.tilar-mazzeo.com

Rebecca McClanahan www.mcclanmuse.com

Fritz McDonald www.create20.com

Michael McGregor www.michaelnmcgregor.com

Christopher Merrill www.christophermerrillbooks.com

Brenda Miller http://myweb.facstaff.wwu.edu/~millerb/index.shtml

Dinty Moore www.dintywmoore.com

Honor Moore www.honormoore.com

Maureen Murdock www.maureenmurdock.com

Daniel Nester www.danielnester.com

Robert Root www.rootwriting.com

Malina Saval www.malinasaval.com

Brandon Schrand www.brandonrschrand.com

Mimi Schwartz www.mimischwartz.net

Sandra Scofield www.sandrascofield.com

Mary Kay Shanley www.marykayshanley.com

Ashley Shelby www.millcitywriters.com

Sue Silverman www.suewilliamsilverman.com

Natalia Rachel Singer www.nataliarachelsinger.org

Michael Steinberg www.mjsteinberg.net

Suzanne Strempek Shea www.suzannestrempekshea.com

Ned Stuckey-French www.english.fsu.edu/faculty/nstuckey-french.htm

Susan Tiberghien www.susantiberghien.com

Thrity Umrigar www.umrigar.com

David Vann www.davidvann.com

Sandy Wisenberg http://slwisenberg.blogspot.com

Ira Wood www.irawood.com

Xu Xi www.xuxiwriter.com

ACKNOWLEDGMENTS

Heartfelt appreciation to my editor, Gabrielle Moss, and to all the authors who contributed writing exercises to this book.

CREDITS

"Life in One Page" by Barrie Jean Borich © 2010 by Barrie Jean Borich.

"The Composite" by Kathryn Deputat © 2010 by Kathryn Deputat.

"Anna's Shrapnel: Recognizing the Revelatory Detail" by Celeste Fremon © 2010 by Celeste Fremon.

"The Five Stages of Grief" by Denise Gess © 2010 by Denise Gess.

"Your First Kitchen" by Robin Hemley © 2010 by Robin Hemley.

"Writing Your Way in the Back Door: The Painting as Entry" by Christine Hemp © 2010 by Christine Hemp.

"The Dying Goat" by Jay Kirk © 2010 by Jay Kirk.

"The One-Inch Window" by Gretchen Legler © 2010 by Gretchen Legler.

"Writing About Images" by Tom Lutz © 2010 by Tom Lutz.

"Stepping into Photographs" by Robert Root © 2010 by Robert Root.

"What Am I Going to Say?" by Myra Sklarew © 2010 by Myra Sklarew.

"Words as Inspiration" by Kathleen Spivack © 2010 by Kathleen Spivack.

"Three Things That Stopped Me in My Tracks: An Exercise in Discovery and Reflection" by Michael Steinberg © 2010 by Michael Steinberg.

"The Brain Map" by S. L. Wisenberg © 2010 by S. L. Wisenberg.

"Riffing" by Lee Zacharias © 2010 by Lee Zacharias.

"'What Was That Like?' Or, How to Find a Subject" by Madeleine Blais © 2010 by Madeleine Blais.

"Breaking from 'Fact' in Essay Writing" by Jenny Boully © 2010 by Jenny Boully.

"Creativity and Authority" by Rebecca Blevins Faery © 2010 by Rebecca Blevins Faery.

"Beyond a Shadow of a Doubt" by Philip Gerard © 2010 by Philip Gerard

"Worth 1,000 Words" by Judith Kitchen © 2010 by Judith Kitchen.

"The Collage Essay" by Shara McCallum © 2010 by Shara McCallum.

"Just Add Water: An Experimental Mini-Essay in a Can" by Dinty W. Moore © 2010 by Dinty W. Moore

"Finding Truth" by Maureen Murdock © 2010 by Maureen Murdock.

CREDITS

"Creating an Intentional World: Using Place in Your Nonfiction" by Eric Maisel, Ph.D. © 2010 by Eric Maisel, Ph. D.

"Walking Through It" by Lia Purpura © 2010 by Lia Purpura.

"Sense of Place" by Suzanne Strempek Shea © 2010 by Suzanne Strempek Shea.

"Landscape and Memory" by Natalia Rachel Singer © 2010 by Natalia Rachel Singer.

"All Work and a Little Word Play" by Marilyn Abildskov © 2010 by Marilyn Abildskov.

"Can You Hear Me Now?" by Philip Graham © 2010 by Philip Graham.

"Starting from Solitude" by Richard Hoffman © 2010 by Richard Hoffman.

"The Artful 'I': Exercises in Style and Voice" by Carl H. Klaus © 2010 by Carl H. Klaus

"The Music of Sentences" by Rebecca McClanahan © 2010 by Rebecca McClanahan.

"Hanging Around Time" by Michael McGregor © 2010 by Michael McGregor.

"He Said What?" by Christopher Merrill © 2010 by Christopher Merrill.

"Permission to Eavesdrop" by Malina Saval © 2010 by Malina Saval.

"Innocence & Experience: Voice in Creative Nonfiction" by Sue William Silverman © 2010 by Sue William Silverman.

"Starting with Dialogue" by Ned Stuckey-French © 2010 by Ned Stuckey-French.

"Can You Smell What [Your Name Here] Is Cooking?" by Ira Sukrungruang © 2010 by Ira Sukrungruang.

"Whose Voice Is Telling the Story?" by Thrity Umrigar © 2010 by Thrity Umrigar.

"The Relationship of Words to Characters and Landscapes" by Ishmael Beah © 2010 by Ishmael Beah.

"The True Disclaimer" by Janet Burroway © 2010 by Janet Burroway.

"Don't Just Describe It . . . Evoke It . . . Make It Real!" by Bruce Dobler © 2010 by Bruce Dobler.

"Zigzags and Leaps: Ways of Locating Our Real Subjects" by Barbara Hurd © 2010 by Barbara Hurd.

"Are We There Yet? How to Create a Structural Road Map" by Leslie Lehr © 2010 by Leslie Lehr.

"The Power of Present Tense" by Mimi Schwartz © 2010 by Mimi Schwartz.

"Crafting Truthful Scenes in Memoir" by Sandra Scofield © 2010 by Sandra Scofield.

"The WHY of Taking Smaller Pictures" by Mary Kay Shanley © 2010 by Mary Kay Shanley.

ABOUT THE EDITOR

Sherry Ellis's first book of writing exercises, *NOW WRITE! Fiction Writing Exercises From Today's Best Teachers and Writers* (Tarcher, 2006), was recognized as one of the best writing books of 2006 by *The Writer* magazine. Her author interviews have been anthologized in *Illuminating Fiction* (Red Hen Press, 2009) and have appeared in literary magazines. She is a personal writing coach and a former writing teacher, who has used writing exercises and prompts in her classes to provide structure and stimulation.

DISCOVER THE ART OF FICTION WITH TODAY'S MOST ACCLAIMED FICTION WRITERS AND TEACHERS

Now Write! Fiction Writing Exercises from

Today's Best Writers and Teachers

This treasure of personal writing exercises from some of today's most acclaimed names in fiction—including Steve Almond, Amy Bloom, Robert Olen Butler, Jill McCorkle, Alison Lurie, Jayne Anne Phillips, and Virgil Suarez—covers everything a fiction writer should know, from creating a believable scene to jump-starting a stalled story, and much more.